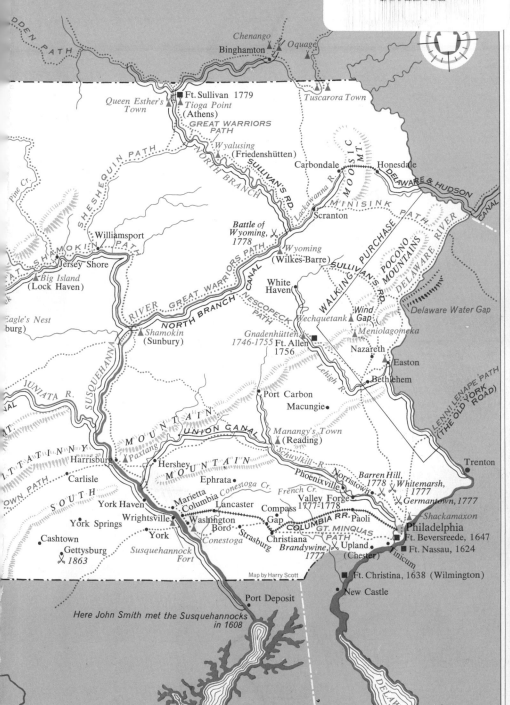

DDEN PATH

Chenango
Binghamton   *Oquage*

Ft. Sullivan 1779
*Queen Esther's
Town*   *Tioga Point
(Athens)*   *Tuscarora Town*

*GREAT WARRIORS
PATH*

Wyalusing
(Friedenshütten)

Carbondale   Honesdale

DELAWARE & HUDSON CANAL

SHESHEQUIN PATH

NORTH BRANCH

SULLIVAN'S RD.

MOOSIC MT.

MINISINK

Lackawanna R.
Scranton

Williamsport

Pine Cr.

SHAMOKIN PATH

Jersey Shore

*Big Island
(Lock Haven)*

*Eagle's Nest
burg)*

*Battle of
Wyoming,
1778*

Wyoming
(Wilkes-Barre)

White
Haven

GREAT WARRIORS PATH

NORTH BRANCH CANAL

RIVER

NESCOPECK PATH

Wechquetank

WALKING PURCHASE PATH

SULLIVAN'S RD.

POCONO MOUNTAINS

*Wind
Gap*

DELAWARE RIVER

Delaware Water Gap

Meniolagomeka

*Gnadenhütten
1746-1755*   Ft. Allen
1756

Nazareth

*Shamokin
(Sunbury)*

SUSQUEHANNA

Lehigh R.

Easton

Bethlehem

JUNIATA R.

CANAL

Port Carbon
Macungie

Manangy's Town
(Reading)

LENNI LENAPE PATH
(THE OLD YORK ROAD)

MOUNTAIN

UNION CANAL

MOUNTAIN

Schuylkill R.

Trenton

TATINNNY

OWN PATH

Harrisburg   *Paxtang*

Hershey

Ephrata

Phoenixville   Norristown

*Barren Hill,
1778*   *Whitemarsh,
1777*

Germantown, 1777

Carlisle

Conestoga Cr.

French Cr.

Valley Forge
1777-1778

Paoli

Shackamaxon

SOUTH

York Haven

Marietta

Columbia

Lancaster

Compass
Gap

COLUMBIA RR.

Philadelphia

Wrightsville

Washington
Boro

Conestoga

Strasburg

Christiana

GT. MINQUAS
PATH

Ft. Beversreede, 1647

Ft. Nassau, 1624

York Springs

York

*Brandywine,
1777*

Upland
(Chester)

Cashtown

Gettysburg
1863

*Susquehannock
Fort*

Tinicum

Map by Harry Scott

Ft. Christina, 1638 (Wilmington)

New Castle

Port Deposit

*Here John Smith met the Susquehannocks
in 1608*

DELAWARE

PENNSYLVANIA

BOOKS BY PAUL A. W. WALLACE

PENNSYLVANIA: SEED OF A NATION

INDIANS IN PENNSYLVANIA

THIRTY THOUSAND MILES WITH JOHN HECKEWELDER

THE MUHLENBERGS OF PENNSYLVANIA

THE WHITE ROOTS OF PEACE

CONRAD WEISER, FRIEND OF COLONIST AND MOHAWK

REGIONS OF AMERICA

*A series of books that depict our natural regions,
their history, development, and character*

Edited by Carl Carmer

PENNSYLVANIA: *Seed of a Nation*
by Paul A. W. Wallace

Already published
THE HEARTLAND: *Ohio, Indiana, Illinois*
by Walter Havighurst

LOVE SONG TO THE PLAINS
by Mari Sandoz

MASSACHUSETTS: *There She Is—Behold Her*
by Henry F. Howe

SOUTH CAROLINA: *Annals of Pride and Protest*
by William Francis Guess

YANKEE KINGDOM: *Vermont and New Hampshire*
by Ralph Nading Hill

VIRGINIA: *A New Look at the Old Dominion*
by Marshall W. Fishwick

PENNSYLVANIA

Seed of a Nation

PAUL A. W. WALLACE

A REGIONS OF AMERICA BOOK

Illustrations by Jerome Paul Witkin

HARPER & ROW, PUBLISHERS, NEW YORK AND EVANSTON

B-N

LIBRARY OF CONGRESS CATALOG CARD NUMBER: 61-6446

To

WILLIAM E. LINGELBACH,

Professor Emeritus of History, University of Pennsylvania,

Librarian Emeritus of The American Philosophical Society,

and an initiating spirit for

the redevelopment and conservation of Old Philadelphia

Contents

Foreword

This is the story of a land, a people, and an idea.

The land is a former ocean bed that now goes by the name of Pennsylvania. During the earth's troubled youth, a cycle of geologic revolutions lifted high above the surface of the water a vast expanse of sedimentary rocks that had once formed the ocean floor. A thrust of unimaginable power from the southeast, where the lost continent of Appalachia lay submerged, bent the rock strata into mountain waves of limestone and sandstone. Since that time these Himalayan-like forms have been worn to a gentler condition by the eons-long action of water and ice. Today over all this mountain landscape, as also over Pennsylvania's piedmont and coastal plain, "The Air . . . is very delicate, pleasant, and wholesome; the Heavens serene, rarely overcast," as Gabriel Thomas wrote some 260 years ago.

The people who now inhabit this land are, as they have always been, a heterogeneous lot: the Indians (they were here first), Europeans of all kinds—Dutch, Swedish, Finnish, English, Welsh, German, Swiss, Scottish, Scotch-Irish, straight Irish, French, Italian, Jewish, Greek, Austrian, Hungarian, Polish, Czechoslovakian, Armenian—with an infusion of African and Oriental. Pennsylvania has never had, as far back as the record goes, a homogeneous population.

That was Penn's idea: the melting pot. When he came in 1682 to "plant a country," it was his belief (which he proposed to test in a "Holy Experiment") that man is a better creature when he is free and that freedom flourishes best in a diversified society. He brought into his province men differing in race, language, and religion. James Madison was to give fresh currency to the idea at the Constitutional Convention of 1787 when, to meet criticism of so extensive a union as was proposed, he suggested that democracy could be more easily safeguarded in a large country than in a small one. In a large country there would be greater differences among the people, and the collective power of minority groups would prevent the tyranny of any one section.

The early Quakers, visiting the Puritans of New England, saw how easy it was for a homogeneous people to deny to others the freedom they demanded for themselves. Penn, in establishing his community, went to work another way.

"We must *give* the liberties we *ask*," he said.

That was the heart of the Holy Experiment.

Henry Adams, looking back on Pennsylvania's past, found her "neither picturesque nor troublesome." He thought her "the ideal American state" and "the only true democratic community then existing [1800] in the eastern states." The popular images her name brings to mind are homely: Benjamin Franklin walking up Market Street in Philadelphia with a bread roll under each arm; the soldiers in their huts at Valley Forge; young Daniel Boone on the farm at Oley; the "plain people" in their bonnets and buggies.

Pennsylvania has contributed to America no supreme revolutionary, no transcendent philosopher, no flaming evangelist. She has contributed instead William Penn, the apostle of fair play, and Benjamin Franklin, the apostle of common sense. Moreover, through the leaven of her early Friends and German Pietists, she has helped to create that large part of America in which, as James Reston has expressed it, "the family, the church and the community are still the foundations of a generous and simple life."

In this attempt to express the distinctive quality of Pennsylvania and its contribution to the nation, the author owes a debt to many libraries and librarians—in particular, to the staffs of the Pennsylvania State Library at Harrisburg and the Historical Society of Pennsylvania and the American Philosophical Society at Philadelphia. Particular acknowledgments are due to Dr. S. K. Stevens, Executive Director of the Pennsylvania Historical and Museum Commission, and to Donald H. Kent, William A. Hunter, and other colleagues on the staff of the Commission, as well as to friends all over the state.

I could say much here in Praise of that sweet Tract of Land, but having spoken so largely and particularly thereof in the Book itself, I shall forbear the least mention in this place.

—GABRIEL THOMAS, *An Historical and Geographical Account of the Province and Country of Pennsylvania* (London, 1698)

5th of 1st Mo. 1681

. . . this day my country was confirmed to me under the great seal of England, with large powers and privileges, by the name of Pennsilvania, *a name the king would give it in honour of my father. . . . 'Tis a clear and just thing, and my God that has given it to me through many difficultys, will, I believe, bless and make it the seed of a nation. . . .*

W. PENN

PENNSYLVANIA

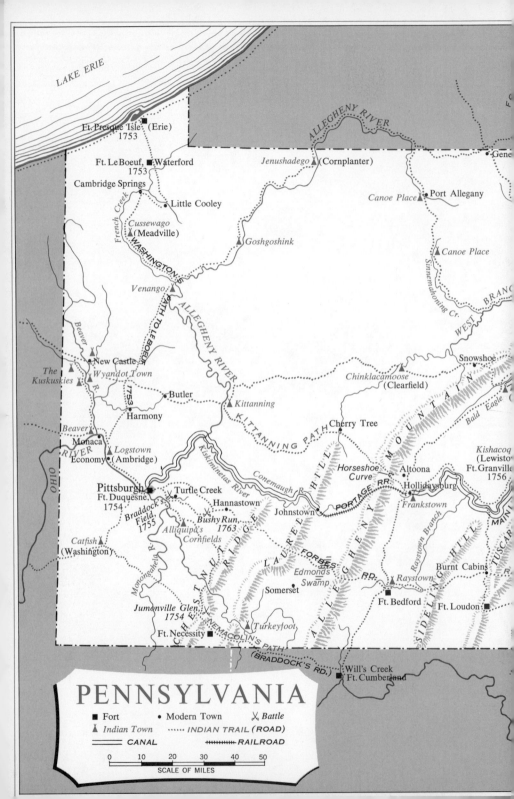

LAKE ERIE

Ft. Presque Isle ■ (Erie)
1753

ALLEGHENY RIVER

Gene

Ft. LeBoeuf, ■Waterford
1753
Cambridge Springs

Jenushadego ▲ (Cornplanter)

Canoe Place ▲ • Port Allegany

Little Cooley

Cussewago
▲ (Meadville)

Goshgoshink ▲

▲ Canoe Place

French Creek

WASHINGTON'S PATH TO LEBOEUF

Venango ▲

Sinnemahoning Cr.

WEST BRANC

Beaver

ALLEGHENY RIVER

The Kuskuskies ▲

■ New Castle
▲ Wyandot Town

Chinklacamoose
(Clearfield) ▲

Snowshoe □

Bald Eagle

1753

• Butler

KITTANNING PATH

Kittanning ▲

Cherry Tree □

MOUNTAIN

• Harmony

Beaver

RIVER

Monaca
Economy •

▲ Logstown
(Ambridge)

Kiskiminetas River

Conemaugh R.

Horseshoe
Curve

PORTAGE R.R.

Altoona □

Hollidaysburg □

Kishacoq
(Lewisto
Ft.Granville
1756

OHIO

Pittsburgh ■
Ft. Duquesne,
1754

• Turtle Creek

Braddock's
Field
1755

Hannastown •

Bushy Run,
1763 ✕

Johnstown •

Frankstown ▲

Raystown Branch

MAIN

Alliquipa's
Cornfields ▲

LAUREL HILL

FORBES RD.

Edmond's
Swamp

Raystown

Burnt Cabins •

SIDELING HILL

TUSCA

Catfish ▲
(Washington)

Monongahela R.

CHESTNUT RIDGE

Somerset •

ALLEGHENY

Ft. Bedford ■

Ft. Loudon ■

Jumonville Glen ✕
1754

Turkeyfoot ▲

Ft. Necessity ■

NEMACOLIN'S PATH
(BRADDOCK'S RD.)

Will's Creek •
Ft. Cumberland ■

PENNSYLVANIA

■ Fort   • Modern Town   ✕ Battle

▲ Indian Town   ······ INDIAN TRAIL (ROAD)

▬▬ CANAL   ┿┿┿┿ RAILROAD

0   10   20   30   40   50

SCALE OF MILES

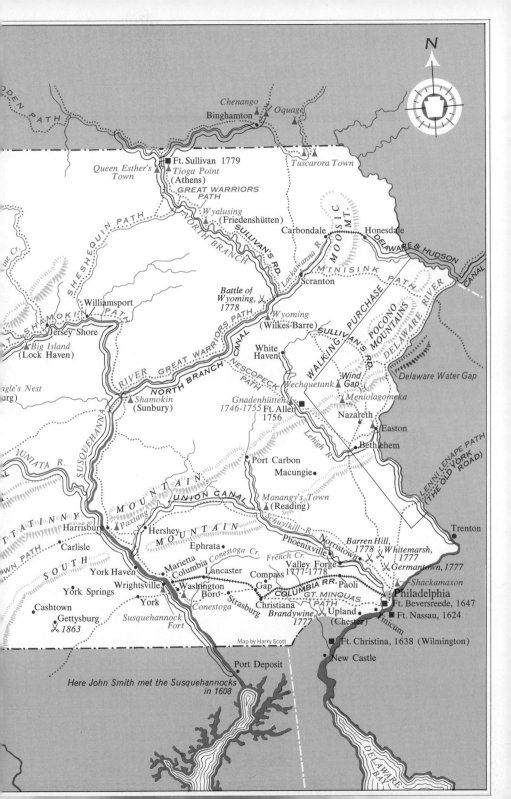

N

Chenango
Binghamton
Oquage

Ft. Sullivan 1779
Queen Esther's
Town
Tioga Point
(Athens)

Tuscarora Town

GREAT WARRIORS
PATH

Wyalusing
(Friedenshütten)

Carbondale
Honesdale

MOOSIC MT.

MINISINK

Scranton

DELAWARE & HUDSON CANAL

SHESHEQUIN PATH

NORTH BRANCH

SULLIVAN'S RD.

Battle of
Wyoming,
1778

Williamsport

SHAMOKIN PATH

Wyoming
(Wilkes-Barre)

WALKING PURCHASE PATH

POCONO MOUNTAINS

Jersey Shore

RIVER

GREAT WARRIORS PATH

NORTH BRANCH CANAL

White
Haven

SULLIVAN'S RD.

DELAWARE RIVER

Delaware Water Gap

Big Island
(Lock Haven)

NESCOPECK PATH

Wechquetank

Wind
Gap

agle's Nest
urg)

NORTH BRANCH

Shamokin
(Sunbury)

Gnadenhütten,
1746-1755 Ft. Allen
1756

Meniolagomeka

Nazareth

Easton

SUSQUEHANNA

JUNIATA R.

MOUNTAIN

UNION CANAL

Lehigh R.

Bethlehem

Port Carbon
Macungie

LENNI LENAPE PATH (THE OLD YORK ROAD)

AL

Manangy's Town
(Reading)

TTATINNY

TUSCARORA MOUNTAIN

Harrisburg

Paxtang

MOUNTAIN

Schuylkill R.

Norristown

Barren Hill,
1778

Whitemarsh,
1777

Trenton

WN PATH

Carlisle

Hershey

Ephrata

Phoenixville

French Cr.

Valley Forge
1777-1778

Germantown, 1777

SOUTH

Marietta
Columbia Conestoga Cr.

Compass

Paoli

Shackamaxon

York Haven

Lancaster

COLUMBIA RR.

GT. MINQUAS PATH

Philadelphia

Ft. Beversreede, 1647

York Springs
Wrightsville

Washington
Boro

Gap

York

Strasburg

Christiana

CONESTOGA

Brandywine,
1777

Ft. Nassau, 1624

Cashtown

Conestoga

Upland
(Chester)

Tinicum

Gettysburg
1863

Susquehannock
Fort

Map by Harry Scott

Ft. Christina, 1638 (Wilmington)

New Castle

Port Deposit

Here John Smith met the Susquehannocks
in 1608

DELAWARE BAY

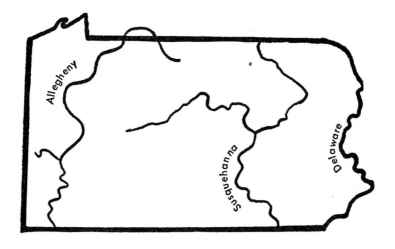

1 *Three Rivers*

White dust rising from her limestone quarries is a reminder that Pennsylvania's physical foundations were laid on the ocean floor. In Paleozoic times the waters that covered the southeastern borders of Pennsylvania washed the shores of a great land mass which geologists call the continent of Appalachia. The rivers of Appalachia, pouring down off her mountains, brought with them the debris of aging rocks and, as they discharged themselves into the sea, clouded its waters with sand, which settled slowly to the bottom. This process, uninterrupted for millions of years, brought about such massive accumulations of sand grains that, under the intolerable pressure, they were turned into sandstone. Similar pressures turned deposits of mud into slate.

When erosion had finished its work on Appalachia and had worn her mountains down to a plain, the rivers lost their momentum, the sand ceased to flow, and the coastal waters cleared. Then myriads of minute sea creatures appeared. Dying, they left their skeletons to accumulate on the sea bottom as the sand had done. Lime beds were thus formed of such thickness and weight that they solidified into limestone, which is now one of the state's most valuable rocks, found in most of the valleys of southern and central Pennsylvania.

The earth, meantime, was cooling; and as it did so, its skin, like that of the proverbial apple, wrinkled and puckered and cracked. Molten rock poured out and, solidifying, produced the quartz and jasper outcroppings found in the Lehigh Hills round Bethlehem and the South Mountains farther west.

As a result of the earth's continuing convolutions, Appalachia sank beneath the sea and after an interval rose again. At one time her coastline lay approximately along the southeastern edge of Lebanon and Cumberland valleys. Then the sea, retreating, exposed most of what is now Pennsylvania to air and sunlight. The miracle of life arose. Vegetation appeared in the vast reaches of what we now call coal swamps, which once covered most of Pennsylvania. Trees sprouted, matured, and died in countless generations. Their decaying remains accumulated. When the land sank again beneath the sea, the pressure of marine sediment (as in the case of sand and lime) helped to turn these carbonaceous deposits into coal.

> There rolls the deep where grew the tree.
> O earth, what changes hast thou seen!
> There where the long street roars, hath been
> The stillness of the central sea.
> ALFRED, LORD TENNYSON, *In Memoriam*, cxxiii

There came a period of peculiar stress for Pennsylvania. Lateral pressures of unimaginable strength from the southeast—corresponding in time with the final subsidence of old Appalachia—caused the earth's rock skin to crease and wrinkle. Horizontal strata many thousands of feet thick—sandstones, limestones, shales, and coal measures—were compressed, bent, and forced upward to immense heights in long parallel ridges. That was what is known as the Appalachian Revolution, when a new range of Appalachian Mountains—the one travelers see today when they cross Pennsylvania by the Turnpike—rose at the death of the elder continent. As a consequence of the extreme pressures that then seized Pennsylvania's coal measures, the Commonwealth now possesses almost all the anthracite (hard coal) in the United States.

The direction from which the thrusting power came is revealed by the fact that all these newer ridges face southeast, and also by the fact that the first ridge, the Kittatinny or Blue Mountain, has the sharpest angle of inclination. The folds grow less abrupt as we follow them north and west and see them decline in the gentle synclines and anticlines of Laurel Hill and Chestnut Ridge.

The elements attacked the new ranges as they had formerly attacked the old. The earth is a great leveler. "Something there is that doesn't love a wall," wrote Robert Frost. No sooner were Pennsylvania's mountains created than erosion started to unmake them; and it was not long (speaking in terms of geologic time) before they were worn down almost to a plain—the peneplain of which there are vestiges today in the ruler-straight tops of our mountain ridges. The highest spot in Pennsylvania today is Mount Davis in Somerset County, 3,213 feet above sea level. In Wayne County, Mount Ararat touches 2,654 feet. But these are nothing compared with the heights Pennsylvania's mountains reached in their youth.

Erosion is still very active. Three great rivers now contend for first place in the scouring of Pennsylvania's land surface: the Susquehanna, which runs a course of 444 miles from Otsego Lake in New York to Chesapeake Bay, draining 46.4 per cent of the state; the Allegheny, which runs some 300 miles from Potter County to Pittsburgh and, with the Monongahela and Ohio, drains 34.5 per cent; and the Delaware, which rises in the New York Catskills and runs 375 miles to the sea, but captures only 14.3 per cent of Pennsylvania's drainage. The Potomac gets most of the remainder with its 3.5 per cent. A little goes into Lake Erie. But it is the three big rivers—the Delaware, Susquehanna, and Allegheny-Ohio (the Indians quite properly regarded these last two as but one stream, the Great or Beautiful River, the Delaware word for which was *Allegheny* while the Iroquois word was *Ohio*)—that have emerged victors in the age-long struggle for supremacy.

The part played by rivers in carving up Pennsylvania's peneplain into our present hilly landscape is as striking as the role these waterways have played in man's history. They have been prime agents in erosion, carrying off debris in the form of sand, pebbles, and even boulders, and using all these as cutting tools in the work of further destruction. Most of the coal measures were thus eaten and washed away, although it is estimated that, when commercial coal mining began in Pennsylvania, there were still close to a hundred billion short tons available.

Everywhere about the state can be seen what the streams have done: in river terraces; in flat valleys widened by meandering streams; in the so-called wind gaps, which are the dried beds of ancient rivers; and in those curiosities of nature, the potholes—commonly called "Indian mills"—which were made by pebbles and stones grating in an eddy. A slight lifting of the peneplain on an axis near the center of the state compensated in part for erosion, but at the same time speeded it up by giving the streams a better headway and encouraging them in the depredations known as "stream piracy."

This geological banditry is mainly responsible for Pennsylvania's present stream pattern. Streams have a natural tendency to eat back into their hills of origin. In this process of "heading," a stream may eat its way into and up and even across the divide that separates it from another stream. In any such breakthrough, gravity being what it is, the lower stream captures the waters of the higher stream and takes them into its channel.

Competition of this sort was encouraged among Pennsylvania's streams, not only by the many breaks that occurred when the folds were made in her stratified rocks, but also by the variety of rock substances that made up her covering. In one place there was the toughly resistant sandstone; in other places, the more yielding limestone, the still softer shale, or the coal measures that put up scarcely any resistance.

The story of the Susquehanna River, especially of its West Branch, as told by Dr. Richmond E. Myers in *The Long Crooked River,* shows how stream piracy operated.

Once upon a time (geologic time) there were four good streams—Loyalsock, Lycoming, Larry's, and Pine creeks—all flowing seaward through an area now bounded on the east by the town of Muncy and on the west by the town of Jersey Shore. They ran in parallel courses, a little east of south, cutting through Bald Eagle, Nittany, and other mountain ridges. Of these four, the Loyalsock was the fastest worker, cutting its channel deeper than the others because it crossed a head ridge only once. Out of it grew a small tributary that headed westward through soft shales and limestones until it captured Lycoming, then Larry's, and finally Pine Creek, drawing their waters eastward into the Loyalsock channel, which thus made tributaries of its three rivals. But its triumph was short. A few miles east of where the Loyalsock made its spectacular break through the Bald Eagle Moun-

STREAM PIRACY

makes the West Branch of the Susquehanna

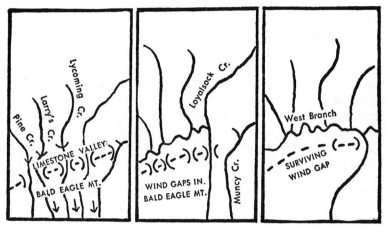

Five independent streams	The Loyalsock captures Lycoming, Larry's, and Pine creeks	Muncy Creek captures the Loyalsock and becomes the West Branch of the Susquehanna

Courtesy Richmond E. Myers, *The Long Crooked River* (Boston, 1949)

tain, another small creek was eating westward into the height of land that separated the Loyalsock from Muncy Creek. When at length the Muncy Creek tributary broke through the divide, it diverted the Loyalsock waters round the eastern end of Bald Eagle Mountain into Muncy Creek's channel. The resulting large stream, which carried the waters of Loyalsock, Larry's, Lycoming, and Pine creeks through the Muncy Creek gap in the Bald Eagle Mountain, now goes by the name of the West Branch of the Susquehanna River.

In this unending struggle the rivers, even the strongest and most acquisitive of them, met their match in a new antagonist that appeared during the Ice Age. Glaciers, formed of sheets of

ice sometimes miles in thickness, moved across Pennsylvania's
northern borders, grinding the land surface beneath them and
breaking off splinters of rock with which they raked and gouged
the country over which they passed. When their progress was
arrested, their towering ice fronts served as dams against which
lakes formed. Often, as a result of these obstructions, the natural
drainage of a whole region was reversed. When at last the glaciers retreated, they left their mark all over the landscape in the
form of lakes and swamps and boulders spilled from glacier
moraines. Four times the glaciers invaded northern Pennsylvania,
and four times they retreated. The last to leave was the Wisconsin Glacier, some twelve thousand years ago.

Many of the most striking features of the Pennsylvania landscape are the result of glacier action. Spanish Hill, a morainal
deposit near Athens, Pennsylvania, has for centuries stirred the
imagination of men—Indians and white men alike—to attempt
an explanation of its origin. For long, it was believed to have
been built by human hands, as Carl Carmer says in *The Susquehanna*—some supposing it to have been erected by the
Mound Builders; others giving credit to the Spanish, the French,
or the Susquehannock Indians.

The terminal moraine of the Wisconsin Glacier gave George
Washington a good ford across Muddy Creek on his journey to
Venango and Fort Le Boeuf in 1753. The sand terraces of the
Wyoming Valley (in the vicinity of Wilkes-Barre) are thought
to be the result of glacier action. In northwestern Pennsylvania,
the gentle contours of the plateau country of Lawrence, Mercer,
and Crawford counties, with their many lakes and swamps, flat
valleys, and odd-shaped hills, are legacies of the glaciers. The
pattern is repeated with variations in the Pocono region of northeastern Pennsylvania. Differences in rock formation and the rate
of erosion help to explain the narrow gorges and vertical waterfalls that distinguish this latter region.

So the struggle went on, the war of the elements—earthquake,
wind, and frost; the rise and fall of mountains; stream piracy;
glaciation—until in the goodness of time the land surface of
Pennsylvania was turned out, finished and exquisite, very much
as it is known and enjoyed today. Forests covered the remains of
once great mountains, and wild animals made homes in the long
valleys. Bear, deer, and in some places bison wore pathways over

the ridges. Men followed them, settling in the valleys of the three great rivers—the Allegheny, the Susquehanna, and the Delaware —which had conquered and made tributary most of the streams in Pennsylvania.

Man, the newcomer, took up the story and carried it on in much the same way. When the first white men settled in Pennsylvania, they found the Indians on the Susquehanna in process of conquering and making tributary the Indians on the Allegheny and the Delaware.

2 "We Came Out of this Ground"

Pennsylvania was far from a barren, trackless wilderness when the first white man arrived. The Indians, according to the latest estimates, had been cultivating the land for well over three thousand years. Their corn fields on the river bottoms and in places where (as modern forestry research discloses) prairie grasses formerly intruded were prizes much coveted by European settlers. Good Indian paths were the means by which explorers "discovered" the hinterland. The Indians of Pennsylvania did not have a civilization as advanced in the material sense as that of the Aztecs, Incas, Chinese, or Europeans, but it was sufficient to give them a good life, with dignity and freedom.

When the white men arrived in search of these same good things, the Indians explained their prior right to the soil with the words, "We came out of this ground." But in truth, man did not originate on this continent. The American Indian's ancestors came from Asia. Thirty or thirty-five thousand years ago Asiatic bands began to cross the Bering Strait to Alaska, whence their descendants drifted down to the tip of South America and across the mountains and plains to the Atlantic seaboard. They were savages, those early immigrants, like the people of Asia and Europe behind them. They brought with them only the rudiments of civilization: speech, a knowledge of fire, a few stone tools, and a social organization based on ties of kindred. Until comparatively recent times their development in the two Americas was roughly parallel to, but very little influenced by, that of Europe and Asia.

8

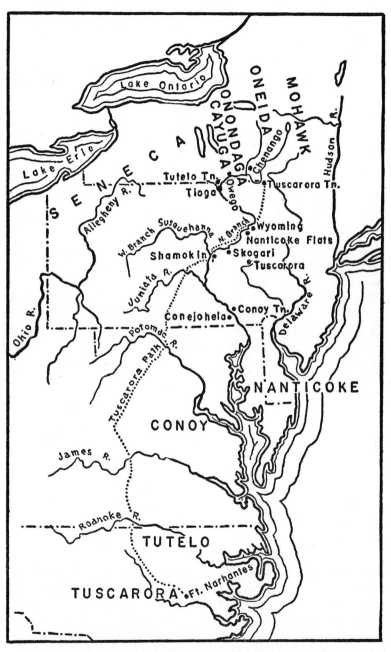

Movement of Refugee Peoples to the Iroquois Country

So it was that when the first white-skinned voyagers stepped ashore from their "winged canoes" on the Atlantic coast, they found a race of men a little behind them in material culture, a little ahead of them in social adjustments, and quite apart from them in some fundamental matters such as one's attitude to the land. The white man thought of land as a chattel, something to be bought and sold like butter and eggs. The Indian looked upon land as a common good, like air and water, as insusceptible to private barter as the mother who bore him.

When the white man arrived, there was more variety and greater division among the Indians in North America than among the peoples in Europe of that day. In Pennsylvania alone by 1600 there were at least three principal cultures—four, if the Eries are included—with further divisions of language and perhaps also of nationality within these cultures.

The first of Pennsylvania's Indians to receive any considerable attention from Europeans were the Susquehannocks. In 1608 Captain John Smith, leader of the Jamestown colony, met a party of sixty Susquehannock warriors near the mouth of the Susquehanna River. Smith, who was by nature an adventurer and also a raconteur, did not conceal his delight at what he saw.

"Such great and well proportioned men are seldom seen," he wrote, "for they seemed like Giants to the English . . . yet seemed of an honest and simple disposition, with much adoe restrained from adoring the discoverers [John Smith and his crew] as Gods."

The early Maryland historian George Alsop took Smith's description of these warriors to mean that the Susquehannocks were seven feet tall—a romantic error that the public has found too pleasing to let die. However, archaeologists who have examined Susquehannock skeletons say these people were no taller than other Indians.

These are the most strange people of all those Countries, both in language and attire [Captain Smith continued]; for their language it may well beseeme their proportions, sounding from them, as it were a great voice in a vault, or cave, as an Eccho. Their attire is the skinnes of Beares and Woolves; some have Cassacks made of Beares heades and skinnes that a mans necke goes through the skinnes neck, and the eares of the Beare fastned to his shoulders behind, the nose and teeth hanging downe his breast, and at the end of the nose hung a Beares Pawe: the halfe sleeves coming to the elbowes were the neckes of Beares and the armes through the mouth, with pawes hanging at their noses. . . . They can make neare 600 able and mighty men, and are pallisadoed in their Townes to defend them from the Massawomekes their mortall enimies.

The Susquehannocks were of Iroquoian stock, akin in language and many of their customs to the Indians of the Iroquois

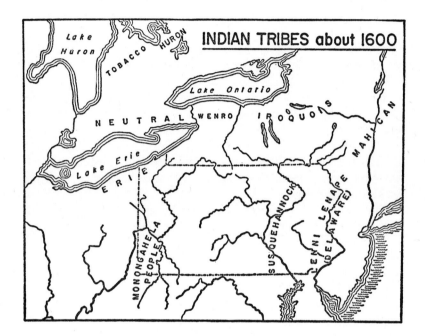

Confederacy as well as to the Eries and Hurons west and north of the latter and to the Tuscaroras and Cherokees in what are now North Carolina and Georgia. They lived in longhouses, eighty, a hundred, or more feet in length, with bunks lining the sides, partitions separating family from family, and a passageway down the middle. Dotting the passageway were stone hearths, one for each family. In every longhouse the Indians were of one lineage and lived under the authority of an elder matron.

The Susquehannocks' principal town in John Smith's day was on the east bank of the Susquehanna River, just south of Washington Boro, near Lancaster, Pennsylvania. They were comparative newcomers to the region, having migrated thirty years or so earlier from the North Branch of the Susquehanna in the vicinity of Tioga Point (Athens, Pennsylvania), where others of their people apparently remained for another generation or longer before following them south.

They were a proud, vigorous people, splendid warriors (as witness their long war with the Iroquois Confederacy), and astute traders. When Smith met them in 1608, he observed that they already had a few European goods, which very likely may have come from Canada, and they were soon to monopolize the fur trade over a large area, subjugating, dispersing, or annihilating all Indian competitors in Pennsylvania.

Out in western Pennsylvania during the opening years of the seventeenth century lived a mysterious people (mysterious because so little is known about them) whose very name has been lost. For convenience, archaeologists call them the Monongahela People, after the river on which the greatest concentration of their remains has been found. They also had considerable settlements on the upper Ohio, the Allegheny, the Beaver, and the Kiskiminetas rivers.

They were highly advanced, living by agriculture, with hunting, fishing, and berry-picking to spice the diet. Their villages were surrounded by palisades and often set on high, commanding positions. Their houses were round "beehive" structures, some twenty feet in diameter, covered with bark or mats. They were good craftsmen and lovers of the beautiful, as may be seen from the remains of their pottery, their carved pipe bowls, and their many small ornaments.

Their history can only be surmised. Some think they should be identified with the Massawomekes who, as Captain Smith said, were the mortal enemies of the Susquehannocks. Others think they may have been the ancestors of the Indians now known as the Shawnees. But one thing is certain. Some time during the middle years of the seventeenth century they disappeared from Pennsylvania. Whether they were destroyed by disease (perhaps an epidemic spawned by a ship's crew on the Atlantic coast), or were dispersed as a consequence of war with the Susquehannocks, the Iroquois, or with both, cannot be determined. After their disappearance, the upper Ohio River and its tributaries reverted to the wilderness. Not until the early eighteenth century, when Indian refugees swarmed in from eastern Pennsylvania and the south, did that country come back into settled occupation.

South of Lake Erie lived a people of Iroquoian stock, the Eries, after whom the lake was named. Scholars are not agreed on the sites of their villages nor on the extent of their hunting grounds, but the generally accepted view is that their territory extended along the southern shore of Lake Erie from Ohio into, and perhaps beyond, Pennsylvania's Erie triangle to near Buffalo, New York.

No white man visited their country until after their dispersion by the Iroquois in 1654-1655, but a good deal is known, through the *Jesuit Relations,* about their impact on neighboring peoples. In particular, the Jesuit missionaries tell us, although at second hand, about the war they waged with the Iroquois Confederacy to the east. It was said that the Eries had over two thousand warriors, which was more than the Iroquois could muster.

The Eries' chief defense in war was the poisoned arrow and the palisaded fort. The Iroquois who besieged them were equipped with guns, but this was not an overwhelming advantage, since apparently the Eries could discharge eight or ten arrows during the time it took an Iroquois warrior to reload his gun. When the Iroquois finally stormed and captured the principal Erie fort, they used canoes as shields under which to approach the walls, and then set them up as scaling ladders to swarm over.

It was with the Indians of eastern Pennsylvania that the colonial province had most contact. The banks of the Delaware and Schuylkill rivers, with their adjoining streams, were the home of the Lenni Lenape (the "Original People"), now referred to as the Delawares. They were extravagant lovers of liberty, virile but for the most part peaceable. They were, indeed, ill organized for war. They liked William Penn and gave him what he and his successors might not have found anywhere else on the Atlantic coast: seventy years of peaceful coexistence in which to conduct the Holy Experiment and lay solid foundations for Penn's dream of a democratic society.

The Delawares were of Algonkian linguistic stock, related to the Mahicans, Shawnees, Chippewas, Crees, and a great number of other Indian nations scattered throughout the United States and Canada between the Atlantic coast and the Rocky Mountains, most of whom honored the Delawares with the title "Grandfather."

The Delawares were not as fortunate as the Susquehannocks

in their literary introduction to the world. Not until William Penn arrived (seventy-four years after John Smith had entered the Susquehanna River and seventy-three after Henry Hudson had entered Delaware Bay) did the Delawares receive a good press. Earlier observers wrote about them with smug, ignorant fastidiousness and contempt. Johan Printz, the Swedish governor who gave the first detailed description of them, was not a man of imagination. In letters to Oxenstierna and Brahe, he wrote as an administrator with a sharp eye to profits from the fur trade and a fat hand on the sword. He was impressed by the Indians' physique (interesting praise from a giant of a man who weighed over four hundred pounds). "Tall, strong, well built," he called them. But he pronounced them also "cowardly and fearful." They had sufficient cause to be fearful, because the Susquehannocks of Printz's time were making ferocious raids on the Delawares to capture the important trading routes, such as the Great Minquas Path, between their own country on the Susquehanna and the European colony on the Delaware River.

Printz was well enough pleased with their wood carving and their skill in working "lead, copper and tin"; but he was shocked to discover that they colored themselves "terribly in the face" and that in summer they wore nothing but "a piece of cloth about one-half an ell wide around their middle."

"They let it be understood," he said with impatience, "that they are a free people, subject to no one, but do what they please."

If love of liberty was the distinguishing mark of Indians in general, an excess of that passion distinguished the Delawares. They had, as a people, little cohesion and almost nothing that could be called a central government. The effective unit of control among them was the local community. Large-scale undertakings, whether in peace or war, were in Penn's day almost unthinkable to them.

In the smaller concerns of daily living, on the other hand, the Delawares had attained a balance of freedom with social responsibility that is astonishing.

" 'Tis admirable," wrote Penn in 1683, "to consider, how Powerful the Kings [chiefs] are, and yet how they move by the Breath of their People." Penn observed them with surprisingly modern eyes, for he was himself experimenting with the problems of democratic government. "Their Government," he wrote, "is by Kings. . . . Every King hath his Council, and that consists of all the Old and Wise men of his Nation [i.e., community], which perhaps is two hundred People: nothing of Moment is undertaken, be it War, Peace, Selling of Land, or Traffick, without advising with them, and which is more, with the Young Men too."

Penn in his younger days had been an expert swordsman, and he responded eagerly to the sight of athletic people. "For their Persons," he wrote, "they are generally tall, streight, well-built, and of singular Proportion; they tread strong and clever [nimbly], and mostly walk with a lofty Chin."

Their language [he continued] is lofty, yet narrow, but, like the Hebrew; in Signification full, like Shorthand in writing; one word serveth in the place of three, and the rest are supplied by the Understanding of the Hearer. . . . And I must say, that I know not a Language spoken in Europe, that hath words of more sweetness or greatness, in Accent and Emphasis, than theirs; for instance, *Octorockon, Rancocas, Ozicton, Shakamaxon, Poquessin,* all of which are names of Places and have grandeur in them. . . . they do speak little, but fervently and with Elegancy. . . .

Their Houses are Mats or Barks of Trees set on Poles, in the fashion of an English Barn, but out of the power of the Winds, for they are hardly higher than a Man; they lie on Reeds or Grass.

Penn speaks of their "long houses." These were much like the Iroquois longhouses, except that the Delawares built theirs with peaked roofs instead of the low-arched roofs of the Iroquois.

"Their diet," he said, "is Maize, or Indian corn, divers ways prepared: sometimes roasted in the Ashes, sometimes beaten and boyled with Water, which they call Homines; they also make Cakes, not unpleasant to eat."

What impressed Penn most of all about these Delawares was their generosity—a virtue that was unhappily to bring about their most serious misunderstandings with white men. Instinctively they let the European share with them the use of the soil, expecting to receive friendly treatment in return. At first they took what the white man gave them in the land treaties (a few guns, iron kettles, woolen blankets, needles, novelties, and such things) not as payment but as expressions of friendship. They did not easily understand that the white man supposed himself to have gained by these treaties not merely an invitation to share the land's produce—"to eat out of the same bowl," as they said—but also the right, which he soon invoked, to keep it to himself and drive its former owners away. It was partly because William Penn understood and respected their attachment to the land that he got along so well with them.

In Liberality they excell [he went on], nothing is too good for a Friend; give them a fine Gun, Coat, or other thing, it may pass twenty hands, before it sticks; [they are] light of Heart, [with] strong Affections, but soon spent; the most merry Creatures that live, Feast and Dance perpetually; they never have much, nor want much; Wealth circulateth like the Blood, all parts partake; and though none shall want what another hath, yet [they are] exact Observers of Property. Some Kings have sold, others presented me with several parcels of Land; the Pay or Presents I made them, were not hoarded by the particular Owners, but the neighbouring Kings and their Clans being present when the Goods were brought out, the Parties chiefly concerned consulted, what and to whom they should give them? . . . Then that King sub-divideth it in like manner among his Dependents, they hardly leaving themselves an Equal share with one of their Subjects. . . . They care for little, because they want but little. . . . if they are ignorant of our Pleasures, they are also free from our Pains. They are not disquieted with Bills of Lading and Exchange, nor perplexed with Chancery Suits and Exchequer-Reckonings. We sweat and toil to live; their pleasure feeds them, I mean, their Hunting, Fishing, and Fowling, and this Table is spread every where; they eat twice a day, Morning and Evening; their seats and Table are the Ground.

Comparative religion was not a very reputable field of study in those days, and contemporary accounts of Indian religion suffered much from the lack of it. Men who worshiped God under any other names than those found in Scripture were denounced as devil-worshipers. Governor Printz, who was not himself a model of Christian piety, reported to his superiors that the Indians "know nothing of God but serve Satan with their Kintica and sacrifices to him," and he advised that they be exterminated.

Penn was more understanding. While regretting their ignorance of Christian theology, he recognized that the object of their highest worship—the Great Spirit, or the Creator, as they preferred to call Him—was none other than the Christian's God under a different name.

These poor people [he wrote] are under a dark night in things relating to religion . . . the tradition of it. Yet they believe [in] a God and immortality without the help of metaphysics. For they say there is a great King that made them . . . and that the souls of the good shall go thither where they shall live again.

In the Big House Ceremony of the Delawares, when the Celestial Bear came down to earth, the center post of the building represented the World Tree, denoting contact between heaven and earth. Of course variants of the symbol are found all over the world, as in the Cosmic Tree of India, the Iroquois Tree of Peace, and the Christian Cross.

To the Indian, everything in nature was sacred, possessed of a living soul—plants, animals, birds, waters, winds, the sun, the moon, even rocks and stones. Everything had its manito, or spirit power, and these powers were the realities. His sense of the sacredness of things did not, however, prevent him (as it does the Hindu) from taking life. He killed animals for food. But when hunting, he killed no more than sufficed to meet his need. He never killed for sport. When he found a cluster of medicinal plants in the forest, he did not dig them all up but left some to propagate their kind. It was his custom to leave the first plant alone, placing beside it a small gift of tobacco. In a word, he felt himself not in combat with nature but in harmony with it. To him, the universe was friendly. He could count on it, provided he did not abuse it. What to the white man seemed the Indian's improvidence was often simply a measure of this harmony.

The Delawares believed that above the earth there were twelve heavens (twelve was to them a sacred number), eleven of them presided over by demigods with functions assigned to them by the Great Spirit, the Creator, who dwelt in the twelfth and highest heaven. John Jacob Schmick, a Moravian missionary stationed at Wyalusing on the North Branch of the Susquehanna during the 1760's, listed these eleven delegated deities as the Sun, the Moon, Earth, Fire, Water, House, Corn, and the Four Quarters: East, West, North, and South. Among some groups a place was made for the two Thunders, who brought the rain and helped the crops.

Prayers to these manitos—prayers of intercession, or more frequently of thanksgiving—were expressed through dance, song, and the burning of ceremonial tobacco. Tobacco smoke, as it ascended, whether from a campfire where it had been sprinkled or from the bowl of the peace pipe, carried prayer to heaven.

If the word religion means a formal belief in certain written articles of Faith [wrote Conrad Weiser in 1746] . . . then we can truly say . . . the Indians . . . have no religion. . . . But if by the word religion we understand the knitting of the soul to God, and the intimate relation to, and hunger after the highest Being arising therefrom, then we must certainly allow this apparently barbarous people a religion.

In short, the Delawares and other Indians were not rootless, wandering savages and were certainly superior to the diseased white riffraff whom all too often the Indians had to endure on the frontier. It is true that they were technologically primitive, living in the Stone Age as far as tools were concerned; but they were for the most part intelligent and sensitive people, warm-hearted, and capable of deep attachments (such as they evinced for William Penn) and proud resentments (such as they directed against Penn's heirs after the Walking Purchase). They were patriotic, feeling toward their nation and the land of their fathers a passionate devotion. They did not talk much about this with strangers, but they did among themselves. They loved their country—not its flag nor a totem but (something that the white man is in danger of losing) the soil itself, the deep woods and the clear streams that marked the bounds of their hunting territories. William Penn understood this. He was shrewd enough to see also that there was a dark side to their love of country. If at any time they should find themselves excluded by sharp practice from their homeland, they would not easily forgive and would need only a little fanning by political agitators to be turned into vengeful and dangerous enemies.

Penn cautioned his people: "Don't abuse them, but let them have justice and you win them."

3 *Enter the European*

Heare is a grete differance beetwixte the Swede and the Dutch Bouthe of them striving for to bee Masters of the River.

—Thomas Doxey to John Winthrop, June 7, 1651

The arrival of the ship *Welcome,* bringing William Penn to New Castle, October 27, 1682, seemed nothing out of the ordinary to the Indians, who had been, beyond memory, in contact with white men. It was 184 years (nearly as long a span as now separates us from the Declaration of Independence) since John Cabot of Bristol on his second voyage had sailed down the North American coast to the thirty-eighth degree of latitude, "taking possession" of the land he sighted in the name of England's King Henry VII. It was 124 years since Verrazano had brought the *Dauphine* with its Norman crew past the entrance to Chesapeake Bay. Since that time, hundreds of small trading vessels had put in at various Atlantic coves to trade with the Indians; and for some fifty years the Dutch, Swedes, and Finns had been living among the Indians on the Delaware River.

What had started the movement of Europeans to America was the search for a short route to India. What kept it alive, after the first hope for quick fortunes from gold, jewels, and spices had failed, was the fur trade. It was Captain John Smith who, from what he learned on the Jamestown expedition, first made the truth plain to London merchants that America offered a return on their money, not as a short cut to India nor as a source of gold and jewels, but as an apparently inexhaustible source of furs. Following his advice, London sent out traders, with farmers to support them, and so made Jamestown the first successful English colony in the New World.

From that time on, furs were a staple of English commerce. It has been estimated that by 1620 there were close to a hundred traders bartering with the Indians on Chesapeake Bay alone. In 1632 it is said that William Claiborne at the head of the bay exported forty thousand gold crowns' worth of beaver skins at a thirty-fold profit. Up and down the North American coast little English colonies, whatever the motive of their origin,—religious or economic—found their lifeblood in the pelts of beaver, marten, otter, deer, bear, and whatever other animal commanded a price in the rapidly expanding European fur market. The wearing of fur garments, which had formerly been the exclusive prerogative of princes of the church and state, had now become so common that the word *beaver* was synonymous with *hat*.

The American Indians, quick to see the advantages of European cloth, metal tools, kettles, and firearms, and finding the exchange of furs the best means of acquiring them, put their main energies into hunting. When the local forest became exhausted, they traveled vast distances in search of game and turned the trails into endless assembly lines of peltries moving toward the sea.

England's trading and colonizing ventures during the better part of the seventeenth century were confined almost wholly to the coast. It was the Dutch, Swedes, and Finns who first exploited the hinterland of Pennsylvania. Dutch interest in the fur trade was stimulated by the report of Henry Hudson, an English sailor employed by the Dutch, who in 1609 brought his ship, the *Half Moon,* to the entrance of Delaware Bay, and also by the report of

Cornelius Hendricksen, who a few years later ascended what Henry Hudson had named the South River (Delaware), possibly as far as the site of Philadelphia, and traded with the Indians for beaver. In 1621 the Netherlands States-General founded the Dutch West India Company, and three years later the one-eyed Dutch captain Cornelius Jacobsen Mey built Fort Nassau on the Jersey side of the Delaware opposite the mouth of the Schuylkill River. Twelve years later, land was purchased for the West India Company on the Schuylkill River itself. There, in 1647, Fort Beversreede (Beaver Road) was erected at a point on the east bank from which it might command not only the river, an important canoe route, but also the Great Minquas Path, which here had one of its several termini. The Dutch thus captured the trade in beaver skins whichever way it came from the Susquehannock country—by land or water.

The site was well chosen, for the Minquas (as the Delawares named the Conestogas or Susquehannocks, *minqua* meaning "treacherous") had made themselves masters of the Indian trade in this part of North America. They would allow no rivals. In a series of raids they drove the Delawares across the river into New Jersey and made them tributary. By barter they acquired supplies of European guns, armor, and even cannon for the better defense of their palisaded fort on the banks of the Susquehanna. In time they came to dominate, both as hunters and as middlemen, the fur trade of Pennsylvania's three great waterways: the Delaware, Susquehanna, and Ohio-Allegheny. With their allies, the Hurons, the Eries, and the French in Canada, they were in a fair way to monopolize the fur trade not only of Pennsylvania but also of vast regions to the west. Only the Iroquois, the Five United Nations of the Mohawk Valley and Finger Lakes region, whose country was by 1640 almost completely denuded of beaver, stood against them.

Meanwhile, the Dutch had encountered a European rival on the Delaware. In 1624 the Swedes organized the South Company, and in 1638 began seriously to contest Dutch predominance on the South or Delaware River. In that year, under Peter Minuit, they entered the river and purchased land (which they named New Sweden) from both the Lenni Lenape and their overlords, the Susquehannocks. Here and there on the large tract thus acquired, which extended from Cape Henlopen to the head of navigation at Sankikans or the Falls (Trenton, New Jersey), they established small permanent settlements. To offset Dutch control of the Minquas Path, the Swedes built Fort Christina (Wilmington) in 1638 at the mouth of the Minquas Kihl (Christina Creek). This creek was the terminus of a path from the Susquehanna River to the Delaware which was somewhat shorter though less convenient than the Great Minquas Path.

In the contest for the beaver trade, Queen Christina of Sweden played an ace in 1642 when she sent Johan Printz to be governor of New Sweden. He was chosen for the post not only because of his military experience but more particularly because he knew Finland, which was then a part of the Swedish kingdom and from which many of New Sweden's settlers were beginning to come. Formerly it had been largely city folk, interested in trade, who had come to New Sweden, but by 1643 the policy had changed. That year farmers and artisans with their families were brought out, most of them Finns. Johan Printz, who had served in the Finnish cavalry and knew the Finnish language, had been sent into Finland to collect suitable young people, skilled workmen and agriculturists, and to head them as their governor in what was to be the real founding of the colony.

Printz is best remembered for the fort he built, called New Gothenburg, on Tinicum Island, which became the first colonial capital in what is now Pennsylvania. This was an excellent spot from which to control the Delawares, for at that time Tinicum Island extended farther into the river than the promontory of that name (it has ceased to be an island) does today. New Gothenburg virtually commanded the Dutch Fort Nassau, and the fact that Tinicum was an island made it safe from Indian attack.

But Printz's belligerence on behalf of New Sweden was more than met by the audacious Peter Stuyvesant of Dutch New Amsterdam. On a peninsula near the present New Castle, Delaware, Stuyvesant in 1651 built Fort Casimir, a formidable structure, 210 feet in length and mounted with twelve guns, a few of which were brought down from the outfaced Fort Nassau. In 1655, some time after the return of Governor Printz to Sweden, Stuyvesant took possession of the entire river.

A few years later fortune deserted him in his turn, but this time it was not the Swedes who were the gainers. With the surrender of New Amsterdam in 1664, Dutch possessions in the

New World passed into the hands of the English, who already claimed the continent by virtue of John Cabot's discoveries more than 160 years before. King Charles II of England presented the provinces of New York and New Jersey, with the lands to the west of them, to his brother James, Duke of York. The South River was renamed the Delaware in honor of Thomas West, Baron De La Warr, who in 1609 had been appointed governor and captain-general of Virginia. In 1673 the Dutch recovered their New World possessions for a few months, but in 1674 these were restored to the English, who retained them for another 102 years.

Among the records of this curious, three-cornered, hot-and-cold war, one document stands out for its importance in the subsequent history of Pennsylvania. This is the royal *Instruction* for Governor Printz, given him before he sailed for America in 1642. It was, as Dr. Amandus Johnson calls it, "the first constitution or supreme law of the states of Pennsylvania and Delaware." More than that, it laid good foundations for the experiment William Penn was soon to undertake on the same soil and among many of the same people.

Several items in the *Instruction* are of special interest. One is the promise of religious tolerance, which was to be the very foundation of Penn's Holy Experiment. Dutch settlers, who were members of the Dutch Reformed Church, were not required to conform to Swedish Lutheranism and were allowed to worship in their own way.

In the matter of Indian land rights, the *Instruction* was explicit and enlightened. It recognized that the original inhabitants had good title to their land. Swedish title was to be obtained only by honest purchase from the native owners.

A third item dealt with the general treatment of those who "came out of this ground." "The wild nations," so ran the *Instruction*, ". . . the Government shall know how to treat with all humanity and respect, that no violence or wrong be done to them by the people of [Her] Royal Majesty." Despite Printz's hot temper and his occasional wish that the Indians (who sometimes got on his nerves) might be liquidated, the Swedes—and the Dutch, too, in this particular area; Governor William Kieft's atrocities had spoiled their record in New York—left behind a tradition of mutual trust between white men and brown to

which some of the success of Penn's experiment must undoubtedly be attributed. The reflections of the Swedish engineer
Lindeström is evidence of that trust: "The savages are honorable
enough in their conversation with the Christians. . . . The one
who knows how to associate rightly with the savages [will find
that they] are a trustworthy and good-hearted folk, when they
are not angered, and even brave-hearted [enough] to risk death
for their good friends."

In fact, the Swedes and Finns, and to a lesser extent the Dutch,
who were interested mainly in the fur trade, left three valuable
legacies for William Penn. The first was a sturdy body of settlers,
who pleased Penn mightily when he saw them: "a plain strong
industrious people . . . they have fine children and almost every
house full. I see few young men more sober and industrious."
These were the people who formed the backbone of the colony,
and who provided what has since become the symbol of the
American frontier: the one-room log cabin "made according to
the Swedish mode," as the Dutch travelers Danckers and Sluyter
described it in 1679, "being nothing else than entire trees, split
through the middle or squared out of the rough, and placed in
the form of a square upon each other . . . the ends of these
timbers are let into each other, about a foot from the ends, half
of one into half of the other. The whole structure is thus made
without a nail or spike."

The second legacy, profoundly important for the security of
Penn's Quaker colony, was the tradition of friendly dealing between Indian and white man.

The third was the tradition of religious liberty, which has been
called "the corner-stone of our modern civilization."

4 The Beaver Wars

Seven years before William Penn set foot in America, the scene of his Holy Experiment came under the Iroquois aegis. Their confederacy, the Five Nations, defeated and dispersed the Susquehannocks in 1675 and established over their enemy's former empire their own "Great Law" or "Great Peace." Their word for it, *Kayenerenkhowa,* may be translated either way, for their language did not distinguish between "law" and "peace," the two concepts being, to their way of thinking, inseparable. The stability that Iroquois dominance gave to Indian affairs in Pennsylvania—though that stability was based on a principle alien to pacifism, namely, that law can be effective only if there is physical power behind it—was to be another contributing cause of Penn's success. With their doctrine of "Peace and Power" the Iroquois kept Penn's Woods virtually undisturbed for over seventy years (1681-1755) and gave the province time to grow to manhood.

James Fenimore Cooper, most of whose Indian verdicts were romantic absurdities, has nevertheless by his narrative skill largely determined the popular attitude to the Indian. He painted the Iroquois, in particular, as demons with an unslakable thirst for blood. It is true enough that, by the time the white man came to know them, the Iroquois were rightly feared by their enemies. Their superior cohesion as a people had brought them almost unparalleled military success. It is true also that they accepted the general Indian code with regard to scalp-taking and the torturing of prisoners. But it is not true that they were mere death-dealing monsters. In the field of government, they were the most creative Indians on the continent. Benjamin Franklin, in a letter to James

25

Parker of March 20, 1750, praised them for showing the way (by the example of their own union, which "has subsisted ages and appears indissoluble") to the union of the British colonies which he so much desired.

The strange thing (considering the stereotype of the Iroquois which is imprinted on the public mind) is that at heart they were a peace-loving people. The anthropologist Horatio Hale, who knew the Iroquois intimately, found in their society a gentleness that reminded him of nothing so much as the quietist sects of India. They produced statesmen of high vision, and their institutions embodied an idea that the Free World today likes to think of as distinctively modern: that of free societies deliberately organized for peace. Their religion was based on the theme of a Messiah who had come to earth to teach them how to organize such a peace—one that would stand up in the wilderness of this world—a peace with power behind it.

Of all the Indian legends none is more profoundly beautiful or more pertinent today than that of the founding of the Five United Nations, the Iroquois Confederacy (later known as the Six Nations after the Tuscaroras had come in). It tells how the Creator, Tarachiawagon, Holder of the Heavens, sent to earth Deganawidah (De-ka-nah-wi-deh), who brought to men the "Good Word of Peace and Power." He showed them how to organize an effective league of nations, giving security to an enlarging circle of peoples. As an Iroquois of historic times expressed it, "The land shall be beautiful, the river shall have no more waves, one may go everywhere without fear."

Deganawidah first converted to his vision a notorious murderer named Hiawatha (Longfellow got the name but nothing else from this Iroquois figure). The two together—Deganawidah with his high vision and Hiawatha with his eloquence—persuaded five warring nations strung out along the warpath that ran from the Hudson River to the Genesee (now the general route of New York State's Thruway) to "take hold" of his message of Peace and Power. On the shore of Onondaga Lake (at modern Syracuse, N.Y.), so the legend runs, Deganawidah put antlers, the symbols of authority, on the heads of forty-nine or fifty chiefs of the Mohawks, Onondagas, and Senecas (called the three Elder Brothers) and the Oneidas and Cayugas (called the Younger Brothers). He planted the Tree of Peace, a great white pine "which pierces the sky and reaches the sun," with branches (the law) wide enough to shelter all mankind. Being a realist, he placed on the topmost branch the Eagle That Sees Afar, symbol of watchfulness and military preparedness.

Beneath the embroidery of myth and folk tale, the legend has a foundation of truth. The essential fact was this: the drawing together of several independent peoples (probably through a long, intermediate process of local confederations) into a union known as *Kanonsionni,* that is, the Longhouse or Completed Cabin. In other words, the Five Nations lived together like related families in a longhouse, each with its own separate fire, but all bound by ties of kindred and a common loyalty.

It was a loose union, each nation preserving its sovereignty virtually intact; but the Great Council at Onondaga, where their common concerns were aired, served to give them a measure of unity, despite their many differences, which has lasted through wars and dispersion down to our own time. "The Six Nations," they say, "will never die."

What is important for the history of Pennsylvania in the legend of the founding of the Iroquois Confederacy is the effect it had on the minds of those who accepted it. Like the Christian *Bible,* it seized men's imagination and directed their conduct.

One of the best things in the legend is the Iroquois variant of the widespread Indian story of the Great Stone Face. It is said that Hiawatha's conversion was brought about by seeing a reflection in the water of Deganawidah's face. Supposing it to be a reflection of his own face, Hiawatha was struck by the possibilities of human nature—his own nature—disclosed in it. He threw away the meal of human flesh he was preparing and resolved thereafter to be more true to himself. When Deganawidah then appeared and explained the Good Word of Peace and Power, Hiawatha "took hold of the message" and became his disciple.

In the same way the Iroquois people took to heart the words of Deganawidah when they heard them repeated in the solemn ceremonies that accompanied the installation of chiefs—words such as these: "This is to be of strong mind, O chiefs: Carry no anger and hold no grudges. Think not forever of yourselves, nor of your own generation. Think of continuing generations of our families, think of our grandchildren and of those yet unborn, whose faces are still coming from beneath the ground."

They were moved especially by words which came at the

solemn climax of the legend: "I am Deganawidah, and with the Five Nations Confederate lords I plant the Tree of the Great Peace. . . . If any man or any nation outside of the Five Nations shall show a desire to obey the laws of the Great Peace . . . they shall be welcomed to take shelter beneath the Tree. . . ."

Those last words were never forgotten by the Iroquois people. The history of Pennsylvania is full of records of Indian refugees, dispossessed Shawnees, Tuscaroras, Conoys, Nanticokes, Delawares, Tuteloes, moving singly, in bands, or as national units, up the Susquehanna Valley to take shelter under the Iroquois Tree of Peace. If aliens were sometimes dragged in unwillingly and placed a little roughly under the Tree, one need only recall the Christian Crusades to understand. The Iroquois desire to make the Great Peace prevail was one of the dominating facts of early American history.

Many have wondered how the Iroquois managed so long to preserve their land and institutions intact amidst hostile populations many times their size. Some attribute their success to the driving force of economic necessity after their beaver supply had been exhausted. Others think it was owing to their advantageous military position among the hills of upstate New York. Still others give the credit to their superior political organization and their wise diplomacy, which enabled them to hold the balance of power between England and France in America. Yet one explanation is too often forgotten. They had a strong sense of mission, a belief in their destiny, which held them together and nerved them to action.

With them, as with the ancient Romans, virtue (*virtus*) meant valor in the service of their country. "High honor and love of country that made nothing of torture and death," writes Edith Hamilton in *The Roman Way*, "was what the Romans set first as the greatest thing of all." So it was with the Iroquois. Their noble legend of Deganawidah and Hiawatha embodied for them an ideal of organized and universal human brotherhood which they believed attainable. They believed also that it was their responsibility to bring this brotherhood about, no matter what hardships the effort might cost. It was, of course, too vast an ideal for their time—with the aggressive white man about to step ashore with his rum and firearms and hideous diseases. They fell far short of achieving it, but the striving for it held them together.

The *Jesuit Relations* for 1660 states that their "ambition" was so lofty that "they think and say that their own destruction cannot occur without bringing in its train the downfall of the whole earth." For those who are heirs of a continent-spanning "manifest destiny," that spirit is not difficult to understand.

It was the Susquehannocks who brought the Five Nations into Pennsylvania history. The coming of the Europeans with their guns and iron kettles and steel traps made every Indian nation's standard of living, and even survival, seem to depend on possession of the white man's weapons and tools. The only commodity the Indian could use to exchange for these things was peltry, for the white traders would take nothing else. The Iroquois, in their haste to get what they needed, soon hunted out their own territory. By 1640 there was scarcely a beaver to be found between the Hudson and the Genesee. They turned, accordingly, to their Indian neighbors, asking for hunting privileges on their lands or passage through them to better hunting grounds. Failing in this, they sought to become middlemen—to buy furs from the far nations and transport them to their own fur market at Albany. They made this last proposal earnestly to the Hurons, a great trading nation to the north, who were at first inclined to share the trade with them. But the French in Canada, who wished to preserve their monopoly of northern furs, found means to prevent the Hurons from granting the Iroquois such accommodation. In desperation the Iroquois took to piracy, waylaying Huron fur fleets on their way to Montreal, very much as British privateers were doing with treasure-laden galleons on the Spanish Main.

The French and Hurons countered by tightening their Indian alliances, in particular with the Susquehannocks to the south. The Neutrals, the Tobacco Nation, and the Eries prevented the Iroquois from reaching the vast hunting grounds to the west, while the Mahicans on the Hudson closed the door to them in the east. The Iroquois had to break out of this hostile circle or perish.

The Beaver Wars started the year after the Treaty of Westphalia (1648) ended the Thirty Years' War in Europe, and they lasted nearly as long as the European war. In 1649, less by massacre than by dispersion, the Iroquois destroyed the Hurons, whose populous towns lay south of the Georgian Bay in Canada.

Later in the same year they destroyed the Tobacco Nation, west of the Hurons; next year, the Neutrals, who adjoined the Senecas ("Keepers of the Western Door of the Long house"); and in 1654-1655, the Eries, who were south of Lake Erie. The Mahicans, who lived on the Hudson River east of the Mohawks ("Keepers of the Eastern Door") were wary and tough and took longer to dispose of; but they, too, were decisively defeated in a battle at Hoffman's Ferry in 1669. Peace was made with them in 1673.

The Susquehannocks were another matter. When the Iroquois, after the defeat of the Eries, sent hunting parties west into the Ohio country, the Susquehannocks waylaid them and stole their furs. The Iroquois countered by sending out whole armies—as many as six hundred warriors at a time—to conduct these hunters home. The war dragged on for years. The Susquehannocks, living in populous, well-fortified towns, seemed unconquerable. Their great fort on the lower Susquehanna was equipped with bastions and mounted artillery. The colony in Maryland, anxious to preserve trade with them, supplied them with the guns and powder they needed. In 1663 the Susquehannocks turned back a Seneca attacking force of eight hundred men.

But out of this long war, as out of all the others, the Iroquois in the end wrested victory. There are no adequate records on how the end came. Perhaps the Susquehannocks had been unduly weakened by war and disease. It is known that they had been deserted by Maryland, their former ally, who in 1674 declared war on them, though it is not known if she took aggressive action against them. There is a tradition that the Iroquois in 1675 stormed, captured, and burned the great Susquehannock fort.

"Since these Barbarians [the Iroquois] have at last succeeded in Exterminating the Andastoguetz, who have held out against them for over 20 years," ran a Jesuit report from Onondaga, the Iroquois capital, in 1676, "they have become so insolent that they talk only of breaking the missionaries' heads."

The Susquehannocks were not "exterminated." They were broken up and dispersed. "The Andastes," wrote Perrot in his *Mémoire*, "were entirely ruined, and the few who remained surrendered themselves by private agreement. They were received among the Tsonontouans, where they are at the present time." Actually they mingled with, and were absorbed by, various Indian nations. A few were permitted to settle in their old haunts on the lower Susquehanna, especially at the Indian town of Conestoga near Lancaster. But as a military power the Susquehannocks had ceased to exist.

Among the highly interesting consequences of this conquest is the fact that the destruction of the Susquehannocks left the Susquehanna Valley open to infiltration by white settlers. The Iroquois tried to save it, however, as Indian country, without incurring the danger of actual war with their English allies, by bringing in a stream of Indian refugees from Maryland, Virginia, and North Carolina.

The conquest also brought the Delawares, who had formerly been tributary to the Susquehannocks, into the Iroquois orbit as "women." How this picturesque (but to the white man's ears insulting) title came to be applied to the by-no-means effeminate Delawares, and what exactly the title meant, is a matter of scholarly debate. The Delawares themselves in the eighteenth century were unsure. Some resented the title, believing it to be an expression of Iroquois contempt for a tributary people. Others took *woman* to mean "peacemaker," suggesting the role they were expected to (and sometimes did) play in international affairs. Today many Delawares living on what is known as the Delaware Line in the Six Nations Reserve in Ontario accept the title as one of honor, denoting a stage of adoption in the Iroquois commonwealth like Dominion Status in the old British Empire.

The Iroquois had several words from which to choose in speaking of woman. The one they applied, and still apply, to Delawares is an old-fashioned term of great dignity, like our words *matron, dame* (as in Dames of the British Empire), or even *queen*. The Iroquois woman held a higher position among her people than the white woman did among hers. Descent among the Iroquois was reckoned in the female line. Blood money (payment to avoid a blood feud following a murder) for a woman was double that for a man. Women appointed the *royaners*, or civil chiefs, and had the right of recall. But white men in the woods mocked at Indian warriors who allowed themselves to be called "women," until the Delawares themselves learned to despise the word. Such, at least, is the explanation some historians give of the changing connotation of the word *woman* in Indian ears and the international disturbances that ensued.

A third, and perhaps the most important, result of the Iroquois conquest of the Susquehannocks was the fact that it placed a responsible power, the Iroquois Confederacy, in control of Penn's Woods. The government of Pennsylvania in the early eighteenth century wisely recognized Iroquois authority over the Indians within her bounds and left it to the followers of Deganawidah and Hiawatha (in default of any military power granted by the Quakers) to preserve order in the forest. This, Pennsylvania's famous Indian policy, was to be one of her main contributions to the development of the American nation.

5 William Penn

. . . know that after many waitings, watchings, solicitings and disputes in council, this day my country was confirmed to me under the great seal of England, with large powers and privileges, by the name of *Pennsilvania,* a name the king would give it in honour of my father. I chose *New Wales,* being as this, a pretty hilly country, but *Penn* being Welsh for a *head,* as *Penmanmoire* in Wales, and *Penrith* in Cumberland, and *Penn* in Buckinghamshire, the highest land in England, called this *Pennsilvania,* which is the high or head woodlands. . . . 'Tis a clear and just thing, and my God that has given it me through many difficultys, will, I believe, bless and make it the seed of a nation. I shall have a tender care to the government, that it will be well laid at first: no more now, but dear love in the truth.

Thy true friend,

W. PENN

"I do judge William Penn as fit a man as any in Europe to plant a country," wrote James Claypoole. Looking back now from a distance of nearly three hundred years, one is compelled to give William Penn top ranking among the founders of Utopian societies. There have been many such projected, but few have survived. Some failed because they were not grounded in human nature; others, because the founder was too inexperienced in government to get the experiment beyond the initial stages. Even Plato, whose *Republic* ranks as the greatest contribution ever made to the literature of Utopia, was a failure when he tried to put his theories into effect at Syracuse.

William Penn, on the other hand, made a practical success of his brain child, Pennsylvania. For one thing, the time was propitious: political experimentation was in the air. For another, Penn himself possessed what was needed for a political entrepreneur. He had money, friends, and principles. He had already, at the age of thirty-six when he received his charter, wide and intimate experience with politics and the law. To the knowledge thus acquired he brought a clear head, a gift for language, the instincts of a gentleman, and sound judgment. *"Knowledge,"* he wrote, "is the *Treasure,* but *Judgment* the *Treasurer* of a Wise Man."

Penn was well prepared, both by family inheritance and by environment, for the role he was to play in Pennsylvania. He was born in London, October 14, 1644, the year of Parliament's great victory at Marston Moor during the Civil War. He was five years old when the office of king was abolished and England became for a time a republic.

His father was a young naval officer, Captain William Penn (soon to be promoted by Cromwell to the position of Rear Admiral of the Irish Seas), who is said to have had Welsh as well as English blood in his veins. His mother was Margaret Vanderschuren Penn, nee Jasper, of Irish and Dutch extraction. William was, in a word, a product of the British melting pot.

During the English Civil War and its aftermath, the navy was in the very eye of the political storm. Admiral Penn was suspected (probably with justice) of correspondence with the exiled Stuarts and found himself for a time in the Tower of London, an edifice later to be graced with the presence of his son. When the admiral was released, he returned to the fleet, where his exploits soon made him a popular hero. In pursuit of Prince Rupert, he swept the Mediterranean as far east as Tunis Bay and Malta, and he defeated the Dutch at sea. It is thought that in 1654 he secretly offered his fleet to the exiled pretender, Charles Stuart, but nothing came of it. In the same year he accepted from Cromwell naval command of the West Indies expedition which captured Jamaica. In 1661, when the monarchy was restored, one of King Charles II's first acts on board the ship that brought him to England was to bestow a knighthood on Admiral Penn.

When Charles, some years later, presented William Penn with over twenty-eight million acres across the sea, thus making him the largest landholder, next to the Crown, in the British Empire, it need not be supposed that this was, as announced, merely in discharge of a financial debt of sixteen thousand pounds to his father. It was more likely in return for other loyal services performed by the Penn family for the unlucky Stuarts.

In 1660, the year of the Restoration, young Penn entered Oxford, as other great liberals—John Wycliffe, John Hampden, John Locke—had done before him. Oxford was royalist in its sympathies and politically conservative—"the home of lost causes." Yet it was, as it has always been, a stimulating environment for a young, inquiring mind. "Truth," wrote William Penn afterwards, "never lost Ground by Enquiry."

At Oxford Penn read, among other things, the works of Hugo Grotius, author of *Mare Liberum* ("Freedom of the Seas") and *De Jure Belli ac Pacis* ("The Laws of War and Peace"). Grotius, whom Catherine Owens Peare in *William Penn* calls "the founder of modern international law" and the man who "conceived the idea of an international morality," subjected the current system of dynastic wars to a withering analysis.

William Penn had an eager mind, and he liked to think for himself, as his college reading encouraged him to do. But this soon brought him into conflict with social convention and Oxford discipline. He turned nonconformist, refused to wear the surplice which Oxford required of her students, absented himself from compulsory chapel, and wrote about freedom of conscience. Oxford expelled him.

His father, hoping to save his son for a court career, sent him off on a gentleman's tour of Europe in company with Robert Spencer, the future Earl of Sunderland.

To the impressionable Oxford expellee the European tour was a dazzling and somewhat bewildering experience. It drew out the contradictory impulses of his many-sided character. For one thing, in the great world of fashion in which he now moved delightedly he picked up the manner and speech of the conventional English gentleman abroad; and when later, as a foppish "returned traveller," he ran into an old family friend, Samuel Pepys, the latter confided to his candid diary disgust at "the vanity of the French garbe" Penn had adopted and his "affected manner of speech and gait." At the same time Penn had suffered inward changes of quite a different kind. He brought back from France a bent of mind that was to determine the course of his later work in America.

Penn had moved into Huguenot circles and come under the influence of Moses Amyraut of Saumur. Amyraut believed that the light of God shone in every man's heart to guide him. Penn's reflective mind saw that, if this doctrine were accepted, certain political consequences would have to follow. Since the light of God shone spontaneously or not at all, it followed that liberty of conscience must be a first consideration in any well-ordered state. On that principle William Penn founded democracy in Pennsylvania.

But America was for the time being the last thing in his thoughts. On his return from the European tour he busied himself in preparation for the career in English politics that seemed to lie ahead of him. His father entered him at Lincoln's Inn for the legal training thought necessary for success in the world of high politics. When William left college for a few weeks in order to see active service aboard his father's ship the *Royal Charles* during the war with Holland, Admiral Penn took the opportunity of sending him with a personal message to the King, thus preparing the boy to tap the fount of English patronage.

A year or so later William had a taste of another kind of adventure. He served as a soldier in Ireland under the Earl of Arran and helped to suppress mutiny in the garrison at Carrickfergus. He won such high praise from the military that for a time he thought of making a career in the army.

But it was not to be. In Ireland, where his father had estates, he met some members of the Society of Friends and, going with them to a Quaker meeting at Cork, heard Thomas Loe speak. He had heard him before, at the age of twelve or thirteen, in his father's house at Macroom, where Loe had been invited to hold a Quaker meeting. Now, ten years later, a more mature Penn— already deeply influenced by Moses Amyraut—heard the message of the Inner Light again. This time it overwhelmed him. Suddenly the conflicting elements in his character slipped into place behind a driving resolution. He had become a man with a purpose.

For some time past he had observed, with a distaste slowly growing into revulsion, the persecution of nonconformists of all sorts, but particularly of Quakers. There had been the so-called Quaker Act, which made it a criminal offense for more than five Quakers to assemble "under pretence of worship." There had also been the Act of Uniformity, which made it mandatory for all clergymen conducting services to follow the English Prayer Book. And there had been the Five-Mile Act, which forbade nonconformist ministers to come within five miles of a corporate town. The feeling of peace that warmed Penn when he was among Quakers now became blended with a more militant mood. He would *fight* for the protection of Quakers, and he began his campaign by publicly joining them.

The strengthening of Quaker ranks by so well-connected a recruit did not go unnoticed among the apostles of uniformity. They welcomed religious heresy as a prime weapon to use in political infighting. When in 1668 Penn published a religious tract in which he subjected certain items of current theology— in particular, a narrow interpretation of the Trinity—to objective analysis, he was arrested and clapped into the Tower of London, where many of the best brains of England had spent their last days.

His confinement there was rigorous and brutal, even for that time; but, when the Bishop of London offered him the alternatives of recantation or imprisonment for life, Penn, a superb fighter, replied tersely, "My prison shall be my grave before I will budge a jot."

Prison confirmed his Quaker "convincement" and hardened his resolution. It did him good in other ways unsuspected by the authorities. It gave him a period of quiet contemplation, cut off from family and friends, during which his mind grew clear and he saw exactly what it was he believed in and what he must do about it. For the younger Penn, as for his father the admiral, the moment of danger was the moment of decision.

He was released from the Tower after pleading his own case, without recantation, in a pamphlet entitled *Innocency with Her Open Face* which somehow reached the King. Returning to Ireland, he visited Quaker friends there in prison and made it his business to free them. It took months of political campaigning to do this—campaigning into which he flung every skill he possessed and used every advantage his high connections opened to him. In the end the Quakers were released. This success further strengthened his resolve and determined the whole course of his life, which was henceforth devoted to giving other men freedom.

The largeness of Penn's mind is seen in the fact that in freeing the Quakers he acted on principles broad enough to free all men. Unlike the early New England Puritans, who demanded freedom for themselves but denied it to others, Penn and the Quakers asked for themselves only what they were prepared to give to all men. Penn put this philosophy into memorable words: "We must give the liberties we ask."

In pursuit of freedom for the Quakers, he became involved in a legal struggle that resulted in one of the English-speaking world's most important victories for civil rights. Arrested in May, 1670, for speaking to a group of London Quakers who had assembled in Gracechurch Street (the Friends Meeting House having been closed by the authorities), he pleaded his case so ably and dramatically that the jury, in defiance of explicit instructions from the bench, brought in a verdict of "not guilty." The magistrate, in a fury, imprisoned and fined the jurymen for contempt of court; but so vigorously did Penn push their defense that the case became a *cause célèbre* and in the end went to the highest court, where it brought a pronouncement from the Lord Chief Justice that a jury may not be punished for its verdict.

If he had done nothing else, William Penn would be remembered today as one of the great architects of freedom. But that was, of course, only the beginning. He advanced from the mere redressing of individual grievances to the creation of a whole society in which freedom should be mandatory.

His mind turned to America. "What so truly sutes with honour and honesty," Captain John Smith had written, "as the discovering things unknowne, erecting Townes, peopling Countries, informing the ignorant, reforming things unjust, teaching vertue."

In 1675 a property dispute in the New World opened the way to Quaker adventures in the field of "honour and honesty." Edward Billings, one of the Friends, having acquired the greater part of what is now New Jersey, appointed three trustees to administer it: William Penn, Gawen Lawrie, and Nicholas Lucas. The *Concessions and Agreements,* which was issued as a constitution for this New Jersey colony, anticipated in part the Frame of Government with which Penn later launched his Pennsylvania experiment. In the Concessions the colonists were promised trial by jury, religious liberty, and democratic government, "for," said the document, "we put the power in the people."

In its treatment of the Indians, too, the New Jersey colony anticipated Pennsylvania. Native rights were recognized. Land was to be bought and paid for before white men were allowed to occupy it, and there was to be no discrimination against Indians in daily intercourse or in the courts of law. If an Indian got into trouble with the white man's law, he was to be tried by a jury of his peers: six Indians and six white men.

Pennsylvania was conceived in 1680 when William Penn petitioned the Privy Council for a grant of land in the New World. The colony was born on March 4, 1681, when the charter was signed.

Penn's purpose in seeking the grant is plain enough. He wanted a haven for the persecuted Quakers. More than that, he wanted a sizable slice of the globe in which to experiment with his theories of government. He wanted a new country, free from European traditions and free from political involvements, where a man could make a fresh start and where he, William Penn, could test out the theories of government with which his mind had been playing ever since encountering Moses Amyraut and Thomas Loe. The Flood had cut off Noah from hereditary entanglements. Why should not the Atlantic Ocean cut off this New World from the prejudices of the Old? Here, guided by the Inner Light, he could experiment with government of the people *by* the people, and find out whether or not it was good *for* the people.

The King's motive in making this extraordinary grant of over twenty-eight million acres to a member of the Whig party—in the face, too, of many court claimants for such plums—is less easy to account for. No doubt one motive, as has been noted, was to discharge a larger debt to the Penn family than the world knew about. No doubt, too, Charles II had other political considerations on his mind, for he was an astute monarch. The King pleased his regular supporters by opening a door for large numbers of the hated Whigs to leave the country. It has been suggested that by this action he may also have saved William Penn's life. Penn had unscrupulous enemies in the now ascendant court party who heartily wished to be rid of him.

Whatever the reason, the grant was made. The King signed the charter March 4, 1681. It was confirmed March 5, and on April 2 William Penn, at the age of thirty-six, found himself proclaimed proprietor and governor of the province of Pennsylvania "to enlarge our English Empire."

Penn explained his own object in other words. It was to "settle a government" by means of which an example might be "set up to the nations." He added, "There may be room there, though not here, for *such an holy experiment.*"

The greatest fault of the charter was its careless definition of Pennsylvania's boundaries. After noting that the new province was to be bounded on the east by the Delaware River, the charter took a leap into the unknown with a simple-seeming passage that for a hundred years was to bathe Pennsylvania's borders in bloodshed: "The said land to extend westward five degrees in longitude, to be computed from the said eastern bounds; and the said lands to be bounded on the north by the beginning of the three and fortieth degree of northern latitude, and on the south, by a circle, drawn at twelve miles distance from New Castle, northward and westward, unto the beginning of the fortieth degree of northern latitude; and then by a straight line westward to the limits of longitude above mentioned [five degrees]."

It was intended that the southern bounds should be about the fortieth degree of latitude. It was not known at the time that the fortieth did not touch the twelve-mile arc above New Castle at all, but in fact lay north of the site of Philadelphia. The complications these geographical howlers were to occasion with Maryland on the south and Virginia on the west were equalled and surpassed by the entanglements that ensued with Connecticut on the north. In time the Quaker colony found itself virtually at war with these neighbors, all three of whom put Quaker pacifism to a disturbing test.

Pennsylvania was given its name by royal fiat and quite contrary to the wishes of William Penn. It had been King Charles' intention from the start to name the new property Penn after his old friend, the admiral. William objected to this on the plain Quaker grounds that such a public use of the family name savored of vanity. He proposed, instead, to call his province New Wales. That name being rejected, Penn suggested a poetic alternative, Sylvania. This the King promptly accepted, but added the prefix *Penn* and declared the matter closed. When William objected to the prefix, Charles, his sovereign, refused to budge a jot. ". . . nor could twenty guineas move the under secretarys to vary the name," wrote Penn to Robert Turner in Ireland, March 5, 1681. He subsequently excused the vain prefix on the ground that after all *pen* was Welsh for "head," so that *Pennsylvania* really meant not "Penn's Woods" but "the High Woodland."

In August, 1682, William Penn went aboard the three-hundred-ton, three-masted ship *Welcome*. From it he sent ashore a final letter dated August 30: "An Epistle Containing a Salutation to All Faithful Friends; A Reproof to the Unfaithful; and a Visitation to the Enquiring, in a Solemn Farewell to Them in the Land of My Nativity." A day or two later (the precise date is uncertain) the *Welcome* set sail with its company of "adventurers and purchasers" for a land which lay, in Penn's happy words, "six hundred miles nearer the sun."

6 *The Holy Experiment*

Because no people can be truly happy tho' under the greatest Enjoyment of civil Liberties, if abridged of the Freedom of their Consciences . . . I do hereby grant and declare, That no Persons . . . who
shall confess and acknowledge One Almighty God, the Creator, Up-
holder and Ruler of the World . . . shall be in any Case molested or
prejudiced, in his or their Person or Estate, because of his or their
consciencious Perswasion or Practice."

— *The Charter of Privileges,* October 28, 1701

It was late October (the 24th or 27th, the exact date being uncertain) when William Penn landed at New Castle, where he was
greeted by his deputy governor, William Markham, and the surveyor general, Thomas Holme. That same day he proceeded to
Upland, which he renamed Chester.

Penn's presence in Pennsylvania was limited to two short
visits. The first was from October, 1682, to August, 1684; the
second, from December, 1699, to February, 1701. He spent
there, all told, about three years. On his first visit, he set the Holy
Experiment in operation under a boldly liberal constitution or
Frame of Government. He returned hurriedly to England in
order to settle the boundary dispute with Maryland and so save
Philadelphia (which Thomas Cresap of that colony called "one
of the Prettyest Towns in Maryland") for Pennsylvania and with
it the economic base of his province. On his second visit, he un-
limbered the Frame from some of its obstructions and signed the
Charter of Privileges. He left again in haste, this time to defend
his proprietorship and the Holy Experiment against a movement
in Parliament to take Pennsylvania away from him and make it
a Crown colony, as had happened once before (1692-1694)
much to the Crown's loss.

Within two or three days of his first landing at New Castle, Penn sailed up the Delaware River to see how well his surveyor general had followed instructions about choosing a site for the capital city. It must be, he said, on the Delaware (that "brave pleasant River," as a contemporary, Thomas Paskell, called it), which Penn knew would always be Pennsylvania's main artery of trade with the rest of the world. With this in view, before leaving England, he had acquired from the Duke of York leases for what were to be the Lower Counties (approximately the modern state of Delaware) in order to secure for his ships the facilities of Delaware Bay and the lower river.

On a sandy beach at the mouth of Dock Creek, near the Blue Anchor Tavern, Penn went ashore to look over the site. The name Philadelphia had been chosen, though not coined, by Penn. This word, which means literally "brotherly love," was already a familiar one in pious circles, where it had come to mean "the communion of God in the spirit," that is to say, the spiritual union of all Christians, whatever their church affiliations or social rank. The word expressed perfectly Penn's hopes for Pennsylvania. The province was to be not just an escape hatch for persecuted Quakers but a place of religious freedom for everyone.

Philadelphia was virtually an alternate name for the Holy Experiment itself and meant nothing less than a Christian democracy in which all men might share. But it meant something else as well. The word had acquired, before Penn selected it, a more particular meaning in face of the widespread persecution of the Quakers. *Philadelphia* meant *"a place of refuge";* and soon to thousands of early immigrants—not only the Quakers but also the German plain sects, the Huguenots, the Scotch-Irish, and others—Philadelphia was the gateway to freedom.

The plan of the city, if not its name, came directly from the head of William Penn. His colony needed a center, for commerce as well as for government, and he proceeded to set up the best one he could devise. His land commissioners were instructed to select a "high, dry and healthy" place on the Delaware River where it was "most navigable." To make sure that there should be in it none of the narrow, crooked, smelly streets and crowded dwellings that had offended him in old-world towns, he gave orders that the streets should be laid out straight, that they should run down to the river, and that every house should be set in a good-sized plot of ground so that the whole community might have the air, as he said with prophetic good taste, of "a green country town."

The site chosen by Holme and approved by Penn when he first saw it that day in late October seemed to possess everything the founder desired. There was a small harbor suitable for schooners and a sandy beach where canoes could run ashore. Above the beach, bluffs rose steeply to high, dry, fertile fields that promised much for the future city's prosperity and health.

The Indians knew the place as Coaquannock. Many trails converged here. Close by was the junction of the Schuylkill River with the Delaware: two great canoe routes from west and north. Indian place names dotted the area: Shackamaxon, Consho-hocken, Kittabakonk, Wicaco, Manayunk. There were only ten houses in Philadelphia when Penn first saw it. Later, for a time, it would serve as the commercial and intellectual center of the Atlantic colonies. Dr. William E. Lingelbach writes: "Although the city may not have been officially declared the capital of the country, it was the seat of government during most of the Revolution and the decade from 1790 to 1800, and the real metropolis of the nation till the second decade of the nineteenth century."

To estimate William Penn's achievement, it is necessary to understand his original intent. Pennsylvania was by no means a timid creation. It represented a vast design to free the human spirit, to unleash human nature with all its faults and extrava-gances (which Penn knew better than most men), and to see if, in the end, the cause of justice might not be better served that way than under the repressions of an autocracy, no matter how enlightened.

If the Holy Experiment is considered in terms of the First Frame of Government, it cannot be called a failure. It was a bold move toward democracy and, whatever deficiencies it may have had, at least it prepared the way for the Charter of Privileges, which was undoubtedly one of humanity's longest steps forward.

It is a mistake to suppose that the Holy Experiment was simply an experiment in pious living and that the objective of Penn's various frames of government was to achieve a political atmos-phere as quiet as a Quaker First Day meeting. If the dissemination of small pieties was his main intent, and if the sanctification of all Pennsylvania politicians, then and now, is to be the criterion of his success, then the author of *No Cross, No Crown* will have to be adjudged a loser. During his lifetime the noise of faction—the quarrel, for instance, between the followers of James Logan and those of David Lloyd—much oppressed him. "I am a man of sorrows," he wrote to the Council, "and you augment my griefs, not because you don't love me, but because you don't love one another."

But Penn was not beaten. He was not a timid soul living in perpetual fear lest he make a mistake. "A man like a Watch is to be valued for his *Goings,*" he wrote in *Some Fruits of Solitude* (one of the best books in the world), which he composed while in hiding from political enemies who wanted him dead. He was neither a fanatic nor a sentimentalist. He knew the world from top to bottom—knew it too well to expect to reform it overnight. He believed that a free society, one in which liberty of mind and body was within the reach of all, provided essential conditions for man's best development and happiness. The opportunities which Americans enjoy today are a measure of his success.

He called his government an "experiment" because he had set himself to find out whether the Inner Light in man was strong enough to light his intellectual as well as his moral pathway.

He called it "holy" because, as he wrote in the preface to the First Frame, "Government seems to me to be a part of religion itself, a thing sacred in its institutions and end."

That he looked on the Holy Experiment as essentially an experiment in democracy is seen from his letter of April 8, 1681, addressed to the inhabitants of Pennsylvania, most of whom at that time were Swedes, Finns, and Dutch. It was written to relieve their natural anxieties at the change of government. He did so by touching on the main object of the experiment:

"I hope you will not be troubled with your change. . . . You shall be governed by laws of your own making, and live a free and, if you will, a sober and industrious people."

Freedom, it will be noticed, was promised unconditionally: "You shall be governed by laws of your own making." As it turned out, the very success of the Holy Experiment, insofar as it meant the setting up of a workable democracy, came at the expense of certain of the lesser virtues. Meekness and sobriety (among some people, at least) are more easily cultivated under a dictatorship. In a democracy, where all men share the pains as well as the privileges of government, there is inevitably a kind of bloodless warfare. In national debate tempers are lost, actions become irrational, and the ideal best is lost in necessary compromise.

It was because Penn achieved so large a measure of democracy in the government of Pennsylvania that the political uproar became so loud. He himself was subjected to ungentle attack, to which he was tempted (sometimes beyond his power of resistance) to reply in kind. But the clamor of controversy did not mean that the Holy Experiment had failed. It meant rather that its success had brought out into the dust and sweat some of the least cloistered but most manly virtues.

In his preface to the First Frame he explained what he meant by free government: "any government is free to the people under it . . . where the laws rule and the people are a party to those laws."

In the same preface, he quoted Scripture: "Let every soul be subject to the higher powers, for there is no power but of God. The powers that be are ordained of God."

For this last he has been violently attacked as presenting what C. E. Vulliamy calls a "purely traditional concept of authority" and as accepting "the divine right of government." It is true that Penn believed government to be necessary for the survival of any society. He believed, in fact, that government *in principle* was part of God's will for man. However, it was in this sense only that he believed in the divine right of government. He did not believe in the divine right of any particular man or body of men to rule. He believed in free government, and he experimented in Pennsylvania to find the best means of producing one and keeping it free. He was feeling his way, and he wisely left his First Frame open for amendments. As a matter of fact, it fell short of fully democratic government as we understand it today. It even fell short of the Charter of Privileges that he himself was to grant Pennsylvania a few years later.

The Frame of Government was presented to the first Assembly, which opened at Chester, the temporary capital, on December 4, 1682. Listed below are the central provisions of the First Frame and the Great Law which accompanied it.

GOVERNMENT

1. A *governor,* the proprietor, or his deputy, the lieutenant governor, with power (a) to appoint judges; (b) to preside over the Council (in which he had a triple vote); (c) to call and dissolve the Assembly; (d) to veto legislation.

2. *A council,* consisting of seventy-two members elected by the freemen of Pennsylvania for a three-year term, one third of the members being elected each year. Executive responsibility rested with the governor and Council. Legislation originated with the Council, but approval by the Assembly was required.

3. *An assembly,* consisting of two hundred members elected annually by the freemen for a one-year term.

THE ELECTORATE

The vote was open to all male inhabitants who (a) met moderate property qualifications; (b) acknowledged the Deity.

RELIGION

There was to be no discrimination against anyone for his religious beliefs, with the following exceptons: (a) Atheists were disqualified from voting. (b) Only Christians were permitted to hold public office. Even with these qualifications, Pennsylvania had, in C. E. Vulliamy's words, "the most complete form of [religious] toleration in existence."

JUSTICE

Trial by jury was guaranteed. The courts were open to the public, and English was the language used in them. The death penalty was abolished except for two crimes: murder and treason. This was a great advance over current practice in most parts of the world, where even petty thefts were commonly punished with death.

AMENDMENTS

The Frame of Government could be amended at the wish of six-sevenths of the members of the provincial Council or of the Assembly, with the consent of the governor.

It is obvious that this was not full-grown democracy, but the door was opened to it. Penn's greatness is seen in the flexibility of his mind, which enabled him to accept the possibility of amendments made by the freemen of his province—the persons who actually operated the Frame.

Changes appeared in the Second Frame, dated April 2, 1683. The governor gave up his triple vote in the Council. To prevent the rise of a landowning aristocracy in Pennsylvania, the laws of primogeniture and entail were abolished. Immigration was encouraged through a provision that the lands of aliens could be inherited by their heirs. Inhabitants were permitted to hunt on unenclosed lands.

Further changes were enacted in 1696 in what is known as Markham's Frame of Government (named for Lieutenant Governor William Markham), which was adopted in William Penn's absence but with his approval. In Markham's Frame, the Assembly was given the right to initiate legislation, sharing that privilege with the Council. Markham's Frame also provided that in the law courts affirmation might be accepted in place of the oath. This made legal the witness of the "plain people," who were forbidden by their religion to take an oath. "Let your yea be yea and your nay be nay."

However, on October 28, 1701, the great triumph for the democratic system in colonial Pennsylvania came with the Charter of Privileges, which virtually ended proprietary rule and gave self-government to Pennsylvania. The proprietor, it is true, still selected the lieutenant governor. The latter appointed the judges and retained the power of veto over legislation. But the Council was abolished (except as an advisory body), so that the colony was then governed by a unicameral legislature, the General Assembly. This body had the power to call and dissolve its own meetings, to initiate legislation, to ease the suffrage restrictions, to make appointments, to control (if not to appoint) the judiciary, and to levy taxes. The governor had no power over it except his veto.

Penn had not sought to hold power in his own hands longer than was necessary to get the seed of the nation well planted. He had the good sense to allow others to cultivate the ground. His was an experiment in free government, and he kept it free, recognizing that in honest—if noisy—discussion lay the best hope for political growth.

"The greatness of Penn as a colonial administrator," writes Dr. S. K. Stevens, "lies not in his *First Frame of Government,* representing his own advanced ideas, but in his ability to go beyond it and to accept a second and even a fourth frame of government embodying ideas of others. That is why the *Charter of Privileges* of 1701 is a great document in the history of human liberties."

In 1751, to celebrate the fiftieth anniversary of William Penn's Charter of Privileges, a bell carrying the words "Proclaim liberty throughout the land unto all the inhabitants thereof" was hung in the State House at Philadelphia by act of the provincial Assembly. It hangs there still, in the building now known as Independence Hall. Today the Liberty Bell, as it is called, carries one's imagination back to 1776. It should, in fact, carry one back another twenty-five years to 1751, when the bell was inscribed in honor of William Penn, and then back a further fifty years to October 28, 1701, when Penn signed the great Charter of Privileges.

William Penn, who knew the "dust and sweat" of active life even better than Cromwell's foreign secretary John Milton did, should be honored today as the most creative statesman in American history. Not only did he found Pennsylvania on principles that have since nourished the life of the whole United States, but he also gave to the founding of his colony an élan that inspired other men and drew out their best inventive genius to supplement his own. It is appropriate that Pennsylvania has named her new state museum and archives building the William Penn Memorial.

7 *Peace without Pacifism*

William Penn recognized the danger of war confronting his province, and he sought to be prepared for it if it came; but first he tried to forestall such an emergency by peaceful methods. "Let us then try what *Love* will do," he wrote, "for if Men did *once see* we love them, we should *soon find* they would not harm us." The men he selected to guide the affairs of the young colony were in sympathy with the objectives of the Society of Friends, but they were by no means doctrinaire pacifists.

Next to the Charter of Privileges, the best fruit of Penn's second visit to his province was the introduction of James Logan. This combative Scottish Quaker had come on the same ship that brought William Penn in 1699, but he did not return to England with the proprietor. Instead, he remained in Pennsylvania in a multiple capacity as Penn's chief proprietory agent, the secretary of the province, the best informed colonial administrator of his time on Indian affairs, a distinguished scholar and patron of learning, and a leading merchant who achieved a near monopoly of Pennsylvania's Indian trade.

James Logan (1674-1751) had a largeness, and at the same time an acuteness, of mind that made him one of the leading figures in colonial America. Though a classical scholar, he found himself as much at home in the politics of his own time as of Cicero's. A member of the Society of Friends, he was nevertheless too much of a realist to accept pacifism as an absolute rule of state. In that respect, as his fellow Quakers put it, he was not a "strict professor." He believed that all government rests ultimately on force.

Benjamin Franklin told an illuminating, if apocryphal, story

50

about Logan's voyage to America with the proprietor. An approaching ship was sighted and believed to be a pirate. The captain of Penn's ship prepared to put up a fight. Most of the Quakers went below, but James Logan remained on deck and was quartered to a gun. When the danger was past (the suspected pirate having turned out to be a friend), Penn rebuked his secretary for his military conduct. Logan replied, "I being thy servant, why did thee not order me to come down, but thee was willing enough that I should stay and help fight the ship when thee thought there was danger."

Logan was refreshingly frank and uninhibited. He made friends and enemies with equal finality. He called John Moore "that composition of wormwood and vinegar." David Lloyd, the fiery Welsh leader of the popular party in the Assembly, loved him so little that he tried to have him indicted for treason. But Logan, in the rough and tumble of provincial politics, gave as good as he got. He kept his neck out of the noose, and by the very jealousies he inspired—which deepened political cleavage —he assisted at the birth of the party system in Pennsylvania and thereby in the long run helped to make democracy work the better.

Penn, the ex-soldier, and Logan, the businessman, had no illusions about war or about Pennsylvania's precarious situation as a province poor in military manpower, rich in natural resources, and surrounded by acquisitive neighbors who were not pacifists. Penn and Logan knew very well that war is not a garment that one puts on and off at will. It is a disease like smallpox. To escape infection requires more than the exercise of a tender conscience. It demands the organization of a league of nations. In 1793 Penn published *An Essay towards the Present and Future Peace of Europe,* in which he proposed that the imperial states of Europe send deputies to a general parliament, which should have power to make and enforce laws for the restraint of disorderly powers; but nothing came of it. Failing such restraint, the best antiseptic against war, as Penn knew, was to have friends on the colony's borders.

However, he was too much of a realist not to understand that Pennsylvania, being part of the great world in which France, Spain, and England were contending for place, could not isolate itself. He therefore saw to it that his deputy governors (with the one exception of Thomas Lloyd) should not be Quakers. He appointed men who had no conscientious scruples against military defense.

There were many prospective threats to Pennsylvania's peace: the French in Canada, sea pirates in Delaware Bay, the border disputes with Maryland and Connecticut (whose charters seemed to give them large slices of Pennsylvania), and the Indians all around.

Against the French danger, there were the Allegheny Mountains and the province of New York to help keep them off Pennsylvania's back. Against the pirates, Penn relied on the British navy; and against colonial competitors, he relied on the British Parliament. As for the Indian danger, should it actually mature, he counted on the friendship of the Iroquois, who had vast influence in the Indian world. James Logan, his adviser in such matters, staked everything on an Iroquois alliance. "If we lose the Iroquois, we are gone," he said.

Penn did not understand all the fine points in Indian politics, bound up as it was with kinship and religious sanctions of a kind unknown to Europeans. But the Golden Rule and his own generous instincts led him to adopt the right approach to his brown brethren. Even after Penn had left the province, the memory of his visits remained to sweeten Indian relations. It was only after long experience with some of Penn's successors that the Delawares and Shawnees finally left the province in disillusionment and anger.

Penn was as frank as he was friendly. When he needed land from the Indians, he said so; and he paid what the aboriginal owners thought they should have for it. The Indians did not at first understand that he was purchasing an exclusive right, nor did he fully understand that they regarded land the way the white man regarded the sky (until the advent of the airplane)—as a common good to be shared and not expropriated. But these misunderstandings produced no bad blood at the time, for neither party was impatient, neither was malicious, and each trusted the other's good intentions. Under such conditions, peace could and did exist for many years. During William Penn's active concern with provincial affairs, race relations in Pennsylvania were very nearly what they might have been if Eve and her progeny had remained in Eden.

It has been suggested that what brought Penn and the Indians together was their religion—their similar concept of the Divine and of man's duty toward it. Certainly the letter which Penn addressed to the Indians, dated October 18, 1682, a few days before his arrival in America, opened the door to friendly understanding on the grounds of a shared belief:

MY FRIENDS:

There is one great God and power that hath made the world and all things therein, to whom you and I and all people owe their being and well-being, and to whom you and I must one day give an account, for all that we do in the world; this great God hath written His law in our hearts, by which we are taught and commanded to love and help, and do good to one another, and not to do harm and mischief one unto another. Now this great God hath been pleased to make me concerned in your parts of the world, and the King of the country where I live hath given unto me a great province therein; but I desire to enjoy it with your love and consent, that we may always live together as neighbors and friends. . . . I shall shortly come to you myself, at what time we may more largely and freely confer and discourse of these matters; in the meantime, I have sent my commissioners to treat with you about land, and a firm league of peace; let me desire you to be kind to them and the people, and receive these presents and tokens which I have sent to you, as a testimony of my good will to you, and my resolution to live justly, peaceably and friendly with you.

I am your loving friend,

WILLIAM PENN

There was no hypocrisy in the letter—no appeal to religious sentiment as a means of softening the Indians for intended land seizures. Penn was honest and open. Like other Europeans, he wanted land; but unlike most others, he wanted to enjoy it with the "love and consent" of the original inhabitants.

It is unlikely that Penn had thought through the problems of colonialism, which have been so well assessed in recent times. Yet Penn understood well enough the injustice of what was going on in the Americas, where Europeans denied or ignored the Indians' right to their own lands. He would have understood Cornplanter's declaration, made many years later, that it was wrong for the King of England to claim ownership of North America merely because a sailor of his (John Cabot) had "found" it.

At the same time, Penn knew that, if he did not enter upon the Pennsylvania lands, others more ruthless would. He believed he could handle his proprietorship in such a way as to benefit both the Indians and the white people. He believed, too, despite evidence to the contrary all over the colonies, that he could develop his Holy Experiment without bloodshed.

Penn found it no effort to make himself at home among the Indians. He visited their communities, joined in their young men's sports—in which he could hold his own—and delighted them with his kindness, humor, respect for age, and comfortable acceptance of their unhurried way of doing business, the Indians being, as they said, "unacquainted with hours." Though he was naturally communicative and could be voluble, experience at Quaker meetings had taught him the value of silence, another trait which the Indians found commendable.

It was a rule among these kinship-oriented people to address a friend not by his personal name but by the degree of kinship he bore to the speaker. They affectionately addressed William Penn, whom they had taken to their hearts, as Brother Onas (*onas* meaning "quill" or "pen"). After his death, every governor of Pennsylvania was known among them by the title, Brother Onas, and the name came to be synonymous with Pennsylvania.

The Indians were great travelers. It pleased them to visit Philadelphia and there hold treaty with Brother Onas. It pleased them as much to welcome him when he visited their country. In April, 1701, a band of some forty Susquehannocks, Shawnees, and Conoys, under Six Nations (Iroquois) sponsorship, held a council in Philadelphia at which they proclaimed a lasting friendship with William Penn and his people. In June of the same year, Penn visited the Shawnee settlements. He traveled west over the Great Minquas Path, stopping at what has since become known as the Shawnee Gardens, near the Gap in Lancaster County. He went on to be entertained "nobly," as Isaac Norris wrote, "at the King's palace on Conestoga." He returned by the water route: up Conestoga Creek and down French Creek to where it entered the Schuylkill some thirty miles above Philadelphia.

His purchases were made correctly—that is to say, in accordance with Indian custom and etiquette. He bought family tracts (their hunting territories) by agreement with the head men of the families or communities concerned and their immediate neighbors. The first purchase, at Pennsbury, was made by Deputy Governor William Markham in advance of Penn's arrival. Between 1682 and 1684, William Penn held nine Indian "treaties" at which he purchased, piece by piece, the greater part of southeastern Pennsylvania. By these and later purchases, Penn and his agents slowly rounded out his domain, with the willing consent of the Indian occupants.

On his last visit to Pennsylvania (1699-1701) Penn was accompanied by his second wife, Hannah Callowhill Penn, and his daughter Letitia. This time he completed his estate of Pennsbury Manor and held Indian conferences there. While he was in Philadelphia, his residence was the Slate Roof House on Second Street north of Walnut. Here his son John, the future governor of Pennsylvania, was born.

In 1712, eleven years after his return to England, Penn suffered a severe stroke. He remained an invalid until his death in 1718. During his illness and after his death, Hannah carried on successfully, assuming full powers as proprietor for fourteen years. On the other hand, his sons—John, Richard, and Thomas —left the Society of Friends for the more congenial atmosphere of the court. After their mother's death they played the role of absentee landlords most of the time, thus contributing to the unimpeded development of democracy in Pennsylvania.

A fitting epitaph for the founder has been written by Catherine Owens Peare in *William Penn: A Biography*. It occurs in a brief appraisal of his work: "He is eternally our contemporary, holding before us the finest traditions of Anglo-Saxon law, showing us the fruits of liberty of conscience, pointing the way to lasting freedom through individual dignity and endowing us with the example of a workable peace among men. William Penn speaks to the condition of our times."

8 The Melting Pot

It was a Quaker idealist who conceived the Holy Experiment, but it was a worldly-wise proprietor who set it going.

The first thing to be done was to get people into the province. In 1682 the European population of its twenty-eight million acres was only about five hundred, including Swedes, Finns, Hollanders, and English. This was much too small a number for Penn's purpose, which was to test the twin principles of popular government and religious liberty in a laboratory large enough to reflect the conditions of a good-sized European state.

He therefore organized a campaign of promotion, appointing agents in different parts of England, Scotland, and the Continent to advertise his liberal land policies and to persuade those whom he called "first adventurers" to emigrate. Some of these adventurers were well-to-do people. The Jasper Farmers, for instance, whom he had known in Ireland, took up five thousand acres at Whitemarsh. To encourage such persons to bring their households with them, he offered to each master fifty acres for every servant he brought along, and to each servant he offered fifty acres at the end of his term of indenture.

Pamphlets advertising Pennsylvania were circulated in England, Wales, Scotland, Ireland, Holland, and Germany. One of these bore the title: "Some Account of the Province of Pennsylvania in America; Lately Granted under the Great Seal of England to William Penn. &c. Together with Priviledges and Powers necessary to the well-governing thereof. Made publick for the Information of such as are or may be disposed to Transport themselves or Servants into those Parts."

In Holland and Germany such advertising stirred memories

of the pleasing impression Penn had made when he traveled there in 1677 with Benjamin Furly, who later helped Penn write the First Frame of Government. The result was that a stream of emigrants from Europe joined the larger movement from the British Isles. In eighteen years (1682-1700) the population of Pennsylvania increased fortyfold—from five hundred to twenty thousand—and Philadelphia, with a population of ten thousand, was well on its way toward becoming the largest city in the American colonies—a position it held up to the Revolution.

In 1683, Penn wrote a letter from Philadelphia to the Earl of Sunderland (with whom he had made the grand tour of Europe a few years before), boasting about his new country and what he was doing with it. The soil was good, he said, and the "aire sereen (as in Languedock) & sweet from the Cedar, Pine & Sarsefrax." The capital city had been laid out "a mile long & two deep—has a Navigable River on each side, the least as broad as the Thames at Woolwych, from 3 to 8 fathom water. There is built about 80 houses, & I have settled at least three hundred farmes Contiguous to it. We have had with passengers 23 Ships, & tradeing 40 great & small since the last Summer, not amiss for one year."

The hope of religious freedom and economic opportunity was what drew most immigrants to Pennsylvania. She was free, furthermore, from Puritan intolerance, from the South's slave-owning aristocracy, and from the Indian wars that tore at the vitals of colonies north and south.

Penn's land policy was enlightened and attractive to small farmers. The lands were sold not to big speculators but to settlers. The terms of the charter required Penn to charge a small quitrent (an annual rental in lieu of feudal service), but the proprietor did little or nothing to collect it. The terms, in short, were so liberal that Pennsylvania became a colony of small, independent farmers who were the backbone of a stable economy.

Many of Pennsylvania's immigrants were indentured servants or "redemptioners." They had come to America penniless, unable to pay for their passage except by selling themselves for a term of years, the money being paid at once to the ship's captain. Germans, English, Irish—men of all nationalities—came over this way, making the best bargain they could on arrival with anyone who wanted to employ them. No stigma was attached to redemptioners. They made some of the best citizens. George Taylor, for instance, one of the signers of the Declaration of Independence, began his American career as a redemptioner from Ireland. He sold himself to a man who owned a furnace near Easton, shoveled coal and ore for a time, married well, made a fortune, and was elected to the Pennsylvania Assembly in 1761.

Not all indentured servants turned into Horatio Alger heroes. Gottlieb Mittelburger, in his *Journey to Pennsylvania* (1750-1754), described the rules that governed the redemptioners and showed the darker side of the system. When a ship arrived, labor employers came aboard, looking for human livestock. To pay for their passage, men and women sold themselves for a term which depended on their own fitness and the current state of the labor market. Some parents sold their children "like so many heads of cattle" in order to go free themselves. Families were thus broken up and children separated from their parents, sometimes never to see them again.

There were rules to cover all contingencies. If a husband was ill on arrival and unable to work, his wife had to sell herself for ten or twelve years in order to pay for his passage as well as her own. If a wife died on the voyage, her husband had to pay for her passage, doubling the time of his own indenture to do so—provided, that is, she had died after the voyage was half over. If she died short of the halfway point, the husband was not financially responsible for her. Parents were not permitted to sell children under five years of age. These, wrote Mittelberger, "must be given to somebody without compensation to be brought up, and they must serve for their bringing up till they are 21 years old." Children sold between the ages of ten and fifteen had to serve until they were twenty-one.

The early newspapers of Philadelphia carried frequent notices of rewards offered for runaway servants. Few escaped. When recaptured, they were punished by extension of their time of servitude: for a day's absence, an extra week of service; for a week's absence, an extra month; for a month's absence, half a year. A recaptured servant, if his master no longer wanted him, could be sold to a third party.

Immigrants poured in from many countries, but chiefly from England and Wales, Ireland and Scotland, Germany and Switzerland. They came in ethnic waves and settled each in his favorite district, so that to this day, despite a good deal of overlapping, Pennsylvania is divided into three recognizable sections: the English in the eastern counties, the Germans in the limestone valleys of the piedmont, and the Scotch-Irish among the mountains, especially in western Pennsylvania. The much-praised American melting pot is seen in Pennsylvania at its best; but at the same time, in speech, customs, and activities each area preserves a quality of its own.

The first great wave of immigration came from Wales. Hundreds of thick-set, ruddy-faced, bright-eyed Welshmen came in hopes of planting a New Wales under the aegis of William Penn, who was said to be of Welsh descent. Most of these early Welshmen were farmers, but there were also men of wealth and education among them, like the several branches of the Morris family. In the second and third generation the Welsh tended to move to the cities, entering the trades, commerce, and the professions. Before 1730, most of the physicians in Pennsylvania were Welshmen. William Penn's physician was Dr. Wynne; George Washington's, Dr. John Jones. The first medical book printed in America was written by Dr. Thomas Cadwalader.

The hoped-for Welsh barony, with right of self-government, where their customs and language were to have been perpetuated, proved impracticable. County lines were drawn across the Welsh territory north of Philadelphia. In the end, both English and Welsh in Pennsylvania were strengthened by the mingling of the two races. But the Welsh as a distinct people are still remembered in the surnames they have scattered over the state, such as Jones, Cadwalader, Morris, Davis, Richards, Griffiths, Evans, Hughes, Rhys (Reese), and Llewellyn, and in such place names as Gwynedd (which they pronounced "Gwinneth"), Merion, Radnor, Haverford, Bryn Mawr, Bryn Athyn, Penlyn, Cynwyd (pronounced "Kunnith"), Pen Argyl, North Wales, and the Welsh Mountains. Best of all is the strain they contributed to Pennsylvania's manhood and womanhood: intense, artistic, intellectual, and physically vigorous.

The second great wave of immigration was English. For a few years after the founding of the colony, English immigration scarcely kept pace with Welsh; but soon it gathered head, and by 1700 the English were by far the most influential element in Pennsylvania's heterogeneous population. What gave the

English predominance was not so much their greater numbers as their greater adaptability to the American environment. They were already accustomed to the English laws and institutions which they found here, and they were less race-conscious than the Germans, less clannish than the Scotch-Irish.

English Episcopalians (as distinct from the Quakers) had not been driven overseas to escape persecution. They therefore felt no need to keep to themselves but reached out to embrace all the advantages of Pennsylvania's prosperous democracy. Nevertheless it was the Quakers (drawn mostly from the English and Welsh population) who until the Revolution provided the backbone of Pennsylvania's commercial and political life. They were leaders in government, philanthropy, education, and science. No less than five of the nine original founders of the American Philosophical Society were Quakers. Honest but shrewd businessmen, non-belligerent but by no means non-acquisitive, they developed a mercantile aristocracy which made and kept Philadelphia the chief center of American business until the Erie Canal cut into the American hinterland and gave first place to New York.

Not all the English immigrants came directly from England. York County in Pennsylvania was settled largely by people of English stock from Maryland, whence came John Dickinson, Benjamin Chew, and James Tilghman. The late Dr. Wayland Dunaway has reminded us that "Benjamin Franklin came from Massachusetts, Jared Ingersoll from Connecticut, Joseph Reed from New Jersey, Andrew Hamilton from Virginia, Gouverneur Morris from New York, John Moore from South Carolina, and Edward Shippen and Francis Richardson from New England."

The third large body of immigrants in point of time, and the second in numbers, were the Palatine Germans and the German-speaking Swiss. These, with a slight admixture of Huguenot French (of whom Anthony Benezet, who has been called America's first great humanitarian reformer, is a conspicuous example) made up the blend now known as *pensylfawnisch* or Pennsylvania Dutch (from *Deutsch,* meaning "German"). The German and Swiss migration, a trickle at first, grew into a torrent as Mennonites, Lutherans, Reformed, German Baptists, Moravians, Schwenkfelders, and others came seeking freedom and a chance to get ahead.

Most of the German immigrants were farmers, who found in the limestone soil of central Pennsylvania conditions like those to which they had been accustomed in Europe. They erected huge Swiss barns, good stone houses, and solid, blunt-spired churches. They soon made the "Dutch country" such a model of thrift and hard work that it became the granary of Pennsylvania. For a time the Proprietary party saw in this large German bloc, which tended to isolate itself, a danger to Pennsylvania's institutions. But their fears disappeared a few years later when the Pennsylvania Dutch (a happily contentious people) broke up in the province's free political atmosphere, some joining one party and some another, and merged themselves wholeheartedly into Pennsylvania's existing political structure. All in all, their contributions in science, literature, music, business, the trades, and the professions—to say nothing of the agricultural genius that has made the Conestoga Valley in Lancaster County known as the Garden of America—have been magnificent.

There were two distinct cultures within the Pennsylvania Dutch: the "church people" on the one hand—Lutherans, Reformed, Moravians; and, on the other, the "plain people"— Mennonites, Amish, German Baptists (Church of the Brethren or Dunkers), River Brethren (to which President Eisenhower's forebears belonged), and a host of smaller sects.

The church people, who today constitute the majority of Germans in Pennsylvania, entered the main stream of American business and professional life so easily (as did the Muhlenberg family) that they attracted little attention to their national origin. It was the plain people, on the other hand, who drew attention to themselves and who in consequence are now popularly supposed to *be* the Pennsylvania Dutch.

Some of the plain sects, in attempting to keep themselves "unspotted from the world," have preserved a number of the medieval customs which they brought with them from Europe and which seem bizarre to modern eyes. The *Meidung* or "avoidance," for instance, which is practiced by the Amish and others, is said to be one of the cruelest punishments known to anthropologists. When a husband or father (it is usually the man who errs) is "hit by the *Meidung,*" as they express it, his wife is forbidden to eat or sleep with him, his children are forbidden to have anything to do with him, and the whole community is under obligation to ostracize him. There is nothing for him to do but, as they say, "go English," which means to leave the community and enter the world of the unsaved.

For a long time a certain psychological block kept many of the Pennsylvania Dutch from full fraternization with English Americans. It was a survival of their old fear of persecution. In America they were irrationally suspicious of "outsiders" and even of those among their own people who had entered the main stream of American life.

Strange folk customs further helped to isolate them: the practice, for instance, of "powwowing" or healing the sick through magical, but piously worded, incantations, always "in the name of the Father and of the Son and of the Holy Ghost." Books dealing with the occult in a practical manner were popular, offering formulas for curing worms, defeating witches, and raising the dead, for instance. *The Long Lost Friend, The Sixth and Seventh Books of Moses,* and *Albertus Magnus* joined the *Bible* and the *Martyrs' Mirror* to complete the old-fashioned Pennsylvania Dutchman's library.

Even Johann Arndt's beautiful book of devotions, *Paradies Gärtlein* (Garden of Paradise) acquired a reputation for magic in Pennsylvania. One day in 1735, Conrad Weiser and the Reverend Peter Miller, converts to the Seventh-Day German Baptists at Ephrata, became so incensed against competitive religious orthodoxies that they built a bonfire at Gottfried Miller's house on the banks of the Tulpehocken and threw into the flames all the church books they could find. Among them was Arndt's *Paradies Gärtlein.* When, next day, the *Gärtlein* was found among the ashes, scorched but unconsumed, word flashed about the countryside that it was impervious to fire and flood and that anyone having it in his house would be protected from both. The consequent demand for it became so great that Christopher Saur of Germantown brought out a new edition.

There are still people in Berks and Lebanon counties who pay money for white magic, as witness the vogue of *Himmelsbrief* or "Heaven's Letter," a religious charm against lightning, robbers, and bullets—even silver bullets. The following extracts are from a one-page printed copy which was bought a few years ago for twenty-five cents from an old blind man in the mountains north of Annville in Lebanon County. The idiom is not strictly English nor the logic quite of this world, but the general intent is clear: "Buy this and live. If you don't believe in it, try it on your dog and you will see."

In the name of the Father, the Son, and the Holy Ghost, as Christ stopped at the Mount, sword or guns, shall stop whoever carries this letter with him! . . . God will give strength! that he may not fear robbers or murderers and guns, pistols, sword and muskets shall not hurt through the cannon of angel Michael . . . and whosoever carries this letter with him shall be protected against all danger, and who does not believe in it may copy it and tie to the neck of a dog and shoot at him he will see this is true. . . .

I pray in the name of Christ's blood, that no ball shall hit me, be it of gold, silver, lead, or metal. . . .

This letter was found in Holstine, 1724, where it fell from Heaven; it was written with Golden letters and moved over the Baptism of Madaginery and when they tried to seize it, it disappeared until 1791. That everybody may copy it and communicate it to the world. . . . Whoever has this letter in his house no lightning shall strike it and whosoever carries this letter shall bring forth fruits, Keep my commandments which I have sent to you through my Angels in the name of my son Jesus Christ. Amen.

Next to the English and the German, the largest block of Pennsylvania's population was the Scotch-Irish (known elsewhere as Ulster Scots). Like their lowland Scots kin, the Scotch-Irish had unbounded respect for the teacher, the preacher, and the honest penny; but in temperament the Scot from northern Ireland differed much from his blood brother across the North Channel.

In Ireland these men had been for many years virtually without a country. They were Scotsmen whose ancestors had been planted on estates which, to suppress rebellion, Elizabeth I, James I, Cromwell, and William and Mary had confiscated from Irish Roman Catholics. The Scots in Ireland, under attack from the dispossessed Irish, complained that they did not receive the support they felt entitled to from England. Their businesses were ruined by reckless English trade laws, and their farms were excessively burdened by the rack rents of absentee landlords. Starved and made desperate at last by a succession of bad harvests, they came in tens of thousands to Pennsylvania in search of economic freedom.

It is estimated that between the years 1728 and 1776 some eighty-five thousand Scotch-Irish came and that in 1790 (when the first census was taken) there were about a hundred thousand of them in Pennsylvania. They settled first in Lancaster, Dauphin, and Lebanon counties, then crossed the Susquehanna into Cumberland Valley, where by 1750 all but fifty families out of five thousand people were Scotch-Irish. As early as 1740 they were pushing up the Juniata Valley into Indian lands, and after the French and Indian War they crossed the Alleghenies.

They moved across the ranges in full self-reliance, felling trees and Indians with equal aggressiveness, running up log houses, schools, and churches, distilling whiskey as a medium of exchange. Their ministers were educated men, spreading a tradition of learning wherever they passed; but if the folklore of western Pennsylvania has a modicum of truth in it, the Presbyterian minister who could not fell a backslider with one blow of his fist was scarcely fit to mount the pulpit and expound the Word.

The proprietors of Pennsylvania, after William Penn's death, recognized the Scotch-Irish (sometimes known as "the wild Irish") for what they were, a hardy border breed, and encouraged their migration into the western parts of the province (before these lands had been bought from the Indians) in order to forestall Maryland and Virginia, who disputed Pennsylvania's boundaries. From the Cumberland Valley the Scotch-Irish spread into western Pennsylvania, which virtually became their province. There they were joined by a good many English settlers and not a few Pennsylvania Dutchmen, both of whom helped to give stability to the high-strung Scottish strain. But it is only fair to say that it was the Scotch-Irish who, with the *Bible* in one hand, a rifle in the other, and a scalping knife at the belt, put the seal on the trans-Allegheny country for Pennsylvania.

Such were the principal ingredients of Pennsylvania's melting pot. That it provided a strong and invigorating brew for the new nation was demonstrated in the Yorktown campaign of 1781, when General John Peter Gabriel Muhlenberg of German Lutheran stock and General Anthony Wayne of Scotch-Irish Presbyterian stock together followed Lord Cornwallis to Yorktown and there, with the aid of George Washington (of English Episcopalian stock) and his French allies, closed the trap that ended the Revolutionary War.

9 *The Capital and the Frontier*

The story is told of a Roman pilot whose vessel neared disaster in a storm. Uncertain upon which of the gods, if any, it would be efficacious to call, he uttered this prayer: "O Father Jupiter, you can save us if you will, you can sink us if you will. O Father Neptune, you can save us if you will, you can sink us if you will. But O Father Jupiter and O Father Neptune, whether you save us or sink us, I will hold my tiller true."

The words *Dum clavum rectum teneam,* "So I but hold my tiller true," were proverbial among Roman seamen. Classical writers interpreted them to mean that success lies not in external advancement but in holding to one's vision of the right, whatever the outcome. It was appropriate that William Penn's sailor father should have taken this as his motto. His son adopted it in an abbreviated form: *Dum clavum teneam.* His grandchildren restored it to the form which Quintilian had made familiar—*Dum clavum rectum teneam*—not changing the meaning by the ad-

65

ditional word, which means "true" or "steady," but making it more explicit.

In the political rough and tumble of early Pennsylvania, William Penn had need to invoke the spirit of the family motto. The enlightened principles on which he had founded his government survived, but their human instruments were found, to his surprise and regret, to be imperfect in the spiritual awareness which he had hoped to create as a by-product of the Holy Experiment.

The democracy which Penn had created was a lusty, Gargantuan infant, not particularly lovable. The squalling that arose when it began to walk offended him to the soul, and there were moments when he almost despaired. He wrote in 1686 of the "scurvy Quarrels, that break out, to the Disgrace of the Province there is nothing but Good said of the Place, and little thats Good said of the People." Eleven years later he complained, "The Reports are . . . that there is no place more over run with wickedness sins so very scandalous, openly Comitted, in defiance of Law & virtue." It became proverbial to say of an irreligious rascal that he was "of the Pennsylvania religion."

But Penn held his tiller true. He had set out to see whether religious freedom and political democracy were feasible in a modern state, and his disappointment at sight of the inevitable faults of a young democracy did not blind him to its promised strength.

He had planted good seed. The young colony was enjoying a natural and healthy growth. The political foundations, as has been seen, were laid between 1682 and 1701—between the granting of the First Frame of Government and the signing of the Charter of Privileges. During that interval, too, the commercial foundations of the province were laid. Farms were planted throughout the three first counties: Philadelphia, Bucks, and Chester. The same years also saw the beginning of industry in Philadelphia and Germantown and the establishment of a flourishing merchant class in the capital city.

Under the Charter of Privileges Pennsylvania moved smoothly and rapidly ahead to take a position of leadership among the English colonies. Governors came and went, political parties grew up and fought with governors, proprietors, the Assembly, and each other. But there were no changes in government sufficient to impede the development of the province's political life or the ordinary citizen's pursuit of happiness.

The first half of the eighteenth century saw the purchase from the Indians of more lands, extending from the Delaware to beyond the Susquehanna, and consequently a westward rush of settlers, who often moved beyond the purchase line into Indian territory. It also saw the emergence of Philadelphia from a country town into one of the important cities of the world: the financial center of the English colonies in America, as London was of the British Isles.

Philadelphia's prosperity was built on the prosperity of the back country. Town and country were joined by sound fibers of trade and communications. The first postal system in the colonies (a private one) was established in Pennsylvania in 1693 to connect the several settlements on the Delaware. From Philadelphia, roads radiated in a widening arc: north to Whitemarsh, North Wales, Macungie, and Bethlehem; east to Trenton, New Hope, and New York; south to Chester and New Castle; west to Lancaster, Reading, and Harris's Ferry. About 1750 the invention of the Durham boat, which drew only two feet of water while carrying fifteen tons of merchandise, provided cheap transportation on the Delaware River for iron ore from the Durham forges in Upper Bucks County as well as for wheat and lumber. A vigorous foreign trade was conducted through the port of Philadelphia.

Pennsylvania's rapid commercial development was in part the consequence of her comfortable military situation, having the British fleet to safeguard her coast and the province of New York and the Iroquois Confederacy to protect her northern borders from New France. Under this shield, and encouraged by the liberal constitution Penn had given her, she enjoyed a phenomenal prosperity. The grain fields of the Germans and Swiss in the limestone country were second to none in the colonies.

Pennsylvania's ironworks were the best in America. Deep in the forest the ironmaster built his forge and established his village of workmen. They mined the ore, quarried the limestone, and cut the wood for the charcoal furnace which separated the metal from the ore's impurities. Thomas Rutter, a Quaker, built the colony's first iron forge on Manatawny Creek in 1716. By 1750 Pennsylvania was the largest iron producer in the colonies. There were many small iron deposits in the province, and one of gigantic size at Cornwall, where Peter Grubb built the Cornwall furnace in 1742.

Small streams provided water power for grist mills like Edward Farmar's at Whitemarsh on the Wissahickon. Indian paths were widened into roads. Early in the century Conestoga wagons began a pioneering career that would soon take them over the Appalachian Mountains, and later across the prairies. The products of farm, mine, and forest (the fur trade) were brought to Philadelphia; and from there Quaker merchants distributed them up and down the Atlantic coast or shipped them overseas to England or the West Indies.

Against the time when citizens of the United States should begin to take a pride in their past, Philadelphia was piling up for herself an astonishing array of firsts. "It had more firsts and oldests than any other city in the nation," writes Horace Mather Lippincott in *Philadelphia*. Among them were the first circulating library, the Free Library, begun in 1731; the first social and intellectual club, Franklin's Junto, organized in 1727; the first hospital, the Pennsylvania Hospital, founded in 1751; the first volunteer fire company, the Union Fire Company, formed in 1736; the first fire insurance company, the Philadelphia Contributorship, organized in 1752; the first art institution, the Pennsylvania Academy of the Fine Arts, whose first home was erected in 1805; the first medical school (1756) and the first law school (1790), both in the University of Pennsylvania. To these should be added the first magazine in the country, *The American Magazine* (1741), and the first American *Bible* printed in a European language, Christopher Saur's German *Bible* of 1743.

In 1723 Benjamin Franklin, at the age of seventeen, came to Philadelphia to make his fortune—and made hers. He was the initiator of half of the firsts in the list above.

Philadelphia had many other distinguished citizens in those days. James Logan has been mentioned. There was also John Bartram, the botanist, whose *Observations . . . In his Journey from Pensilvania to Onondaga, &c.* (London, 1751) is a travel classic. Other men who contributed greatly to Pennsylvania's culture included David Rittenhouse, who made his own instruments for measuring the transit of the planet Venus; Lewis Evans, the cartographer, who in 1749 produced the first good map of Pennsylvania; and Thomas Godfrey, who invented the mariner's quadrant. The Philadelphia Hospital was founded by Dr. Benjamin Rush and Dr. Thomas Bond. Beautiful buildings were rising in what is now called Old Philadelphia and in the city's environs as well. James Logan's country home, Stenton, completed in 1730 in Germantown, and Hope Lodge, completed about 1750 by Samuel Morris in Whitemarsh, were handsome examples of Georgian residential architecture. The building Governor William Keith had erected near Hatboro as a malt house to provide a market for surplus grain during a time of depression was done over by Dr. Graeme as a home for his family and a charming retreat for Philadelphia society.

A burst of religious poetry came from hundreds of persons in the German churches. Good music was composed and played in the Moravian settlement at Bethlehem and the Seventh-Day German Baptist Kloster at Ephrata. Benjamin West, who was to become one of England's greatest painters, was in 1755 still in his teens but just ready to set up as a portrait painter in Philadelphia. Valentine Haidt arrived in Bethlehem from Germany to begin his career among Pennsylvania's Moravians as "the painting preacher." And Benjamin Franklin launched his career as founder of institutions for the enlargement of men's minds with the Library Company of Philadelphia in 1731 and the American Philosophical Society in 1743. The University of Pennsylvania was an outgrowth of his pamphlet *Proposals Relating to the Education of Youth in Pennsylvania,* which he published in 1749. He was later one of the founders of Franklin (now Franklin and Marshall) College.

William Penn, who desired men to "converse with Nature and Art," as he wrote in *Some Fruits of Solitude,* would have approved of all this. He would have been glad to know that in Philadelphia ("the communion of God in the Spirit") piety did not regard learning as an enemy.

Meanwhile, the formal religious life of the province was advancing. Well-organized bodies like the Society of Friends, the Church of England, and the Presbyterians erected churches and meeting houses; and, though they did not all pull in the same direction, they did manage among them to control the government of the province. Among the early German immigrants, the Great Awakening produced a flowering of strange sects like the Newborn, the New Mooners, and the Seventh-Day German Baptists, whose monastic system established at Ephrata in Lancaster County attracted inquiring minds from overseas. However, such bodies as these, though picturesque and significant of religious trends in their day, did not fairly represent the deep and steady current of religion that guided most of the German-speaking population in Pennsylvania.

The Moravians arrived in 1740. By reason of their numbers, which have always been small (they are not a proselyting church), it has been easy to discount their influence, which during the mid-eighteenth century was very great indeed. They were survivors, under the sponsorship of the German Count Zinzendorf, of an ancient Protestant church founded in 1457 and known as the Bohemian Brethren or United Brethren. Their Church was one of the sanest and steadiest products of the early Reformation. They were a small body when they first established themselves on the banks of the Lehigh in 1741 at a place which Count Zinzendorf named Bethlehem, because he spent Christmas Eve in a two-room cabin listening to the cattle in the adjoining room. They developed a model community at Bethlehem that devoted itself to producing missionaries, not primarily to win members for their own Church, but to deepen the spiritual life of all churches in the province. They avoided the religious disputes of the time, and with their sound organization and happy clear-headedness they achieved a reconciliation of piety with common sense that gave them great influence for good in the colony. It was the Moravians in England who brought John Wesley to his second and most significant "conversion." It was the Moravians in Pennsylvania who, through their great mission among the Delawares and Mahicans, made the most enlightened attempt this country has seen to solve the native race problem.

The Swiss Mennonites and the Church of the Brethren (German Baptists or Dunkers) brought with them to Pennsylvania a stable organization and a tradition of industry and strict living which provided a healthy counterbalance to the restlessness of an immigrant population in a strange land. The early Lutherans in Pennsylvania came under the guidance of Henry Melchior Muhlenberg. He was by nature a shy man, but he proved a worthy fighter in the interdenominational jungle of the time. He drew the scattered and often hysterical Lutheran congregations together, resolved "confusions," established a sound ministerial order, and got rid of the religious pretenders then roaming the countryside with eyes on the fair sex and hands in the collection plate.

The Anglican community shared with the Quakers (though

they usually pulled in opposite directions) the political leadership of the colony. When the Quakers, temperate in all things except pacifism, slipped out of the main stream of American life, it was the Episcopalians in the east and the Presbyterians in the west who led the colony. Two-thirds of the signers of the Declaration of Independence were Episcopalians.

The Baptists and Methodists came on the scene somewhat later. So did that distillation of Reformed and Mennonite, the United Brethren in Christ (not to be confused with the Moravians). The Church of the United Brethren in Christ was the first large church born in Pennsylvania. It began to take form in 1767, when Martin Boehm of the plain folk—a Mennonite—and Philip Otterbein of the more liturgical Reformed Church, shook hands at a revival meeting in Long's barn near Lancaster and said, in good Pennsylvania Dutch, "Mir sin' Brüder (Wir sind Brüder), "We are brethren."

The German plain sects, being suspicious of "worldly" education, retarded the development of public instruction in Pennsylvania. But Quakers, Episcopalians, Presbyterians, Moravians, Lutherans, the Reformed, and others did what they could to promote it. The Church of England, to which Penn's heirs as well as many of the government officials and merchants of Philadelphia belonged, assumed leadership in the cause of higher education. They strongly backed Franklin's nondenominational institution, which opened in 1751 as "the Publick Academy in the City of Philadelphia," with Franklin as president, became a "college" in 1755, and emerged in 1779 as the University of the State of Pennsylvania. The brilliant but prickly-dispositioned William Smith of Aberdeen University became first rector of the academy, then provost of the college, and later of the university.

Pennsylvania's first schools were the offspring of her churches. The Quakers and Moravians were alike in advocating education for all who desired it, without cost to the student. The Moravians led all others in providing education for girls and women. Such well-known Moravian girls' schools as the Female Seminary at Bethlehem and Linden Hall at Lititz show how well they put their educational theories to work. Education was, indeed, a Moravian tradition. The seventeeth-century Comenius, who is often called the "Father of Modern Education," was for many years the leading bishop of the United Brethren.

"Many of the pedagogical procedures which the twentieth century would claim as the products of its original thought," wrote Mabel Haller in *Pennsylvania History* in 1958, "were the accepted practices of the eighteenth-century Moravian schools: parent-teachers' meetings, school-community associations, educational and vocational guidance, student participation in school management, the homeroom, the adviser, teacher-training . . . adult education, evening schools, medical services, and other seemingly modern practices." Since the Moravians were not afraid of the English language, as were some others among the German-speaking groups, their stimulating influence on American life was greater than might have been expected from their small numbers.

While all this development was going on in and around Philadelphia, what was happening to the soil's original owners, whose friendly response to William Penn's overtures had saved the colony from the fear of Indian war and so made possible its phenomenal and uninterrupted growth?

Indian "right of soil" in a wide arc about Philadelphia had early been extinguished. The settlers, as they felled trees, built log cabins, and sowed their seed, had no thought of the hardship their coming inflicted on the Indians, nor of the sacrifices the latter were making to accommodate their white friends. But the continued uprooting of Indian communities and the destruction of hunting grounds (often in advance of any purchase) deprived the Indians of the very blessings the white man had come to America to find: freedom, dignity, and the good life.

William Penn's sons did not know how to handle the problem posed by restless settlers and aggrieved Indians. Settlers continued to occupy Indian lands without asking leave, and some Indians, even after lands had been purchased and paid for, continued to ask for satisfaction. William Penn had promised that no land should be taken without the Indians' consent, but this involved the slow process of negotiation, while the twin problems of white squatters and Indian blackmail called for an immediate solution.

Penn's heirs looked for a short cut. They thought they found one in what came to be known as the "Walking Purchase."

The "walk" involved, to begin with, the showing of a deed (or rather, a copy of that document, for the original was never produced) by which, many years before, some Unami Delawares were said to have sold a hunting tract to Penn, extending from a point near Wrightstown in Bucks County back into the woods for a distance to be measured by a common Indian formula: the distance a man walks in a day and a half. As rendered in English, this formula read, "as far as a man can walk in a day and a half."

The trick lay in the word *can*. By training walkers, cutting a path through the woods, and stretching *can* to the limit of human endurance (three walkers started, two fell out, and the third endured until noon of the second day), the Penns increased the intended twenty-five or thirty miles to more than sixty. Then a survey was made that, by a manipulation of angles, struck off in a quite unintended direction and comprehended another sixty miles. Consequently, by deception, the white man made the tract include not only the original Unami village hunting territory but all the lands in Pennsylvania occupied by the Munsee Delawares and those inhabited by a considerable body of Shawnees as well. It was almost as if a man had bought a farm in Pennsylvania and surveyed it to include the state of Maryland.

When the Delawares appealed to their "uncles," the Iroquois, for justice, the latter were persuaded by government agents that the Delawares had already disposed of all the land concerned by private sale—as indeed they had disposed of some of it. The Iroquois accordingly ordered Delawares and Shawnees to leave the disputed territory and retire to the Wyoming Valley on the North Branch of the Susquehanna, on the assurance that these lands would be preserved for them forever.

It seemed to Penn's heirs that they had got rid of the Indian problem at a cheap price, but this was not so. When the Indians at Wyoming Valley learned in 1754 that the Susquehanna Company of Connecticut had purchased (or claimed to have purchased) this valley from the Iroquois and proposed to establish settlers therein, a fire was lighted in their hearts. It smoldered for some years and then flamed into the two massacres at Wyoming. Many of the Delawares and most of the Shawnees left for the Ohio country. A few remained with Teedyuscung, who had been appointed by the Iroquois to hold the valley for the people of his race. The propaganda value of all this chicanery was apparent to the French on the eve of the French and Indian War.

In 1755, the year of Braddock's defeat, there were other explosive elements in the Indian situation. For many years the Iroquois had been concerned with the plight of Indian refugees— an international problem with which Pennsylvania and the other English colonies were totally unprepared to cope. Indeed, in that age of European expansion the problem was but little understood. Even the enlightened Spanish priest Las Casas, who had pro-

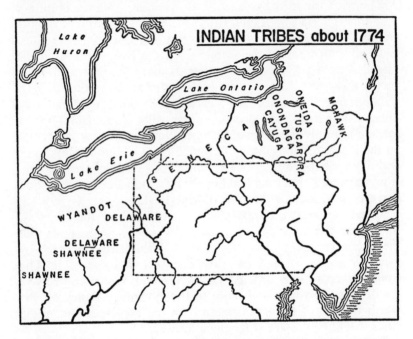

tested about it throughout a long life, found himself unable to move his native country to translate his liberal views into effective action.

It was the Iroquois who found a solution. They remembered certain words spoken by their founder, Deganawidah, that had been handed down in the legend of the planting of the Tree of Peace: "Roots have spread out from the Tree of the Great Peace. . . . If any man or any nation outside the Five Nations shall show a desire to obey the laws of the Great Peace . . . they may trace the roots to their source . . . and they shall be welcomed to take shelter beneath the Tree." Following this precept, the Iroquois encouraged dispossessed Indians to take refuge with them and become, as their phrase ran, "props to the Longhouse."

The Six Nations showed by their use of the word *props* that they were aware of advantages to themselves in thus providing aid to refugees. They invited Indians of various nationalities to settle in the Susquehanna Valley, which had lain virtually unoccupied since the defeat and expulsion of the Susquehannocks in 1675. By this means they delayed for many years—without

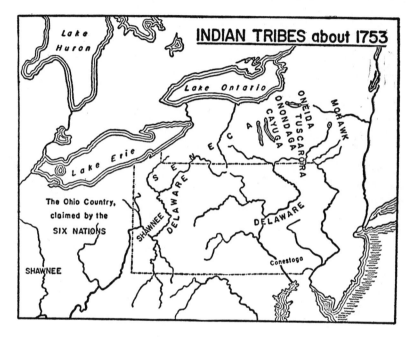

going to war about it—the final absorption of these lands into white settlements.

So it came about that, throughout the first half of the eighteenth century and a little longer (until the signing of the Fort Stanwix Treaty of 1768), there were movements of refugee Indians from the southern colonies up into the Susquehanna Valley as they retreated slowly before advancing English settlements. By non-violent rearguard action, bands of Shawnees, Conoys, Tuscaroras, Nanticokes, Tuteloes, Delawares, and Mahicans defended the southern approaches to the longhouse.

The Iroquois sent agents to arrange for the transportation of these people to their new homes. The plan seems so very modern that one may wonder if it could have happened so long ago and among a people whom white men have traditionally regarded as "savages." But it is all on record—in the printed archives of Pennsylvania and New York as well as in the correspondence of Conrad Weiser, Sir William Johnson, and the Moravian missionaries. From Maryland, Virginia, and North Carolina Indian messengers came north to the Iroquois country, requesting asylum; then back to the south went Iroquois agents to welcome the refugees and help them on their way. John Jacob Schmick, a Moravian missionary in an Indian town at Wyalusing on the North Branch, told how in 1766 Iroquois emissaries traveled down the Susquehanna, requesting the Indians in the towns they passed to send canoes down-river, fetch the sick and aged belonging to a band of Tuscaroras moving north, and have food ready for them when they arrived. At Wyalusing the Tuscaroras broke their journey and stayed for several weeks as guests of the Moravian Indians.

In 1759 Christian Frederick Post, a Moravian missionary who married a Shawnee wife, prepared for the Pennsylvania government a clear statement of Iroquois policy: "They settle these New Allies on the Frontiers of the White People and give them this as their Instruction. 'Be Watchful that nobody of the White People may come to settle near you. You must appear to them as frightful Men, & if notwithstanding they come too near, give them a Push. We will secure and defend you against them.'"

The Nanticokes, who found themselves in trouble on Maryland's eastern shore, were invited by the Iroquois to settle in the Wyoming Valley at what is now the city of Nanticoke. They arrived in 1748. Five years later they were withdrawn by the Iroquois and settled farther up the river at Chenango (near Binghamton, New York). Teedyuscung and a band of Delawares and Mahicans then took their place in the Wyoming Valley.

When the Connecticut "purchase" of the Wyoming Valley became known, Teedyuscung or "Old Teddy," as some of the Quakers liked to call him, prepared to live up to his name, which has been said to mean "He Who Makes the Earth Tremble." The Iroquois, who were responsible for the presence of the Delawares in the valley, were no less angry. John Shickellamy (better known to history as Logan) was the Six Nations' representative in this area at the time. He made a statement on the subject, March 1, 1755. Pennsylvania's Indian interpreter, Conrad Weiser, wrote it down:

That whosoever of the white Should venture to Setle any land on Woyumock or thereabout belonging hitherto to the Indians will have his Creatures killed first, and then If they did not desist they them Self would be Killed, without distinction, let the Consequences be what it would.

Within a few months of this warning, the French and Indian War flamed out. The further story of that unhappy valley, through the Massacre of Wyoming, July 3, 1778, was recorded in blood.

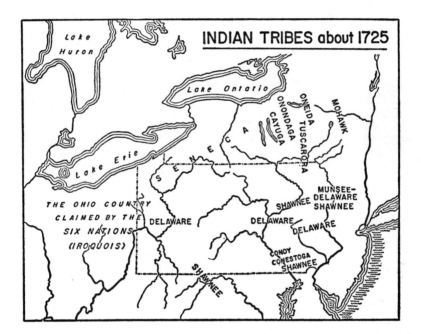

Long before the Indian War the Quakers had become a minority in the province; but the support given them by the German plain people helped to preserve their control of the Assembly. Pacifism, which William Penn had recognized as an ideal to aim at rather than as an absolute rule of government, had become a shibboleth among Quakers in the Assembly. Pennsylvania, in consequence, found herself at the outbreak of war without a military establishment.

The illogic of the situation was concealed from Pennsylvania's citizens by the existence of military barriers conveniently disposed about her by her friends and neighbors: the British fleet to the east, the province of New York to the north, and the Iroquois to the north and west. These all were meant to stand between her and her great trade rival, the French in Canada.

Moreover, James Logan, who had a near monopoly of the province's fur trade, held on to this business not only for the money and prestige it brought him but also for reasons of high policy. The fur trade helped to keep the Indians quiet and (attaching them by economic ties to Pennsylvania's traders) withdrew from the French potentially powerful allies. Thanks to the British fleet, which made French contact with Canada precarious, English goods could also be sold in the Ohio country much more cheaply than French.

The Quakers were so successful in this trade war (which lay under no Scriptural ban) that they brought upon themselves war of the forbidden kind.

10 *George Washington Wins His Spurs*

Virginia brought George Washington into the world and gave him a place in society, but it was Pennsylvania that first shaped him for his national career. The journey to Fort Le Boeuf in 1753 brought him into the public eye and trained him for the job that lay two decades ahead. It introduced him to the great world of international politics, drew out the resilience of his character, and demonstrated his capacity to hold firm to a purpose while at the same time accommodating himself to people and circumstances. This last quality, immensely steadying to those around him in time of crisis, did much to determine the outcome of the Revolutionary War.

When the French landed some two thousand men on the south shore of Lake Erie in 1753, built forts at Presque Isle (Erie) and Le Boeuf (Waterford), and established an advanced post on the Allegheny River at Venango (Franklin), Pennsylvania felt a bitter shock. Her Assembly's Quaker conscience, however, was too sensitive to permit a military reply. Therefore Conrad Weiser, whose successful treaty with the Ohio Indians at Logstown (Ambridge) in 1748 had been indirectly responsible for drawing the French into this military adventure (they too claimed these lands), proposed that the colony of Virginia—undeterred by pacifist scruples—should step in and, as he said, "knock the French on the head."

That was what the Old Dominion began preparing to do. The first step was to send the French a warning just one degree short of an ultimatum. George Washington, a spirited and ambitious

79

young man, offered to carry it. To the authorities at Williamsburg he appeared to possess just the right blend of courtesy and assurance to impress the French—the British Empire's most gallant but also most formidable opponent.

Young Major Washington (he was twenty-one years of age) received his instructions at Williamsburg on October 31, 1753. He assembled horses and baggage with men to look after them, hired Jacob van Braam to serve as his French interpreter, and at Will's Creek (Cumberland, Maryland) engaged the irreplaceable Christopher Gist to serve as guide and mentor. Gist, who was settler, trader, explorer, all in one, was wise in the ways of the woods. He understood the Indians, coached Washington in their diplomatic procedures, and explained the problems peculiar to this western region where the Iroquois maintained political authority of a kind that was difficult for a mind trained, like Washington's, in the European tradition to understand.

Rain, which later turned to snow, menaced the party from the start. It swelled the streams and made them unfordable. At the mouth of Turtle Creek the party borrowed a trader's canoe to get their baggage across while they swam the horses. When, on November 30, they set off from Logstown, where the party had been joined by an escort of three Iroquois chiefs (the Half-King, Jeskakakie, and White Thunder) and a young hunter (probably Guyasuta) to keep them supplied with fresh food, they were informed that the shortest route to Fort Le Boeuf was impassable by reason of the floods. They would have to go round by way of Venango. Between Logstown and Venango, as we now know, they were to have the advantage of the dry ridge (near Portersville) that geologists today call the terminal moraine of the Wisconsin Glacier.

On their way north they passed through three Indian communities: Murdering Town (probably named for an Indian who figured in traders' account books as "the Murdering King"); Venango, where the French had set up a post commanded by the astute Joncaire (who tried to separate Washington's Indians from the party they had come to protect); and Cussewago (Meadville). When they reached the Big Crossing of French Creek (near present Cambridge Springs), the party started to make a raft, but gave it up. The creek was flooding too dangerously. They thought it better to keep on the east side, even though this entailed a long ride round the marsh that stretched back from the mouth of Muddy Creek. They lost half a day making the detour through what is now Little Cooley and another half-day carrying their baggage across a creek on a tree, but by the evening of December 11 they arrived at Fort Le Boeuf.

All Washington had to do was deliver Governor Dinwiddie's message (". . . it becomes my duty to require your peaceful departure") and receive the French commandant's reply. It took five days to get this done. Most of the time was spent in a battle of wits, conducted in accordance with the best traditions of chivalrous courtesy. The French hoped to detach the Indians from Washington's entourage. Washington was determined to keep them with him, fearing that if he left them behind, the Anglo-Iroquois entente might be the loser. Meantime, he observed with anxiety that the rain had turned to snow and was piling up, white and menacing, in the woods. He sent the horses off, fearing that in their weakened condition, if they were further delayed, they might not be able to travel through the snow. For himself, Christopher Gist, and the Iroquois chiefs, he depended on canoes, which the commandant, Legardeur de St. Pierre, promised to provide.

At last, on December 16, Washington set off for Virginia, carrying St. Pierre's rejection of Dinwiddie's demands. This part of the journey turned into pure nightmare. Everything went wrong. Washington's patience, courage, and sheer physical endurance were put to such a test as nothing short of the darkest hours in the Revolution were ever to equal.

The snow had stopped and the water level in the creek was falling. Ice was forming. Sometimes the swift current threw the canoes of Washington's party against the bank, and they were near foundering. Often the light craft grounded, and the men had to get out into the water to ease them over the shallows. In some places the ice was so thick they could hardly break through, and at one point they found it impossible. They had to haul the canoes a quarter of a mile across a spit of land to reach running water again. At Venango they found the horses waiting for them, but the creatures were so worn down that they were unable to make more than a few miles a day, even when their riders dismounted and walked beside them.

Washington, feeling that he held the fate of empires in his

hands, thought it best to leave the slow-moving caravan and, with Christopher Gist, make his way by minor trails or no trails at all through the woods to Frazier's cabin at the mouth of Turtle Creek, where there were fresh mounts. Gist objected. He feared the young Virginia gentleman, who was accustomed to ride, not walk, would never make it on foot through the snow. But Washington had made up his mind and would not be dissuaded. He donned Indian costume—leather leggings and a belted matchcoat—for better convenience in the underbrush and set off on the march that nearly ended him.

They slept the first night in an Indian wayside cabin, got up at two the next morning, and came to Murdering Town (Harmony) on Conoquenessing Creek. There Gist was hailed by an Indian who expressed unbounded pleasure at seeing him again. Gist fancied he had seen him with Joncaire (a bad omen) at Venango, but Washington was taken with the man and thought they could not do better than engage him as a guide to show them the shortest way to the Forks of the Ohio (Pittsburgh).

A few miles out of town the new guide, whom they began to suspect of leading them in a wrong direction, suddenly turned about and fired at them. The shot went wild. The Indian darted behind a tree to reload, but Washington and Gist were on him in a moment. Gist was about to kill him when Washington intervened. They let the man go—making sure, however, that he did not immediately follow them.

It was now night. Fearing lest in the dark the Indian might sneak back and finish his job, they walked all night and all the next day over desolate, broken country. They used a compass, making no effort to follow a trail. It was then that George Washington discovered in himself the enormous reserves of strength and purpose that in later years were to carry an army and a nation through a multitude of disasters to victory. Gist's tenderfoot was shaping himself for leadership.

When at last they reached the Allegheny River a little distance above the Forks, they were disappointed to find that the frost, which had frozen the small streams so solidly that they had scarcely been able to get a drink, had been unable to close over the swift Allegheny River. Ice stretched some fifty yards out from each bank, and in between swept a savage torrent pushing heavy blocks of ice before it. Exhausted though they were, they set about building a raft. With a small hatchet they hacked down some trees, cut them into logs, and by evening pushed off hopefully into the current.

Soon finding that they made no headway against the churning water and ice, Washington in desperation thrust his pole to the bottom on the down-river side, trying thus to stop the raft's course for a moment while he maneuvered it toward the far bank. As he threw his weight on the pole, the raft smashed against it with such force as to knock it and Washington into the river. With his long arms he managed to grasp the logs and pull himself aboard again, but the men had now lost all control of the craft. Nothing but a lucky grounding near a small island saved them. They waded ashore.

The night spent on the island was cruelly cold. Their wet clothes froze on their bodies. But when dawn came, they saw that the cold had been kinder to them than they had known. It had frozen the river solid. They walked safely across to the east bank, picked up a good trail to Turtle Creek, and a few hours later were at Frazier's.

Next day Washington, once more the Virginia gentleman, paid a courtesy call on Alliquippa, the Seneca "Queen" of a neighboring Indian community ("Alliquippa's Cornfields" may still be seen on the banks of the Youghiogheny) and an influential figure in Anglo-Indian relations. Afterwards Gist and he resumed their journey, and on January 16, 1754, exactly one month from the day they had left Fort Le Boeuf, Washington delivered the reply of Legardeur de St. Pierre to Governor Dinwiddie. It ran in part:

As to the summons you send me to retire, I do not think myself obliged to obey it. Whatever may be your instructions, I am here by virtue of the orders of my General; and I entreat you, Sir, not to doubt one moment, but that I am determined to conform myself to them with all the exactness and resolution which can be expected from the best of officers. . . .

I made it my particular care to receive Mr. Washington, with a distinction suitable to your dignity, as well as his own quality and great merit.

Later the same year, 1754, George Washington showed his quality again. But that time he carried on the argument with France in another fashion—by firing the opening shot in the French and Indian War.

11 *The Fight for the Forks*

South of Niagara, the principal key to the interior of the continent was the Forks of the Ohio, Pittsburgh's Golden Triangle. Whoever commanded this river junction, where the Allegheny and the Monongahela unite to form the Ohio, controlled a great waterway, one that descended all the way from Lake Erie (after a short portage) to the Gulf of Mexico. The Forks also controlled the best passes across the Appalachian mountain chain south of the Mohawk Gateway, and since that passage was guarded by the Iroquois, the Forks commanded the best available trade routes

—by way of the Potomac, the Monongahela, the Juniata, or the West Branch of the Susquehanna—into the west.

For ten years—that is, from George Washington's skirmish at Jumonville Glen in 1754 to Bouquet's treaty with the Indians at Coshocton in 1764—three separate powers fought for possession of the Forks: the French, the English, and the Indians. Washington, the Marquis Duquesne, and Pontiac—each understood the importance of the Forks to the future of the people he represented. Hence, Braddock's defeat in 1755, Forbes's capture of Fort Duquesne in 1758, and the Battle of Bushy Run in 1763 —all on Pennsylvania soil—were crucial incidents in the history of the continent.

In still another way the fight for the Forks was decisive. It exposed the fallacy of a doctrinaire pacifism and returned the province to the more judicious policies of William Penn, who interpreted the text, "Render unto Caesar the things that are Caesar's and unto God the things that are God's," with a more generous allowance for the facts of life than some others were disposed to do. Penn, though he strove mightily for peace and tried to create conditions under which it could survive, understood the competitive world of ape and tiger in which his role as founder had been cast.

The Quakers, who during the first half of the eighteenth century controlled the Pennsylvania Assembly, refused to sanction measures of military defense. Key officials, knowing how vulnerable the province was, tried to alert the people to their danger and to get a militia law passed. But the Assembly controlled the purse, and the Quakers (with the help of German and Swiss pacifists) controlled the Assembly.

Men like James Logan had seen clearly enough that this impasse would bring about the end of the Holy Experiment—unless, that is, some way could be found of providing military defense without violating their consciences. Logan thought he saw light on the western horizon. Could the friendship of that amazing little league of nations known as the Iroquois Confederacy be developed to a point of providing this protection? He believed it could, if the French did not steal a march on the English colonies and win the Iroquois themselves.

When Logan heard of the Montreal Treaty of 1701, by which the Iroquois agreed to remain neutral in any French-English war, he was gravely disturbed. He learned later, however, that he need not have been. One of the terms of the treaty was that, in case of such a war, the French should "sit on their mats" as far as the Iroquois were concerned. In other words, they would refrain from crossing Iroquois territory; and this, the Indians understood, included the Forks of the Ohio.

Pennsylvania's Indian policy was a product of James Logan's vision. His vision, in turn, was based on information received from the adopted Mohawk, Conrad Weiser, and from Shickellamy, the Iroquois viceregent at Shamokin. The gist of the policy was Pennsylvania's acceptance of Iroquois jurisdiction over the Indians within her bounds. She would depend on the Iroquois to quiet the Delawares and Shawnees and to keep the French at a safe distance.

For both parties it was, on the whole, a sound policy. It strengthened the Iroquois in the Indian world to have their authority thus recognized by white men, and it satisfied Quaker scruples to have the Iroquois do their police work for them.

The events that led up to Braddock's defeat made a neat chain. Although three powers were involved in the fight for the Forks, a French-English quarrel brought it to a climax. The French had long sought a monopoly of the Indian trade west of the Allegheny Mountains. But early in the eighteenth century Philadelphia merchants, who had already enticed the fur trade of the Susquehanna Valley away from Albany, began to carry low-priced English goods across the mountains to capture the fur trade of the Ohio country from the French. Quaker merchants who were engaged in this business closed their eyes to the probable military consequences. The French, desirous of keeping the trade to themselves and also of protecting their communications between Canada and the Gulf of Mexico, were bound to resist Pennsylvania's intrusion by whatever means they could.

Great numbers of Pennsylvania traders, men such as the Irish-born "prince of traders," George Croghan, led pack trains deep into French-claimed territory. In 1748 at Logstown (eighteen miles downstream from the Forks) Conrad Weiser made a treaty, on behalf of Pennsylvania, with the western Indians. There he met Tanacharison, newly appointed "Half King" or viceroy for the Six Nations in that area, and helped him fill his council bag with wampum. The treaty was a portent the French could neither misread nor ignore. Accordingly in 1749 they despatched Céloron de Blainville to plant leaden plates at the mouths of important tributaries of the Allegheny and Ohio rivers to give warning that this country was claimed by the King of France.

When in that year Virginia formed the Ohio Company with the purpose of acquiring these same lands, the showdown could not be much longer delayed. The Marquis Duquesne in 1752 came to Canada with instructions to erect in the Ohio country forts that would seal off the English from the interior. A start in that direction was made in 1753 when a military force of some two thousand Frenchmen and two hundred Indians built a fort at Presque Isle. Others were erected later at Le Boeuf, near the head of French Creek, and at Venango, where French Creek enters the Allegheny. The bitter competition was no longer a trade war nor a concern only of Pennsylvania. It was a war between two empires.

Virginia took up the challenge for the British. She sent a small contingent to forestall the French at the Forks of the Ohio by erecting British defenses there. When, however, French troops appeared in force before the half-finished fort and demanded its surrender, there was nothing to do but comply. The gallant young Colonel Washington withdrew his covering force a few miles to Great Meadows (not far from present Uniontown) and, to protect it, ran up a stockade which he called Fort Necessity. Thence he launched a surprise attack on a French force at a place that has ever since been known as Jumonville Glen or Jumonville Rocks after the French ensign who lost his life in the skirmish. A few days later Jumonville's brother, Coulon de Villiers, compelled Washington to surrender his new-made fort.

Thereafter events moved swiftly. The British, recognizing the danger to their empire of a French fort at the Forks of the Ohio, raised, supplied, and transported an army sufficient to destroy it. The design was well conceived, bold, and, on the whole, efficiently conducted. The army, commanded by Braddock, achieved an all-but-impossible success in crossing the Allegheny Mountains, range after formidable range, equipped with siege guns, howitzers, six-pounders, twelve-pounders, and great quantities of ammunition and supplies. "I know of no other feat in the annals of the military history of North America that can be compared with it," writes Dr. Lawrence Henry Gipson in *The British Empire before the American Revolution.*

In a blinding flash, however, this overwhelming success was turned into a defeat so catastrophic that it has become the classic American symbol of disaster.

On the morning of July 9, 1755, the French knew they were beaten. Their Indian allies knew it as well and refused to take part in any attempt to halt the British advance. The French held impassioned conferences in which they tried to stir the Indians' martial blood. About noon of this crucial day, some 600 Indians were at last persuaded to join a force of 108 French regulars and 146 Canadian militia in a sally outside to see what could still be done. By every reasonable calculation it was already too late. Early that morning the British had made two crossings of the Monongahela at the last places where the defenders had any real prospect of a successful action. The British were now advancing rapidly along a ridge road toward the fort.

Nine miles from Fort Duquesne, the French and Indian forces met the British vanguard head on. The French were immediately broken and scattered. In the first exchanges of shot, the French commander, Captain Daniel Liénard de Beaujeu, was mortally wounded, the Canadian militia gave way, and the Indians disappeared among the trees.

But the battle was not over. Captain Jean-Daniel Dumas took command and sent his Indians racing through the woods on both British flanks, whence they directed a cross fire that made this a black day in British and American annals.

Captain Dumas—alert, aggressive, magnetic, with something quixotic about him—was born for just such a moment. Four years later at Quebec, he was to lead a body of college boys in another forlorn hope, an attack on the British at Point Levis, aimed at crippling General Wolfe's operations. He failed, and the name of Captain Dumas has gone down in history as the hero not of Quebec but of the Monongahela.

The story of Braddock's defeat has been told so often that it seems like threshing old straw to tell it again. However, recent scholarship has punctured many old misconceptions, giving such a study of the battle as Dr. Gipson's all the impact of a totally new tale.

To begin with, there was no "ambush." The French-Indian maneuver, after the first shock had stunned them, was simply so swift and well-co-ordinated that it had all the effects of an ambush on their startled opponents. When the Virginians and others tried to fan out and fight behind trees like the Indians, they were too late. The concealed enemy, already in position, picked them off. A large part of the British casualties, contrary to popular tradition, were among those who tried to fight backwoodsman-style.

Braddock, whatever his faults, did not play the part in this engagement which tradition assigns to him—that of a stupid martinet, beating back with the flat of his sword those who could have saved the day Indian-fashion. Clear-headed, he did what he could to recover the errors (of which Dumas so quickly took advantage) committed by Colonel Thomas Gage, commander of the British vanguard. This is the same Thomas Gage who, as commander in chief of British forces in America, in 1775 ordered the expedition to Lexington and Concord.

Gage was a careful officer, but he blundered twice at the Monongahela. First, he failed to occupy a small hill overlooking the road on which the British army would pass. No doubt it seemed to him unnecessary, all serious dangers apparently having been left behind at the river crossing. Second, when he met the French and Indians, instead of either pushing ahead to open ground or waiting for reinforcements, he retreated. In that retreat, the men got out of hand. Flinging themselves back against Colonel Burton's eight hundred men, who were hurrying forward to aid them, they threw them also into confusion. As if this were not trouble enough, the baggage convoy, contrary to positive instructions, came up from behind to press against the rear of Burton's force and further impede (during the crucial minutes before panic seized the soldiers) any attempt at orderly maneuver.

By the time Braddock arrived on the scene, everything was in chaos. He tried, unsuccessfully, to move his forces forward into the clear. A body of men who entered the woods in an attempt to capture the hill overlooking the battlefield were shot down by their own troops, half-blinded as these were by the smoke and made stupid by fear.

After two or three hours of this hell, during which Braddock, before he received his mortal wound, had five horses shot from under him, the army broke and ran.

"Of 1,373 non-commissioned officers and privates but 459 were neither killed nor wounded; of 86 officers, but 23," writes Dr. Gipson.

A few weeks after Braddock's defeat, the massacre of settlers at Penn's Creek in the Susquehanna Valley brought home to peace-loving Pennsylvanians the reality of a war they had not sought.

Still the Assembly declined to sanction a militia law. The Reverend John Elder of Paxton (Harrisburg) wrote: "There are within this few weeks upwards of 40 of his Majesty's Subjects massacred on the Frontiers of this and Cumberland Cy., besides a great number carried into Captivity, and yet nothing but unreasonable Debates between the two parts of our Legislature." Under the threat of violence (a mob from the frontier, carrying their dead, having descended on the city), the Assembly at last passed a militia law proposed by Benjamin Franklin and thereby put the province into a position to defend itself.

All this time men wondered what had been going on among the Iroquois, who were supposed to be Pennsylvania's safeguard in the west. The Six Nations as a body had done what they could to maintain the terms of the Montreal Treaty of 1701. They had protested the French invasion. Before hostilities commenced, their "Ladies of the Council" (*dames de conseil*) had come to Presque Isle to demand by what right the French had invaded Iroquois soil. Tanacharison, the Half King, sent what amounted to an ultimatum. He gave the French three successive warnings, the customary Iroquois prelude to an act of war. These warnings being disregarded, he conferred with George Washington at what is still known as the Half King's Rock before dawn on the morning of the skirmish at Jumonville Rocks; and he supported Washington in the campaign that followed—supported him, that is, until Washington (contrary to the Half King's advice) immobilized his forces behind what Tanacharison afterwards called "that little thing upon the Meadows," when the Indians withdrew.

After Washington's defeat at Fort Necessity and the building of Fort Duquesne, the Delaware Indians and their friends in the

west found themselves in a difficult position. Despite their grievances, they had no desire to go to war with Brother Onas. Yet the
French threatened to destroy them if they did not. If they stood
up against the French, would Pennsylvania support them? They
sent emissaries to Philadelphia to find out. They received in
Philadelphia an abundance of kind words and a few gifts (among
other things a supply of "bed lace") but no assurance of active
help in their emergency. They returned to the Ohio disillusioned,
and being under immediate pressure from those who now possessed the Forks of the Ohio, they accepted the French hatchet.
Captain Jacobs and Shingas "the Terrible," Delaware chiefs, led
devastating raids into central Pennsylvania.

The purpose of the French and Indians was to terrorize the
countryside, drive the farmers off the land, and so ruin Pennsylvania's economy. The province's reply was to erect small blockhouses every few miles along the mountain frontier and to have
the garrisons patrol the intervals between. This was insufficient to
prevent Indian raids, but by increasing the danger to the attacking parties, it limited their range. "The Enemy not beat but
scared off" was Conrad Weiser's laconic comment on a typical
skirmish.

The war dragged on, with no large battles and only one regular
siege—that of Fort Granville on the Juniata near present Lewistown, which was captured and destroyed July 31, 1756. The
public mind was soon filled with reports of atrocities all along the
frontier. Farms were attacked, cattle killed, houses burned,
the inmates killed or led off captive.

To restore morale, Colonel John Armstrong led what would
today be called a commando raid against the Delaware headquarters at Kittanning on the Allegheny River. At dawn on
September 8, 1756, he surprised the Indian town. Captain
Jacobs, the Delaware war chief, sent his womenfolk to safety in
the woods but remained in his bark cabin to fight it out. Armstrong's men set fire to the town. Jacobs, warned that he would be
burned alive in his cabin if he did not come out, replied, "I eat
fire," and fought on. In the end he was killed, most of the cabins
were destroyed, and a supply of gunpowder was blown up. Armstrong, though his own losses had been heavy, took his forces
back over the mountains.

Though the raid had not seriously injured the Delaware war

effort, and though Shingas took fearful revenge on the English settlements, the destruction of Kittanning did so much to lift Pennsylvania's spirit that it changed the complexion of the war. It showed that Indians were not supermen, and so made the continuing war of attrition easier for the whites to bear.

As the colonists' will to resist grew firmer, a change came over Indian relations—revealed in the rise and fall of Teedyuscung. Teedyuscung, a Delaware, was friendly to white men. He was angered, however, when he and his family were forced by the Walking Purchase to move from their home to the Wyoming Valley. He was further provoked by the rumor that Connecticut people planned to colonize Wyoming and displace him again. When war broke out, he lifted the hatchet, but at the same time he encouraged peace negotiations, looking forward to a reconciliation. Thus developed the series of peace conferences at Easton in 1756, 1757, and 1758. Indulging in metaphor, Teedyuscung announced himself "king" of (i.e., speaker for) eighteen nations and said his "halloo" could be heard across the mountains all the way to the Ohio country. Resenting the title of "woman" which the Iroquois had given his people, in conference one day he symbolically took off his woman's skirt, flung it at the Six Nations chiefs, and told them to wear it. "I am a man," he said. There were scalps to prove it.

But at Easton in 1758 the Six Nations, who all this time had been working in their own way to clean up the Ohio mess, put Teedyuscung in his place. Over his head they made peace with Pennsylvania on behalf of their wards, the Delawares, and thus brought the Indian war in the province to an end. When Frederick Post, a devout and fearless Moravian, carried this news to the Indians on the Allegheny River, they quietly detached themselves from the French. So it was that when General Forbes brought his expeditionary force to the Forks of the Ohio on November 25, 1758, he found Fort Duquesne in ruins. The French had blown it up the day before and retired, some to Niagara, some to New Orleans. A new fort was erected and named Fort Pitt. The key to the west was in British hands.

12 *Western Pennsylvania*

The movement of population into the "old west," between the Susquehanna River and the Allegheny Front (the mountain wall west of Bedford and Altoona), was a flood that nothing could stop. The craving of European man for adventure, new sights, and land beyond the reach of government interference, drove thousands beyond the limits of settlement and the bounds of Indian purchase. Many of these squatters were indentured servants who had served their term or run away before its expiration.

To young people with the best part of life before them, the forest they entered with or without official sanction promised a world of excitement. First, there was the search for desirable lands, preferably in sheltered valleys where the presence of locust trees, white oak, and black walnut promised a fruitful limestone soil. Then there was the great game of games, the pitting of man against nature, involving the erection of a log cabin for shelter and the clearing of the forest for the planting of fertile acres. While the first crop grew, there were hunting, fishing, and perhaps visits over rough trails to trading posts or Indian villages where food would be generously shared.

The forest, on the whole, was a friendly place. Its groves and streams provided the pioneer with food: fish, flesh, and fowl; berries, nuts, and roots. It gave the newcomer shelter in his notched-end, clay-caulked log cabin. Its smaller wild creatures —the chipmunk, ground hog, raccoon, and porcupine—gave him companionship. Its black bears were not dangerous unless attacked, and even its frightening panthers (or pumas) would rather run than fight.

There were hardship and danger, too, but with them came the loyalty between men that such pressures bring. John Heckewelder made this observation in 1762, when he and Christian Frederick Post, both Moravian missionaries, crossed the Allegheny Mountains in snow over three feet deep. Dead bodies of horses by the wayside showed the extremity of their danger. At nightfall they came to a cabin built by "Saucy Jack" Miller in Edmond's Swamp, a district also known as the Shades of Death because no sunlight filtered through the dense canopy of hemlock and white pine.

Scarcely had we entered [Heckewelder wrote], when the wolves began their dismal howl, which was the hunter's night music all the year round. Jack had no stable; but our horses found tolerable pasture on a piece of land of about three acres, which had been cleared and fenced in by the hunter and his sons. The young men offered to watch our beasts, and protect them from the wolves. A bell was fastened to the neck of each horse, a few fires were kindled, the hunters took their guns, and, followed by their dogs, began their watch, while we tried to refresh ourselves by a good night's sleep. But in this we were disappointed. The howling of the wolves, the barking of the dogs, the tinkling of the bells, by means of which the young men were enabled to tell where the horses were, and more than all the continued shouting of the guard from without, to assure their father of their watchfulness, and the answering cry of the old hunter from within, drove sleep from our eyes. Still we were thankful for the safety in which we were permitted to pass the night; and the next morning we took an affectionate leave of this wild but hospitable family.

As adventurous pioneers moved up into the mountains, they found a forest different from that with which the lowlanders had to contend. They were confronted with pitch pine and laurel on the sandy slopes, and elsewhere with a new breed of hardwoods, such as sugar maple, cherry, beech, and yellow birch. There were occasional groves—sometimes miles in extent—of white pine, the giants among them rising two hundred feet in their search for the sun; but such concentrations were avoided as much as possible until the next century, when lumbermen taught Pennsylvania the value of these mighty stands of "greentop gold."

Before the French and Indian War, settlers from Virginia, the presumed boundaries of which overlapped those of Pennsylvania in the west, moved out to the Monongahela and Allegheny valleys. Christopher Gist, surveyor for the Ohio Company of Virginia, in company with Thomas Cresap and a Delaware Indian named Nemacolin, prospected a wagon road over what came to be known as Nemacolin's Path from Will's Creek (Cumberland, Maryland) to the Monongahela, and a few settlers followed them. The French and Indian War drove them away, but they returned when the conflict was over and made clearings here and there in southwestern Pennsylvania.

The Indian in peacetime was a good neighbor, friendly and compassionate. He drew no color line in sharing his food, shelter, and knowledge of woodcraft. If, as used to be said, he never forgot an injury, it is certain that he never forgot a kindness. Even in wartime he protected those who had been good to his people and dealt honestly with them, as was proved by the escape of Benjamin Chambers and his family at Chambersburg when the Conococheague Valley was ravaged by Chief Shingas and his band.

There was, nevertheless, a chasm between Indians and most white men in some of their thinking. To the American Indian, as to the Hindu, the Chinese, and other Asiatics, there was a measure of divinity in all nature. To the white pioneer, on the other hand, as Paul Brooks writes in *Horizon,* whatever was not useful was evil and was to be either exploited or destroyed. "Whereas the Chinese [and, let us add, the North American Indian] had a religious fervor for wild places, to the primitive western mind they were wastelands inhabited by evil spirits."

Michael Wigglesworth of New England wrote in 1662 that he found everything beyond the settlers' clearings:

> A waste and howling wilderness,
> Where none inhabited
> But hellish fiends, and brutish men
> That devils worshipped.

With such a gospel to rely on, too many of our pioneers found killing Indians in time of peace to be not only a respectable sport but even a religious duty.

Indians befriended individual white men whom they found struggling to find homes for themselves in the woods. But, as the white settlements thickened and the specter of a lost homeland rose again in the minds of Indians who had not forgotten their earlier displacement from eastern Pennsylvania, a resolve took shape that the white man must, in their phrase, be "thrown back" over the Alleghenies. As they understood the Treaty of Lancaster (1744), these mountains had been specified as the limit to which their sale of lands beyond the Susquehanna extended. The sale in that treaty had been of lands west "to the setting of the sun." White men took this to mean west to the Pacific Ocean. Indians said it meant to the highest point of land, i.e., to the summit of the Allegheny Mountains.

The Iroquois, as has been shown, resisted French occupation of the Ohio country and, to this end, welcomed English armies into the region. But when at the close of the war they found the English continuing to garrison their forts and bringing in settlers, they protested. Their protests were received with contempt by General Jeffrey Amherst, commander in chief in North America, who regarded Indians as savages and, to the dismay of competent Indian agents like Sir William Johnson and George Croghan, openly treated them as such, subjecting them to stupid discourtesies and upsetting their economic life by withholding normal supplies of powder and lead for hunting.

Soon the Ohio country seethed with Indian discontent and anger at their old ally, who seemed to be turning against them. Race feeling was inflamed. A temporary union of several western tribes to meet a common danger vented its anger in what Parkman calls the "Conspiracy of Pontiac." Pontiac was the leading spirit among the Ottawas, Wyandots (Hurons), Chippewas, and Potawatamies. The leader of the Senecas, who joined them, seems to have been Gaustarax (Mud-Eater), an important behind-the-scenes figure. With him was Guyasuta, the better known Indian, at least among white men. The western Shawnees and Delawares were drawn in as well.

For three years the plot simmered. It was planned to surprise and capture all English garrisons west of the mountains. How the plan was kept secret is difficult to understand, for here and there through all that time individual Indians, hesitant about risking a final showdown between the races and anxious to save the lives of their white friends, gave intimations of what was coming. Conrad Weiser was thus alarmed in 1760, but he died before he could investigate. At Tuscarawas in 1762 Shingas gave young John Heckewelder veiled hints of trouble approaching, and when Heckewelder failed to heed them, King Beaver made them more explicit. That was only a few months before the war cry sounded. Yet the surprise, when it came, was complete.

In May, 1763, simultaneous attacks on the forts west of Lake Erie destroyed them all except Detroit, which was put under siege. In June the Pennsylvania forts at Venango, Le Boeuf, and Presque Isle were captured, and Fort Pitt was isolated.

The relief of Fort Pitt after the Battle of Bushy Run was one of the turning points of Pontiac's War. The battle was fought on August 5 and 6, 1763, between a British force of over four hundred men heading toward Fort Pitt and a smaller Indian force consisting mostly of Senecas, the "Keepers of the Western Door" of the Iroquois longhouse. The British were led by the gallant Swiss soldier of fortune, Colonel Henry Bouquet; the Indians, by Gaustarax. Guyasuta may have been present, but he was not in command.

The Indian attack was skillful, unexpected (Bouquet had thought he might be attacked in the defiles of Turtle Creek a day later), and well sustained. This was no hit-and-run affair. The battle opened as Bouquet's forces reached a small stream, Bush or Bushy Run, on the site of the present Harrison City. Unwilling to be caught on this low ground, Bouquet managed to pull back about a mile to a slight elevation, where his men formed a circle, protected by wagons and flour bags, with the horses and wounded in the center. How many men Gaustarax had with him is not known. Bouquet made no estimate, but Sir William Johnson afterwards set the number, from Indian reports, at about ninety-five. The figure is probably too low, but certainly there was at Bushy Run a great disparity in numbers—as there had been at Braddock's Field a few miles away.

The Senecas and their Indian allies had one important advantage: mobility. They kept to the woods and poured in a cross fire which was embarrassingly accurate. Bouquet's men, tired after a long day's march, were soon tormented by lack of water. If Bouquet could have found a proper target, he might have charged the Indians with his greatly superior forces and annihilated them. But his enemies were thinly spread, invisible, and quick on their feet. Fighting them was like beating the air.

During the night, some of the bolder spirits got water from a

nearby spring. That helped morale. But the morning's prospects
were bleak. An invisible enemy continued to pour death from the
woods around them. It began to look as if Braddock's defeat
were being re-enacted in slow motion. To find an exit from disaster, Bouquet resorted to a daring stratagem, difficult to execute
on that beleaguered hill. Bouquet had with him parts of two Scottish regiments, the 77th and the 42nd (the latter subsequently
known as the Black Watch), composed of men who were seasoned
and now desperate. Some of them managed to conceal themselves
among the rocks and trees on both sides of Bouquet's circle.
Then, by arrangement, the line of soldiers between these hidden
parties appeared to waver and give way. The Indians took the
bait and poured into the gap thus created, hoping to end the fight
with one quick blow. Suddenly from both sides appeared the
Highlanders in a bayonet charge for which the Indians were
totally unprepared. Many were killed and the rest fled.

Bouquet resumed his march. Still unsure of the outcome, he
reported at night that if the enemy attacked again, he doubted
whether he could carry off his wounded. But the Indians, unwilling to risk their small numbers in another major engagement,
allowed Bouquet and his men to proceed to Fort Pitt.

Next year Bouquet marched an army west to the Muskingum
country and brought the war to an end in a treaty at Coshocton.

For the Indians, defeat in battle was the least of their mis-
fortunes. Fears and hates, stirred up among white frontiersmen
by the events of Pontiac's War, poisoned the interracial atmosphere for a hundred years to come. Gangs like the Paxton
Boys (whom Benjamin Franklin called "white savages"), filled
with a blind hatred that could not distinguish friend from foe,
killed Indians indiscriminately. On December 14, 1763, under
the incitement of the pious but hysterical Lazarus Stewart, they
murdered a number of friendly Indians living at the village of
Conestoga. Those who escaped were brought by the authorities
to Lancaster for safety. A Mennonite, Bentz Hershey, risked his
life by letting officials know that he had overheard the Paxton
Boys plotting to finish the job. But too little attention was paid
to his warning, and on December 27 the Paxton Boys celebrated
the Christmas season by butchering the last of the Conestoga
Indians (most of them old men, women, and children) with axes,
shotguns, and knives. Lazarus Stewart, pronounced an outlaw,

escaped to the Wyoming Valley, where he joined the Connecticut people in the Pennamite Wars and lost his life, July 3, 1776, in the Battle of Wyoming.

There had been a few settlers in western Pennsylvania before the French and Indian War, but the real settlement of that country did not begin until after Bouquet's treaty with the Indians at Coshocton in 1764. The famous Proclamation of 1763, establishing the Appalachian divide as the Indian boundary and forbidding white settlement beyond it, had no more effect on the westward flow of population than King Canute's interdiction had had on the flowing tide. In western Pennsylvania and Virginia there were soon many settlers confident that their squatters' rights or "tomahawk claims" would in time be honored by government. Pennsylvania officials winked at this, hoping that her squatters would provide a counterweight to Virginia's when the boundary dispute came to be settled.

By 1768 the danger of another Indian war seemed (or was made to seem by land speculators) so great that the only way to avoid it was to repeat the old process of legitimizing settlement by belated purchase. In the Fort Stanwix Treaty of 1768, the Six Nations were persuaded to part with vast territories on the understanding that the boundary thus established would be the final one. The Fort Stanwix line ran down the North Branch of the Susquehanna to Towanda, then struck across country to the neighborhood of Williamsport or Jersey Shore (the place of entry to the West Branch being afterwards disputed), then up the West Branch to Cherry Tree, thence by a straight line to Kittanning, and down the Allegheny and Ohio to the Tennessee River. The Ohio was to be the permanent boundary. The history of Indian relations for the next twenty-six years (until, that is, Anthony Wayne's victory at Fallen Timbers in 1794) revolved about the Indians' doomed but gallant attempt to keep this boundary intact.

The growth of Pittsburgh at first mirrored the development of Western Pennsylvania, as the growth of Philadelphia had mirrored that of the eastern counties. By July of 1760, less than two years after General Forbes had found Fort Duquesne a smoking ruin, Pittsburgh had a population (apart from the garrison) of 149 people. In another nine months she had 332. Thereafter for a time she ceased to grow. The fort itself was abandoned in 1772. But settlers continued to pour into the valleys around. There were settlements at Redstone (Brownville) on the Monongahela, at Turkeyfoot (Confluence) on the Youghiogheny, and in the valleys around Bedford and Ligonier.

After the Fort Stanwix Treaty and the "new purchase" in 1768, the Land Office of Pennsylvania was flooded with applications. Terms were easy. Tracts were limited to three hundred acres, the price was five pounds per hundred acres, and payment could be deferred till the patent was taken out—which often meant indefinite deferment. Under such inducements settlers moved onto the new lands in great numbers. Within five or six years southwestern Pennsylvania was comfortably filled. The years 1769-1774 saw what Solon J. Buck and Elizabeth Buck, in *The Planting of Civilization in Western Pennsylvania,* call the "first push of the American people into the great interior valley of the continent."

"All this spring and summer," wrote George Croghan on October 2, 1770, "the roads have been lined with waggons moving to the Ohio." The Bucks estimate that by 1774 there were probably "fifty thousand people living west of the Allegheny Ridge and south of the Ohio, Allegheny, and Kiskiminetas in what is now Pennsylvania." By that same year some of these settlers had begun to move on into Kentucky.

The westward movement was interrupted for a few months in 1774 by what is known as either the Shawnee War, Lord Dunmore's War or the Real Estate War. The war was provoked by several ugly incidents, climaxed by the wanton murder of some thirteen members of the family of Shickellamy's son, Logan, whose memory is preserved in so many Pennsylvania, West Virginia, and Ohio place names.

The war ended in a drawn battle at Point Pleasant—a battle which registered, however, as an Indian defeat, because the Shawnees and their allies had not the numerical strength to continue the contest after it. Large land cessions followed.

The war's best memorial is found in the message which Logan sent to the governor some time after the battle—a message which found its way into Thomas Jefferson's *Notes on Virginia:*

I appeal to any white man to say, if ever he entered Logan's cabin hungry, and he gave him not meat; if ever he came cold and naked, and he cloathed him not. During the course of the last long and bloody war Logan remained idle in his cabin an advocate for peace. Such was my love for the whites, that my countrymen pointed as they passed, and said, "Logan is the friend of white men." I had even thought to have lived with you, but for the injuries of one man, Colonel Cresap*, the last spring, in cold blood, and unprovoked, murdered all the relations of Logan, not sparing even my women and children. There runs not a drop of my blood in the veins of any living creature. This called on me for revenge. I have sought it: I have killed many. I have glutted my vengeance: for my country I rejoice at the beams of peace. But do not harbour a thought that mine is the joy of fear. Logan never felt fear. Logan will not turn on his heel to save his life. Who is there to mourn for Logan?—Not one!

The pioneer and the parson made their way side by side into western Pennsylvania, clearing the forest and building log cabins and log churches. The prime example of a parson was the Reverend John Macmillan, a Presbyterian who was born in Chester County in 1752, was graduated from Princeton in 1772, and went that same year as a missionary to western Pennsylvania, where he settled permanently in 1778. The woods soon rang with his voice. He was a powerful orator and an indefatigable saddle-bag preacher. His vigor of mind and body earned him the popular title of "Pope of Western Pennsylvania." His monuments today are the many churches he founded and what was once known as John Macmillan's Log College (still standing) in Canonsburg. The latter developed into Canonsburg Academy and later into Washington and Jefferson College at Washington, Pennsylvania.

Chauncey Brockway is an example of the typical pioneer. He appeared a little later, it is true, because northwestern Pennsylvania, which was his home, was late in getting settled; but his experiences there were very much like those encountered by earlier pioneers in more southern counties.

In 1817, according to his "Autobiographical Sketch" (*Pennsylvania History,* April, 1958), he moved from New York State to what is now Elk County, Pennsylvania. With him were his wife, their baby, and, for part of the way, a couple of hired men. They traveled by way of Tioga Point (Athens), driving a wagon up

---

* It does not appear to have been Michael Cresap, the son of Colonel Thomas Cresap, who was responsible for the murders, as Jefferson supposed, but Daniel Greathouse.

Towanda Creek and down Lycoming Creek and fording the latter twenty-four times. When he swam the horses across the mouth of Pine Creek, he was nearly drowned. From Lock Haven he proceeded by Indian path along the West Branch of the Susquehanna to Sinnemahoning Creek, where he got a canoe. It was so late in the fall that ice was already forming in the creek. He had to lighten the canoe by leaving most of the food supplies behind.

Their last day's journey (Chauncey, his wife, and the baby were now alone) was made on foot through the snow. No path was visible. All they had to guide them were some blazes on the trees and occasional cut bushes pointing the way. Chauncey Brockway carried the baby; his wife, a small bundle and satchel. Snow falling from the trees melted and soaked into their clothes. Increasing cold froze the clothes on their bodies. They had to clamber over fallen trees, climb steep hillsides, and make painful headway over icy rocks on the edge of swift streams.

Late in the afternoon Mrs. Brockway broke down. Her husband took her bundles and somehow helped her to struggle on. To stop now, without food or fire, would have meant death for them all.

"We got to Josiah Mead's log cabin as the gray twilight of evening set in," he wrote, "and I never was more glad to see a cabin and the smoke of fire."

When at last they reached their own land, Brockway described an experience by no means unfamiliar to thousands of other settlers in western Pennsylvania—settlers whose example still stirs patriotic pride in the old-time pioneers.

Here we were, just ready to begin life for ourselves, and this was our situation, our family and our prospects. We had our log cabin to make out of timber then standing, and provisions enough for 8 or 10 days and some 20 or 25 dollars in cash, and about 100 miles from our base of supplies, or where any provisions could be bought, except some 16 bushels of corn I bought on my way coming up the river, and it was 30 miles down the stream. This looked a good time, or a fair chance, at least, to starve, and not ten days provisions on hand and the creek and river frozen over and no road, or team, if there had been a road. . . . The only thing to be done was to do the very best that we could and take our chances for it. . . .

As to provisions for the winter for myself, Mrs. Brockway and the baby, the hired man, and father Nichol's hired man, five in all, about 13 bushels of unground corn, to be brought 12 miles on our backs, no meat, no milk, no butter, no potatoes or turnips (save some four quarts each that I borrowed and I had helped my father dig 1,000 bushels before I left N.Y. and he was feeding out six bushels per day to his cattle at home. O how we did want some of them). No sugar, but a little tea, had a little salt. This is the way Mrs. Brockway cooked the unground corn, made a clean stout little bag of thick stout cloth, put two quarts of good clean ashes into the bag, then boiled in water until a good, strong lye was made, then take out the bag and put in the corn and boil until the hull, or bran, will rub off, then pour off the lye, and pour in water, and rub and wash until the hull and lye is all off, then boil the corn in clear water until the corn is soft and pulpy, and salt to suit taste, this we called hulled corn. Then boil some good spring water and salt it a little, this we called water porridge, or water broth.

This was our bill of fare for 1½ months, or from the latter part of Dec. until sometime in Feb. For breakfast we had hulled corn and water porridge, for dinner we had water porridge and hulled corn, and for supper we had for a change, water broth and hulled corn. We all stood it very well and worked hard.

13　*1776 and What Came of It*

The "melting pot" is a good metaphor up to a point, suggesting, as it does, the mingling of strangers in new patterns of loyalty and joint enterprise. But the figure must not be stretched too far. Human beings do not undergo a chemical change when they come together. Pennsylvanians had to learn, as the English had learned long before, that it takes many generations to integrate large blocks of population—as, for instance, the Celts, Angles, Saxons, Danes, and Normans in the British Isles—and that differences of one sort or another (race, social class, occupation, regional interest) may just as well increase as diminish with the passage of time. Differences may give health to democracy, but they do not give tranquillity. In producing a balance of stresses in a state, they also produce friction and noise.

The split between patriot and loyalist, as the Revolutionary storm clouds gathered, was only one of many divisions in Pennsylvania. There was the three-part division based on geographic origin: English, German, Scotch-Irish. There was the division between the mobile western frontier and the stable east. There was the occupational division: the farmer against the city man. There were also class divisions: the working man against the capitalist, and the poor settler against the land speculator.

This last division grew out of a contest for lands acquired from the Indians. On the one side were the actual pioneers, at grips with the forest; on the other, the rich landowners with headquarters in the east. Some of these proprietors so manipulated the conditions of settlement that *bona fide* settlers found themselves hopelessly in debt for tools and groceries they had been forced to buy at top prices. As a result, they lost their holdings, together with their improvements, to the absentee landlords.

Equally disturbing was the division between the excitable Scotch-Irish element in the west and the well-established and more conservative elements in the eastern counties. The Scotch-Irish (in those days called "Irish" in Pennsylvania and "Ulster Scots" in Ireland) provide a key to Pennsylvania's peculiar response to the Revolutionary War. The Scotch-Irishman had a grudge against England, but he had a deeper and more immediate grievance against the Quakers in Pennsylvania. He held them responsible for the military unpreparedness that exposed the Indian border to attack. He further blamed them for making it difficult to right the situation—difficult because western Pennsylvania had not been allowed adequate representation in the Assembly. In 1776 the three original counties, holding one-third of the population, elected twenty-four members to the Assembly, while the eight new counties, with two-thirds of the population, elected only fourteen members. The Scotch-Irish saw in the Revolution an opportunity to correct this inequality.

Occasion for the change was provided by the Continental Congress when, in preparation for independence, it called on the thirteen colonies to establish new governments. On July 5, 1776, ninety-six delegates met in the State House in Philadelphia to draw up a new frame of government. Benjamin Franklin took the lead. The work of the delegates was completed in September.

The conflicts that centered about Pennsylvania's Constitution of 1776 provide so good an introduction to her seemingly ambivalent attitude toward the American Revolution that it is profitable to take the state constitution out of its time sequence and discuss it before, rather than after, Concord and Lexington.

The Constitution of 1776, both in its strength and in its weakness, will be better understood if it is remembered that it was composed hurriedly at the outbreak of war. Its main purpose was to extend democracy and to correct the injustice suffered by the western counties. It attained its end by shifting the injustice to the east.

At first sight, the new arrangement seemed equitable enough. All counties were given equal representation in the government. But this meant discrimination against the more thickly populated areas. The new counties now had a total of forty-eight representatives in the Assembly as against the old counties' twenty-four; and the latter were further handicapped by the test laws, which restricted office-holders and even voters to those who took an oath to uphold the constitution. Since the taking of oaths was repugnant on principle to the Quakers, the Mennonites, and other German plain sects, the test laws considerably reduced the voting list in eastern Pennsylvania, where most of the "plain people" were concentrated.

In form the new government consisted of three bodies. For legislation there was a single house, the People's Assembly. It was composed of six representatives from each county, to be elected yearly. Administration was in the hands of a Supreme Executive Council, consisting of one member from each county and one from the city of Philadelphia. They were to be elected every three years.

The third body was the Council of Censors. This institution served as a watchdog. It consisted of two representatives elected from each county and one from the city, whose business it was to keep a check on those who administered the government and to see whether the constitution needed amendment. The censors were to meet every seven years.

This body was not only the most original and the most ambitious but also the most disappointing creation achieved by the new frame of government. Its function, as stated, was "to enquire whether the constitution has been preserved inviolate in every part; and whether the legislative and executive branches of government have performed their duty as guardians of the people, or assumed to themselves, or exercised other or greater powers than they are entitled to by the constitution." The power of amending the constitution rested with the censors. They alone had authority to decide upon the need of change. They alone had the right to call a convention to consider amendments.

The best part of Pennsylvania's Constitution of 1776 was its Declaration of Rights. There was little new in it, but it did include a reinterpretation of William Penn's liberal views and at the same time a mirroring of the new national pattern for which Penn had been in part responsible. It reflected the Declaration of Rights issued by the Stamp Act Congress, the Virginia Declaration of Rights (which it followed in much detail), and the Declaration of Independence. Pennsylvania's rights, as propounded in 1776, have been preserved almost intact to this day.

After drafting man's "indefeasible rights" and noting that all power of government rested in the people, the Declaration of Rights went on to enumerate man's particular rights, among which were: the right to trial by jury, the right to release on bail, the right of an accused person to speak in his own defense, freedom of speech, freedom of the press, freedom of assembly, and freedom of religion.

Religious freedom constituted a considerable extension of the rights granted in Pennsylvania's earlier frames of government. Restrictions imposed on Roman Catholics were now removed. The principal restriction still remaining was the requirement that members of the Assembly take an oath that they professed faith in one God and believed in the divine inspiration of the Old and New Testaments.

The strengths of the Constitution of 1776 were that it settled, for the time at least, the grievance of the Scotch-Irish and that it gave the Commonwealth a sound statement of democratic belief. But its faults were soon evident, faults so great that they set off a counter-revolution of such violence as almost to destroy the new state's foundations.

The principal defect in the constitution was that it provided for no authoritative check on hasty legislation, which the unicameral Assembly, filled with men of little experience, was all too prone to pass. A second fault lay in the Test Oath, which required all voters and all officers of government to swear that they would not "directly or indirectly do any act or thing prejudicial or injurious to the constitution." This was understood by conscientious people either to debar them altogether from the vote or at least to prevent their exposing in any way the manifest imperfections of the new frame of government. In consequence a large part of the electorate (some said nearly half) found themselves dispossessed of the full rights of citizenship.

The Whigs, whose triumph had brought about the Constitution of 1776, were now themselves divided. The radicals or Constitutionalists (defenders of the new constitution) were led by Benjamin Franklin (for a time), David Rittenhouse, and Robert Whitehill of Cumberland County. They were backed by the Scotch-Irish on the frontier. The more conservative or middle-of-the-road men, called Anti-Constitutionalists, were led by John Dickinson, Robert Morris, Thomas Mifflin, and James Wilson.

They were backed by the merchants and lawyers of Philadelphia.

The apathy apparent in some Pennsylvania quarters toward the Revolution sprang from the struggle over the state constitution. Some of its opponents refused to fight the British under its terms. Richard Peters was quoted as saying it was "a sickly Constitution, not worth defending." John Cadwalader, when in 1777 he was appointed a brigadier general of militia, went into temporary exile rather than serve. Some citizens took the oath of allegiance to the United States but refused to subscribe to the state oath.

Such was the political temper of the Commonwealth during the opening phases of the Revolution.

For nearly a hundred years before 1776, Pennsylvania had played a leading role in the humanitarian movement burgeoning on both sides of the Atlantic Ocean. When in the English colonies that movement flamed into revolution, Pennsylvania was still in the forefront. It is true that she had no Sam Adams, Patrick Henry, George Washington, or Thomas Jefferson; but if she allows New England and Virginia credit for sparking the American Revolution, she can make good claim to having provided the gunpowder.

There was, to begin with, the example of William Penn with his Holy Experiment and Charter of Privileges. There were the Quakers with their belief in the Inner Light—the surest foundation for self-government. There were the combative Scotch-Irish in western Pennsylvania, ready and eager to fight for their inalienable rights. And there was Benjamin Franklin, world-renowned, to provide by diplomacy the international friendships essential to final victory. It is no wonder that the Continental Congress as well as the Constitutional Convention gave the Keystone State the honor of their presence when it came to integrating the dreams, ambitions, and grievances of thirteen separate political entities into a viable instrument for human welfare.

The Quakers and German plain sects might object to the violence of the explosion when it came, and the loyalists protest the break with England, whom they believed to be sound at heart; but Quakers, plain sects, and loyalists had all helped to shape the American Dream.

At the Stamp Act Congress in New York, 1765, it was Pennsylvania's John Dickinson who drafted the Declaration of Rights and the Petition to the King. After the passage of the Townsend Acts in England, Dickinson wrote in *Letters from a Farmer in Pennsylvania* that "the cause of one is the cause of all." In 1768 he wrote a Liberty Song, which carried throughout the colonies the words, "To die we can bear—but to serve we disdain." His writings, immensely popular at the time, were to earn him in retrospect the title "Penman of the Revolution."

Dickinson hoped till the end that firm but courteous remonstrance would keep the issue between England and her colonies a matter for the conference table; but he never doubted nor let others forget what the duties of the colonies would be if they were once convinced that the debate could not be settled in peace. In 1776 he voted against the Declaration of Independence; but the decision having been made, he headed the committee that drafted the Articles of Confederation. In 1779 he was elected a member of the Continental Congress from Delaware. From 1782 to 1785 he was president of the Supreme Executive Council of Pennsylvania, and in 1787 he was a member of the Federal Constitutional Convention. It was largely owing to his influence that Pennsylvania and Delaware were the first states to ratify the Constitution.

If Pennsylvania was hesitant about making the break with England irrevocable, she bore her share, and a little over, in making the break effective. Her Scotch-Irish Presbyterian settlers on the Susquehanna and west to the Forks of the Ohio contributed generously to the new nation's army. For one thing, they had brought with them from Ireland an old grievance against England, and the Revolution gave them a chance to even the score. For another, they saw in the Revolution an opportunity to redress the wrong done, as they thought, by the Quakers, who had denied the frontier adequate military protection during the Indian wars. The Pennsylvania Germans also contributed well to the army, not because they had a grievance against England (on the contrary, as a people, they owed her much), but because of their new-found loyalty to their adopted country.

Philadelphia, geographical and intellectual center of the colonies, was chosen first capital of the United States, although for a few months (during the campaign for the city and the British occupation that followed) she perforce yielded to Reading,

Lancaster, and York. Despite the presence of a considerable number of pacifists among the English Quakers and the German plain sects, Pennsylvania gave to the Continental army some of its best generals.

The campaign which resulted in the capture of Philadelphia, September 25, 1777, was a masterly one for both sides in the contest. Sir William Howe, with an excellent army and brilliant commanders, was victorious in every engagement, but he came off second best in the end. As Dr. Henry Pleasants writes, his prime object, when he landed his forces at the Head of Elk, was to cut Pennsylvania off from the southern colonies. This he could do either by destroying Washington's army or by severing it from its base of supplies at Reading. Washington denied him the satisfaction of doing either.

Washington's purpose was to play for time, to prevent Howe from assisting Burgoyne, and to encourage the American people with the spectacle of defiant action—even though in the face of almost certain defeat—without losing his army, his supplies, or his liberty of movement. The game was a risky one; but played as it was with the spirited help of men like Greene, Sullivan, Anthony Wayne, and Peter Muhlenberg, it won enormous stakes: not only the confidence of wavering Americans but also the support of an ally, France. The resilience of Washington's army, according to Dr. Pleasants, in venturing an attack at Germantown so soon after the defeat at Brandywine, was no less influential than the victory at Saratoga a few days later in persuading France to support the new American nation.

After Germantown, Washington regrouped his forces at Whitemarsh in a half-moon on three hills, now known as Militia Hill, Fort Hill, and Camp Hill. Howe brought his army out of the city to probe these positions on December 5, 6, and 7; but finding them strongly held, he withdrew. After Cornwallis had done extensive foraging under cover of Howe's advance, the British army retired into winter quarters.

When Washington called a council of officers at Whitemarsh to discuss the choice of his own winter quarters, Peter Muhlenberg advised a line stretching from Reading to Allentown, where accommodations could readily be found. But Washington, unafraid of risks and trusting the stamina of his men, chose Valley Forge. He chose it not simply because it offered a good defen-

sive position flanked by the Schuylkill River and further protected by a nest of hills but also because it contained the British
more closely to Philadelphia and at the same time protected the
approaches to Reading, thus saving the rich resources of Pennsylvania's hinterland for the American army.

The story of Valley Forge, with its privations and its heroic
resistance to inactivity and boredom—the greatest of all enemies
—has often been told. But the dramatic climax of that vigil has
seldom been noticed. When it became known that Howe was
preparing to leave Philadelphia, Washington permitted the very
young Lafayette, who had been given a place on his staff as a
compliment to France, to cross the Schuylkill River with a force
of 2,100 men and five cannon in order to observe British movements. Barren Hill, where Lafayette established his camp, was
only two miles from British outposts on Chestnut Hill.

There, on May 20, Clinton and Grant, who had marched at
night into position, caught Lafayette in a trap. It has been customary to laugh at General Howe and his army in Philadelphia
for wasting strength in a round of balls and masquerades; but
the tough and lively striking force which drove Lafayette back
across the river does not offer substance for ridicule.

The Marquis suddenly discovered himself cut off from his
communications with the main camp by way of the bridge of
boats at Swede's Ford. It was only by skillful feints and hard
marching that he managed to reach the little-known and very
difficult Matson's Ford at Conshohocken ahead of the British,
who then launched a cavalry attack to catch the men struggling
through the breast-deep river crossing. To protect them, Lafayette left behind him a band of some seventy Oneida Indians who
had recently come down from the Iroquois country to give
George Washington a hand. General Peter Muhlenberg, who
held the advanced lines at Valley Forge and may have seen the
spirited engagement that followed, was a grandson of Conrad
Weiser, Pennsylvania's ambassador to the Iroquois. He reported
the action fully to his father, the Reverend Henry Melchior Muhlenberg, a few days later. The elder Muhlenberg wrote it all down
in his diary for May 23, 1778:

The Indians were the last to get over, and they were surrounded
in a small thicket by the English light cavalry, but they retired behind the trees in accord with their custom and let loose their usual

hideous war whoops, which threw the horses and riders into confusion and sent them flying; whereupon the Indians shot five or six of the cavalrymen and gathered up their cloaks.

Diving into the river, the Indians swam across after the others. One Oneida lad, a chief's son, was found to be missing, and prayers were offered to the Great Spirit for his safety. It is recorded that a few minutes later he climbed out on the bank, unhurt. This was probably the young Oneida whom Lafayette afterwards took to France and educated at his own expense.

Pennsylvania, the Quaker State, is seldom thought of as a breeder of war heroes. But two Pennsylvanians, dissimilar in racial background and in character (good illustrations of the melting pot), joined Washington's staff early in the war and emerged major generals at the end of it, to take their places among the best-loved figures in American history. They were Anthony Wayne and the Reverend John Peter Gabriel Muhlenberg.

Anthony Wayne, of Scotch-Irish extraction, was a man of many moods—all intense—and a mixture of caution and daring. He was confident, aggressive, brave to the point of recklessness, yet subject to moods of almost pathological loneliness—moods in which men found him brooding and quarrelsome. He was ambitious and as jealous as Benedict Arnold, but outspoken and utterly loyal. After Benedict Arnold's defection, Washington, with supreme insight, put "Mad Anthony" in his place at West Point.

On January 3, 1776, Wayne was commissioned colonel and given command of the Fourth Pennsylvania Battalion. This was the unit with which he made the Canada Expedition in support of Montgomery and Arnold. In the defeat at Three Rivers he helped to save the army from rout, as he was again to do at Brandywine and Germantown. Later he headed a force of eight Pennsylvania regiments—really a division consisting of two brigades—and commanded it without the help of a second brigadier or the commensurate rank of major general until the end of the war.

He was daring and he sometimes overreached himself, but he was steady, quick, and resourceful in the face of disaster, as he proved again and again throughout the war. At the Battle of Brandywine on September 11, 1777, Wayne was given the holding operation against Knyphausen, while Muhlenberg and Weedon rushed north to win fame through a stroke that blunted the main British thrust under Cornwallis.

Wayne's resourcefulness was perhaps best seen at the so-called Massacre of Paoli on September 20, 1777. In conjunction with General Washington he had been preparing to ambush General Howe and his army. As Harry Emerson Wildes writes in *Anthony Wayne, Trouble Shooter of the American Revolution*, Wayne had his fifteen hundred men in a good hiding place but, impatient at Washington's slowness to move up in support, decided to attack alone. He moved his men to within half a mile of the British, changed his mind, and moved back—but not without accidentally alerting the enemy. Howe feinted a return to Philadelphia, while Major General Sir Charles Grey, with the Black Watch, planned to surprise Wayne. Lest the British troops betray themselves by firing at shadows, the cartridges (or the flint locks) were removed from their muskets. The bayonet was the only weapon left to them.

Wayne received warning of the attack from his vedettes ten minutes before the British arrived. He alerted the camp, removed the artillery, corrected the errors of some excited officers, got the men into order, and directed an orderly retreat, losing some three hundred men, killed and wounded. A court-martial later examined Wayne's behavior and unanimously exonerated him, declaring he had done "every duty that could be expected from an *active, brave* and *vigilant* officer." He was acquitted "with the highest honor."

At Germantown on October 4 during the disasters that covered the battlefield as thickly as the fog, Wayne's forces penetrated farthest into the British lines and then, retreating for lack of support, fought a good rear-guard action for seven miles, thus enabling the defeated American army to withdraw past Whitemarsh up the Skippack Road to safety.

At Monmouth, it was Wayne's steadiness that saved the day. Deserted by Lee, Wayne held the advanced post in the orchard with two Pennsylvania regiments until reinforcements arrived to turn defeat into victory.

Three years later in the Tidewater Campaign, Wayne and Muhlenberg found themselves together in the field, under Lafayette's general direction, covering Cornwallis' movements. They made a great pair. Daring and resourceful, they converted this swift-darting campaign into a brilliant spectacle of team play between two star performers. Both were eager and aggressive, yet both were aware of the danger if they relaxed for a moment in Cornwallis' neighborhood. Independent though they were, each was quick to help the other at the first hint of alarm. When Muhlenberg on one occasion dangerously exposed himself to one of Tarleton's lightning cavalry strokes, Wayne moved in so quickly that Tarleton thought better of it and veered away. Later at Green Spring, July 6, 1781, Wayne, misinformed about the British position, moved to cut off what he supposed to be an isolated fragment of Cornwallis' forces and found himself engaged with the whole British army. Muhlenberg, on hearing the gunfire, sensed his friend's distress and without orders moved up so swiftly that Wayne, though badly mauled, was able to extricate himself.

When on September 28, 1781, the troops moved up to siege lines at Yorktown, Washington's "Order of Battle" placed Muhlenberg's and Hazen's brigades on the right under Lafayette, while Wayne's and the Maryland brigades were under Steuben in the center. But, as Yorktown was Muhlenberg's show, it belongs to his story.

Peter Muhlenberg was of German extraction, a son of the Reverend Henry Melchior Muhlenberg, "Patriarch of the Lutheran Church in America." Though he was born in Pennsylvania and spent most of his life there, he was serving as an Anglican pastor in Virginia when the war broke out. It was in his pulpit at Woodstock, Virginia, on one Sunday morning in January (probably January 21), 1776, that he doffed his clerical gown, displaying the military uniform beneath it, and said, "There is a time to pray and a time to fight, and this is the time to fight." His career for the next five or six years, though he was with the Virginia line, is one in which Pennsylvania takes equal pride with the Old Dominion. Whatever disputes may have subsequently separated Virginia from the Keystone State, they have always shared, and will continue to share, pride in the Reverend General Peter Muhlenberg.

At Woodstock on January 12, Muhlenberg received a colonel's commission. Five months later he was found to have trained the Eighth Virginia Regiment so well that at Fort Moultrie he won the encomium from General Charles Lee that it was "alert, zealous, and spirited." At Brandywine he moved his men four miles in forty-five minutes to face Cornwallis at Birmingham Meeting, where he and Weedon held the British long enough to enable Sullivan to withdraw his shattered forces. He did signal service at Germantown as well as throughout the war.

However, it was during the fifteen months before Cornwallis' surrender at Yorktown that Muhlenberg made his greatest contribution to American victory. When Charleston fell, May 12, 1781, all Virginia's troops of the line were lost with it. George Washington then turned to the dependable brigadier to build a new army. Muhlenberg built well, but his supplies were short. When in January, 1781, he received orders to oppose Benedict Arnold at Jamestown (with further instructions from Jefferson to take "the greatest of all traitors" alive or dead), he had only three hundred bayonets for his three thousand men, and his artillery consisted of two brass six-pounders. His efforts to draw Arnold into a trap were unsuccessful. When Phillips replaced Arnold and took his men in boats up the James River against Richmond, Muhlenberg could do no more than race him by land to Petersburg and there fight a stiff delaying action before blowing up the Pocahontas Bridge and retiring. Afterwards he joined Wayne, and they kept up a dancing, stabbing attendance on Cornwallis until His Lordship holed in at Yorktown.

While the Yorktown trap was being set, Muhlenberg was given the job of tightening its southern quarter. He poised himself south of the James River, ready to destroy bridges, boats, mills, and provisions if Cornwallis should try to escape by that route. When the trap was finally closed and Washington moved up to siege lines at Yorktown, General Muhlenberg's brigade of light infantry, "the flower of Washington's army," formed the advance guard.

Washington undoubtedly intended that the final honors at Yorktown should go to Muhlenberg, who for fifteen months had been America's principal field commander in the Virginia campaign. With the French fleet in the river and a stout international army in the trenches, it was well known that Cornwallis was done for and that the capture of Redoubt 10 was to be the American army's prime symbol of victory in the Virginia campaign, if not in the war. The capture was assigned to Muhlenberg, who made the necessary dispositions. At the last moment, however, changes were made at headquarters. Lafayette's young friend Alexander Hamilton, who had joined the Virginia troops only a few days before and lobbied furiously for self-advancement, was given the honor of leading the assaulting party. Muhlenberg was still in charge of the whole action and went over the top with his men, but for some unexplained reason the report of the engagement was written not by the commander but by Colonel Hamilton. Hamilton did not mention Muhlenberg at all, and Lafayette, when he sent Hamilton's despatch to headquarters (whence it reached all the newspapers), mentioned Muhlenberg so casually in his own covering report that the public has scarcely associated Muhlenberg's name with the Yorktown action at all. In a recent history of the Revolution he is mentioned at Yorktown only as "Parson Muhlenberg," a picturesque figure somehow associated with the American troops. But Pennsylvanians know that Peter Muhlenberg deserves the military honor George Washington had intended for him.

14   *Constitutional Conventions:*
Federal and State

The United States had won the Revolutionary War, but the greater test of her people lay ahead. Once the pressure of physical danger was removed, conflicts of interest threatened to break up the continental confederacy. Could the people of thirteen sovereign states, separated as they were by geography, historical tradition, and economic competition, make the imaginative effort required to unite them in one citizenship? Advantages of such a union that seem obvious today were arguable then. Would the individual states accept loss of sovereignty in the interests of a wider loyalty? Would the people tolerate the machinery needed to make the union effective? Might not the attempt to bring about a change of loyalties from the lesser to the greater unit stir up old jealousies and destroy even such unity as the recent struggle had created?

Few members of the Constitutional Convention, when they

assembled in Philadelphia, had any confident answers to those questions. So fearful were they of adverse popular reaction that, when Benjamin Franklin at a certain crisis in the discussions suggested that the meetings thereafter be opened with prayer, the proposal was rejected on the grounds that, if the people heard of this, they might think the Convention was unsure of itself and be the more inclined to reject its proposals. It was the successful overcoming of all such fears that constituted the real victory of the Revolution.

Both in the drafting of the proposed constitution and in the winning of popular approval for it afterward, Pennsylvania's part was crucial. Her best minds supported the key terms of the Constitution, and her example (she was the first large state to ratify it, the only one ahead of her being her daughter, Delaware) gave impetus to the decisions of others.

It was fitting that Philadelphia, which had housed the Continental Congress when it issued the Declaration of Independence, should be the birthplace of the federal Constitution. Meetings were held in the State House—not yet known as Independence Hall, although one of its rooms was sometimes given that name.

Chief honors in the deliberations must go to Virginia. It was only to be expected that George Washington, known for his skill as a co-ordinator as much as for his renown as a soldier, should be given the chair. James Madison, in whom the scholar and politician had achieved an almost perfect balance, took the lead in the discussions. But Pennsylvania contributed a strong delegation, men of administrative experience and speculative mind. Of her eight members (the largest delegation in the Convention) seven had been members of the Continental Congress, five had been officers in the Continental army, three had had wide experience in law, and three had held administrative positions in finance. They were Benjamin Franklin, James Wilson, Robert Morris, Thomas Mifflin, George Clymer, Thomas FitzSimons, Jared Ingersoll, and Gouverneur Morris.

Benjamin Franklin, who at eighty-one years of age was the oldest member of the Convention, brought to it the prestige of his career as a scientist, president of the convention that had drafted Pennsylvania's Constitution of 1776, member of the Continental Congress, colonel in the army, and ambassador to

France—in which latter capacity he had done almost as much to win the war as the armies commanded by George Washington. Thomas Mifflin had served as president of the Continental Congress and as a major general in the war. Robert Morris had in 1781 established the Bank of North America, and for three years (1781-1784) held the office of superintendent of finances. Aristocratic man-of-the-world Gouverneur Morris (no relation of Robert Morris) was his assistant superintendent of finances.

Of all the Pennsylvania delegation, James Wilson did most for the Constitution. He had had experience as a member of the Continental Congress and as a successful member of the bar with a good practice in Carlisle. He had been a counsellor in the settling of the Wyoming controversy between Pennsylvania and Connecticut, both of whose charters embraced the Wyoming Valley. He had, moreover, a comprehensive and exact knowledge of constitutions all over the world from the days of the Athenian democracy to his own time. He also had a gift that does not always go with superior knowledge: ability to express himself persuasively in debate. This was one of the few gifts lacked by Benjamin Franklin, of whom Major William Pierce of Georgia wrote, "He does not shine in public Council."

It is easy to understand the anxiety with which the members approached the question whether to present the public with the best constitution the Convention could devise or to issue a watered-down version, innocuous, indecisive, but easy to swallow. Their decision, a noble one, was to offer only the best: to concentrate not on what they thought the electorate would be most likely to accept but on what in the long run of history would be best for the country. The words attributed to Washington, "Let us raise a standard to which the wise and honest can repair," are a measure not only of his courage and wisdom but also of the maturity of the American democracy in accepting what the delegates had fashioned in that spirit.

One question raised early in the debate concerned Pennsylvania's past experience so closely, and its solution (on lines strongly urged by James Wilson) had such an important influence on the future of the United States, that it ranks as Pennsylvania's most essential contribution to the Convention.

Early in the debate Roger Sherman of Connecticut raised the question as to how extensive should be the central government's powers. Sherman's contention was that it was impossible for government to "pervade," as he put it, a large state. Little Connecticut, he thought, was the best size for an effective political entity.

William Penn had not feared geographical nor cultural divisions among his people. The Commonwealth had found that such differences as existed had enriched rather than impoverished, strengthened rather than weakened, the state. But Sherman, discussing what is now called States' Rights, insisted that people were happier in a small state than a large one. Therefore he proposed that the unit on which the citizen's loyalty concentrated should be the individual state, while the central government should have its powers limited to a few definite purposes, chiefly in the field of foreign affairs—defense, treaty-making, and commerce.

James Madison of Virginia countered with an argument that was implicit in Pennsylvania's melting pot, though it had never been so well expressed before. Carl Van Doren in *The Great Rehearsal* summarizes his argument thus:

> There were bound to be factions and interests in any state. But if the state were large enough, then no one interest would be likely at any time to form itself into a majority against the interest of the whole people or of any particular minority.

In other words, the danger of oppression was less in a large republic than in a small one. In his *Notes on the Confederacy* Madison wrote:

> The great desideratum in Government is such a modification of the sovereignty as will render it sufficiently neutral between the different interests and factions, to controul one part of the society from invading the rights of another, and at the same time sufficiently controuled itself, from setting up an interest adverse to that of the whole society. In absolute Monarchies the prince is sufficiently neutral towards his subjects, but frequently sacrifices their happiness to his ambition or his avarice. In small Republics, the sovereign will is sufficiently controuled from such a sacrifice of the entire Society, but is not sufficiently neutral towards the parts composing it. As a limited monarchy tempers the evils of an absolute one; so an extensive Republic meliorates the administration of a small Republic.

James Wilson of Pennsylvania (a "commonwealth" where this principle had been well tested) supported various measures which would guard the national government from encroachment by the states. On the other hand, John Dickinson (attending as a representative of Delaware) recommended that "the accidental lucky division of this country into distinct states" should not be destroyed. Early in the Convention he expressed the hope that in one branch at least of the legislature the states should have equal representation.

There was bitterness between the States' Righters and those who wished to see the principle of proportional representation extended to both branches of a bicameral legislature. Wilson wanted to know whether they were forming a government for men "or for imaginary beings, called *States*." Bedford of Delaware accused the larger states of preparing by means of proportional representation to ruin the smaller ones. "I do not, gentlemen, trust you," he said. ". . . Sooner than be ruined, there are foreign powers that will take us by the hand."

Benjamin Franklin, in the voice of Poor Richard, spoke for compromise. "When a broad table is to be made," he said, "and the edges of planks do not fit, the artist takes a little from both, and makes a good joint. In like manner here both sides must part with some of their demands, in order that they both join in some accommodating proposition." He reminded the delegates that Scotland, in her union with England, instead of being swallowed by her larger partner as the whale swallowed Jonah, had put so many Scotsmen into the government that it might be said Jonah had swallowed the whale.

Compromises were effected. A plan that Dickinson had earlier suggested was brought out again and found to provide a sensible solution. It was decided that in the House representation should be proportioned to population; in the Senate all states were to be equal. It was also decided that Congress should not have the power of veto over state laws. Instead, as Supreme Court Justice Owen J. Roberts wrote in *The Court and the Constitution,* "Controversies arising out of the alleged transgression by one government upon the authority of the other were relegated to the Supreme Court."

All during the Revolution there had been agitation in Pennsylvania to revise and amend the State Constitution of 1776. The Revolution itself settled the conflict between patriot and loyalist by defeating and driving out the latter. But other factions remained: the Whigs, now divided; the radicals or Constitutionalists, backed by the frontier; and the conservative Anti-Constitutionalists with their main strength in Philadelphia.

In the ensuing struggle for constitutional amendment, the Council of Censors was the center of conflict. The censors, ostensibly guardians of the public weal and supposedly responsive to every need for constitutional amendment, were in fact the chief obstacle to revision. Representation on the council, consisting of two members from each county, was so weighted in favor of the sparsely settled western counties (whose interest it was to preserve the *status quo*) that no prospect seemed in sight for any change. The Constitution of 1776 under the guise of democracy seemed actually to have saddled Pennsylvania permanently with not a democratic but a proletarian government.

The Constitution itself proclaimed a contrary principle: "Representation," it said, "in proportion to the number of taxable inhabitants is the only principle which can at all times secure liberty, and make the voice of the majority of the people the law of the land." But in practice the principle was denied. Frederick Muhlenberg wrote to his brother, Henry Ernest Muhlenberg, on June 28, 1784: "Is it just that 1500 Taxables in Washington, Bedford, Westmoreland, or other back counties, who, by the way have paid little or no Tax during this revolution should have as much to say in the Council of Censors as 8000 from Lancaster or 7000 from Philadelphia who bear the burden of the State?"

Benjamin Franklin found the Assembly a biased and incompetent instrument of government. To William Strahan he wrote on August 19, 1784: "It is a fact that the Irish [Scotch-Irish] emigrants and their children are now in possession of the government of Pennsylvania, by their majority in the Assembly, as well as of a great part of the territory; and I remember well the first ship that brought any of them over."

The middle-of-the-road people, who wished to retain the democratic features of the new constitution while revising it to secure more equitable representation, fought a hard battle. New tactics were adopted. Instead of boycotting the government, as many of them had done at first, they resolved to work *within* the constitution for its amendment, and their movement gained ground with the electorate. Robert Morris reorganized the state's finances. John Dickinson returned to Pennsylvania political life and became president of the Supreme Executive Council. Frederick Muhlenberg became speaker of the Assembly and presided over it from 1780 to 1783. The conservatives (Republicans, they called themselves) enjoyed a temporary control of the legislature from 1782 to 1784. When, however, they attempted a revision of the test laws, the radicals absented themselves from the Assembly and caused the bill to fail for lack of a quorum.

But the popular tide was turning. In 1786 the Anti-Constitutionalists came back to power. In 1787 they amended the test laws, making them require no more from the voters than a declaration of allegiance to the state, and two years later they removed even that gentle test.

It was the question of ratification of the federal Constitution that brought the final downfall of the state constitution. The Assembly passed a motion calling for a convention to debate ratification. The radicals (supporters of the Constitution of 1776), to prevent final action on the convention, absented themselves in sufficient numbers to deprive the Assembly of a quorum. Then a Philadelphia mob took a hand. They caught two of the radicals, hauled them back to the State House, and delivered them to the Assembly, where their enforced presence made a quorum. Business was resumed and arrangements were completed for the ratifying convention. Under the leadership of James Wilson, Frederick Muhlenberg, Benjamin Rush, and Thomas McKean, the federal Constitution was adopted by a vote of forty-six to twenty-three.

Ratification of the federal Constitution prepared the way for a similar advance on the state level. A state constitutional convention assembled on November 24, 1789. Albert Gallatin afterwards described it as "one of the ablest bodies" of which he had ever been a member. Certainly its history provides one of the best examples of a mature democracy in action. After the frantic disputes of the past fourteen years, the leaders on both sides, in particular William Findley for the radicals and James Wilson for the conservatives, agreed that the old constitution, however good it might have been in conception, simply did not work. Under their influence the convention agreed by overwhelming vote that the Assembly should have the checkrein of a second chamber, to be known as the Senate; that the chief executive power should rest, not in twelve men but in one, the governor; and that he should have the power of veto.

The Constitution of 1790 did not represent the triumph of any one group—sectional, radical, religious, or economic. It represented the melting pot at its best, all sections of the state making the necessary compromises and adjustments to serve the best interests of the whole. The people of Pennsylvania, after all the shouting and jostling, had achieved a stable democracy. The Constitution of 1790, which, as Harry M. Tinkcom writes, expressed this new stability "in a solid documentary form," may be regarded as the triumph of Penn's Holy Experiment.

Thomas Mifflin, a gentleman of Quaker extraction who had been a major general in the Revolutionary War, had served in the Continental Congress, had been president of the Supreme Executive Council, and was of conciliatory impulse and manner, became the first governor of the Commonwealth.

15 *Some Angle Shots of Benjamin Franklin*

Benjamin Franklin is the only man in Pennsylvania history who can be said to compare in stature with William Penn. They were both men of affairs, both men of creative genius, both citizens of the world. In other respects, however, two men could hardly be more unlike. Penn was an open-hearted, unsuspicious friend of humanity, easily taken in by a pious fraud like Philip Ford, who robbed him of his estate and nearly robbed him of his province. At the same time Penn in a Holy Experiment created Pennsylvania and made it the seed of a nation. Benjamin Franklin, on the other hand, was a shrewd apostle of common sense, Mr. Worldly Wiseman, who brought not philosophy but electricity down out of heaven.

Of the two, Franklin is by far the better known. Despite his giant intellect, he seems always to be one of us. In whatever guise he came—as politician, inventor, scientist, or sage—he talked about things familiar. "Poor Richard" is like the milkman, bringing the simple necessities of life.

It would be tedious to discuss the Benjamin Franklin everyone knows: Franklin the printer, almanac-maker, newspaperman, magazine editor, book publisher, and pamphleteer; Franklin the founder of the American Philosophical Society and the Academy (forerunner of the University of Pennsylvania); organizer of Philadelphia's first street-cleaning and fire department; inventor of the Franklin stove and the lightning rod; architect of the thirteen steps to virtue and the Albany plan of union; postmaster, diplomatic agent, ambassador to France, president of the Executive Council of Pennsylvania, and member of the Constitutional Convention.

The image of Franklin as a public figure has become so familiar that its impression is dulled. He needs to be seen from a new angle: from the Ephrata Cloister, for example, or the Nescopeck Indian Path, or even the Grand Châtelet prison in Paris. Such "candid shots," which give a fresh and intimate view both of Franklin and of his time, do not in the least belittle him, for he was never less vulnerable than when off guard. Perhaps it is because he never assumed the role of the great man that he never looks a small one.

He was always himself and always at home. Among people everywhere he was composed and comfortable. It was the same whether Wedderburn of the Privy Council was on his neck or Madame Brillon was on his knee; whether he was condoling with the Indians on the death of Old Briton of Pickawillany or outwitting a sharper in France trying to employ him as a stool pigeon. To observe him in these incidental contacts (devoid, most of them, of the stimulus to genius that affairs of state provide) is to become sharply aware again of Franklin's "imperturbable common sense" and also of the amazing drive—and no less amazing poise—of his mind, which seems never to have known a moment's drowsiness or discomfort. Everything interested him, and his interest always resolved itself into action.

Take, for instance, Conrad Weiser's beard. When Franklin first saw it, it was long enough to wave in the wind. Franklin was surprised to see a successful farmer, Indian ambassador, county judge, and father of a large family covering chin and chest in this reclusive fashion, for the beard was a sign of retirement from the world. A few years earlier Weiser had burned his Lutheran books of devotion and joined the Seventh-Day German Baptists in their celibate colony at Ephrata in protest against the furious denominationalism he found among the "worldly" churches. He believed with William Penn that "It were better to *be* of no church, than to *be bitter* for any."

When Weiser turned up on August 29, 1743, at Benjamin Franklin's bookshop on Market Street in Philadelphia, Franklin was glad to find the opportunity to turn the Dunker justice's eyes in upon himself, for Franklin believed with William Penn that "A Devout Man is one thing, a *Stickler* is quite another." He sold

Conrad a copy of Butler's *Hudibras,* a satire on the English Puritans. The couplets bounced across the page before Conrad's eyes, making fun of humbugs who

> Compound for sins they are inclined to,
> By damning those they have no mind to,

and reminding the justice of his own growing disillusionment with the Cloister. On becoming a priest "after the Order of Melchizedeck," he had been made all too close a witness to the fact that the flesh is not always tamed by mortifying it. It is hardly a coincidence that five days after his purchase of *Hudibras* Conrad Weiser wrote a sharp letter of resignation from the Cloister.

In Butler's verses Conrad Weiser also saw a replica of his own beard, which

> . . . was canonic, and did grow
> In holy orders by strict vow. . . .

To conclude this Hudibrastic episode in the life of Pennsylvania's Indian ambassador, it should be observed that Conrad in revulsion put scissors to his chin. At Lancaster next year, 1744, the chiefs of the Iroquois Confederacy, in a jovial mood at the close of their treaty with Maryland, Virginia, and Pennsylvania, formally expressed gratitude to Governor Thomas for Conrad Weiser's having cut his beard, which, they said, frightened their children.

One of Benjamin Franklin's best traits was his unfailing presence of mind. No situation was too much for him. He could switch from one milieu to another, change his mood, his language, and his frame of reference, without embarrassment. When catapulted into new surroundings, he was in no time at all in charge of operations, showing the experts how to get things done.

This quality appeared at its best during the French and Indian War. He steadied the Commonwealth at a time when the terrified settlers were driven from their farms and the Quakers in the Assembly found conscientious scruples against providing military protection. Out on the frontier Colonel Conrad Weiser had been managing a body of volunteers that he posted at strategic points to control the Indian paths. By this means he succeeded in making the Delawares and Shawnee war parties cautious, but he could not eliminate their raids on the settlements. The Indians were elusive, striking quickly and vanishing into the forest. The untrained militia were bewildered and undependable. The frontier was caving in.

Into this confusion stepped Benjamin Franklin. As a young man he had devoured Daniel Defoe's *Essay on Projects*. In maturity his reflection, like Defoe's, tended always to action. Studying the situation, although he was without experience as a frontiersman, he quickly came up with a solution. He persuaded the Assembly to pass a militia bill which gave cohesion and permanence to the province's military organizations. He helped to concoct a "Plan of Operations" calling for the erection of forts and blockhouses at intervals along the inner flank of the Blue Mountains. To Colonel Weiser on the battlefront he issued, with as much confidence as if he had been such a noted Indian fighter as Tom Quick or Sam Brady, a paper of "Instructions" on Indian scouting. It reads like a manual:

If dogs are carried out with any party, they should be large, strong, and fierce; and every dog led in a slip string, to prevent their tiring themselves by running out and in, and discovering the party by barking at squirrels, &c. . . . In case of meeting a party of the enemy, the dogs are all then to be turned loose and set on. They . . . will confound the enemy.

He continued as if he were writing a school textbook, liberally sprinkled with *A*'s, *B*'s, and *C*'s:

Suppose a party marching from A intends to halt at B, they do not go straight to B and stop there, but pass by at some little distance, and make a turn which brings them thither. Between B and C, two or three sentinels are placed to watch the track, and give immediate notice at B, if they perceive any party pass by in pursuit, with an account of the number, &c., which enables the party of B to prepare and attack them if they judge proper, or gives them time to escape.

Franklin, though without an official military title, was assigned to the defense of Northampton County, which was in a panic after the killing of Moravian missionaries by enemy Indians at Gnadenhütten (Lehighton and Weissport) on the Lehigh River. With about a hundred soldiers and a body of axmen he set off for that northern county, intending to erect a fort commanding the Nescopeck Path, one of the main warpaths by which the enemy penetrated the English settlements.

The construction of Fort Allen at what is now Weissport was planned and executed with the same methodical competence that had gone into his electrical experiments and the scheme he presented at Albany in 1754 for the union of the colonies. Trees were felled; trenches dug; palisades cut to length, sharpened, assembled, and planted three feet deep. A platform six feet high was erected inside the walls for the musketmen. Within a week the fort was completed, 125 feet long and 50 feet wide. A swivel gun was fired to announce the fact to the enemy. Franklin's scientific curiosity was satisfied, meanwhile, by such things as measuring with his watch the time it took two men to fell a pine tree fourteen inches in diameter. The answer was six minutes.

With all his mechanical precision Benjamin Franklin had also a fund of imaginative sympathy, a quick perception not only of other men's thoughts but also of their mode of thinking. When he needed to, he could bring himself quickly into harmony with alien minds and put himself in the place of those who were most unlike him. He, a city man of the eighteenth-century Enlightenment, had no difficulty in identifying himself with Indians and their way of thought. This is apparent in his *Remarks concerning the Savages of North America,* in which he rebukes his fellow citizens for their false pride, letting them see themselves as the Indians saw them.

Savages we call them [he writes] because their Manners differ from ours, which we think the Perfection of Civility; they think the same of theirs. . . . Having few artificial Wants, they have abundance of Leisure for Improvement by Conversation. Our laborious Manner of Life, compared with theirs, they esteem slavish and base; and the Learning, on which we value ourselves, they regard as frivolous and useless.

His remarkable skill in projecting himself into other men's minds was, in part, what made him so good an ambassador for his country. It also helped to protect him from sharpers like John Schaeffer.

That slippery scoundrel was a brother-in-law of the Reverend Frederick Muhlenberg—much to the latter's grief and consternation, since the relationship imperiled a promising political career. Schaeffer turned up in France during the year that ended so gloriously for American arms at Yorktown, with plans up his sleeve for victories of another kind. He had a formula for making a quick fortune at the expense of his country's allies. His type may still be seen at country fairs, wrapping a piece of soap in a five-dollar bill. The materials for John Schaeffer's sleight of hand were the hull of a sailing vessel, a single-masted lugger (without the mast), and the address of Dr. Benjamin Franklin at Passy. He and his accomplice Bernard (a Frenchman in whom the police were already interested) planned to outfit and sell the lugger as a privateer, the war presenting openings for private enterprise on the high seas. But all this was on speculation. They had no cash. The problem was how, without money, to make this floating shell look warlike with a mast, sails, and guns. They slated Benjamin Franklin for the goose that would lay the golden eggs for them.

Though devious with Franklin, Schaeffer was engagingly frank with his accomplice. It would appear from Schaeffer's letters to this underworld worthy that the good doctor was soon netted. "The people," he wrote, "inquired of my Carracter of doctor francklin he told them what Ever I do with them they may depend upon it that I was a gentellman of fortune and honour and Came well Recommended in the best Manner to him in Consequence the [y] struck Imidattly with me—"

Schaeffer succeeded in selling the putative privateer to a certain M. d'Autun for sixty thousand pounds. But D'Autun made him sign a contract specifying exactly what equipment the purchaser had paid for and putting up security in the form of a cutter—to which unhappily neither Schaeffer nor his accomplice had title. Schaeffer sent quick instructions to Bernard to make the boat "look warlike" and not to let the hurriedly hired captain know anything about their business.

But in the confidence game as in war it is the unexpected that happens. Shortly after signing the contract, Schaeffer perforce wrote an agonized letter to Bernard indicating that D'Autun had smelled a rat. Schaeffer's last advice to Bernard was, "the moment you Recive this Letter . . . Destroy all my Letters" and flee to a rendezvous in Rotterdam.

That the flight proved unavailing is seen in the letter Schaeffer addressed from the Grand Châtelet in Paris, September 21,

1781, to "His Excellency Doctor Franklin," offering that friend of liberty an opportunity to do his stuff:

Sir, I am now in a Strange Country & 4000 Miles from Home No frinds to Vindicate me in my unhappy Situation Not with Standing there in Every Proof of my Inosance I am now fully Perswaded that without the Assistance of your Excellency [I] will Not be relived of Preson. I hope your Excellency will do Every thing that Lais in your Power to relive me of my Distrest Situation.

Schaeffer's lawyer appealed to Franklin in terms intended to wring the ambassador's heart. But Poor Richard did not lose his composure. He had, in fact, a formula of his own for just such occasions: to notify the prefect of police. That official had intercepted all the letters from Schaeffer to his understudy: and when the case ended with the Pennsylvania adventurer cooling his heels in prison, *M. le Préfet* put the dossier into the hands of the American ambassador at Passy. The papers are preserved today in the Historical Society of Pennsylvania. They provide a suitable memorial to those qualities of perspicacity, common sense, and *savoir faire* that endeared Franklin to the French and won for his country a great ally.

16 *Robin Hood Was at Home Here*

The backwash of the Revolution in Pennsylvania produced a crime wave of a curiously unorthodox kind. Highwaymen appeared in picturesque sequences of adventures as if they were conducting rehearsals for amateur theatricals. They were high-spirited fellows, who put into these nocturnal adventures an engaging touch of chivalry, as if they were more interested in the sport than in the rewards.

The best known of these was a group of loyalist sympathizers called the Doane gang—five brothers, all over six feet tall: Joseph, Moses, Levi, Aaron, and Mahlon, with their cousin Abraham. When they saw the war going against them, they resolved their frustrations by attacking and robbing American officials, especially tax collectors. That these officers should have been singled out for attention was natural enough. Not only did tax collectors carry cash rewards for illegal highway prowess but their losses could be expected in some measure to put a drain on rebel resources.

American government authorities had difficulty in apprehending such bandits, not so much because of any fear of reprisals they might have inspired among those best able to inform on them, as because of the sympathies they evoked among the common people. In humiliating tax collectors, they put themselves in accord with one of the most profound and widely held of human prejudices—that which equates all publicans with sinners.

These particular "minions of the moon," furthermore, were averse to violence. They even respected private property, if it was in approved hands, and they possessed a rough chivalry, robbing the rich to help the poor.

Their first robbery was committed in Bucks County three days after the British surrender at Yorktown, presumably in reprisal for that disaster. On October 22, 1781, in company with other loyalists, they robbed John Hart, Esq., the County Treasurer, of 735 pounds in silver and paper money. Soon the "Royal Refugees," as they sometimes called themselves, came to be one of Pennsylvania's best known institutions.

They robbed Captain Ralph Williamson, collector of fines for Wrightstown Township. The fact that they found no more than twenty pounds on this occasion, and none of it state money, did not disturb their chivalrous equanimity. "As they were leaving," records Henry C. Mercer in *The Doanes and Their Times*, "one of the men took a bottle out of his saddle bags and gallantly offered Mrs. Williamson 'something to steady her nerves.' "

In time the going became rough for these "gentlemen of the shade," and a certain acerbity creeps into the record. After the conclusion of the war, the Commonwealth of Pennsylvania set about cleaning up its robber bands, and Frederick Muhlenberg, speaker of the Assembly, signed a proclamation against them which was printed and posted conspicuously all over the state. When Joseph Doane was captured and imprisoned, his brothers, who had hitherto avoided violence, threatened to take a new line. In the empty house in which Moses Doane was captured and killed, a document was found which constituted the Doane Brothers' reply to Muhlenburg's proclamation. In the enforced absence of Joseph Doane, who was by profession a schoolmaster, the orthography of this composition was weak, but its intent was clear:

These May inform Any That It May Concarn that If Joseph Done prisner Now in philadelphia Is not Released And Acquitted Immediately That We Will put Mulinburgh to Death In ten Days Without fail; and take another of your head Man and An other till Wee have taken ten for Every Refugee you put to Death Wee Will put ten to Death. . . . We Are Not your Subjects Neither Will Wee Ever Bee. . . .

THE ROYAL REFUGEES YOUR SWORN ENEMIES
. . .TO MULINBURGHS FRIENDS IF HE HAS ANY

For some time after that, Frederick Muhlenberg did not travel alone. Horses were stolen from his stable at the Trappe (Collegeville). But after a brace of hangings (Levi and Abraham) in 1788, the Doane Brothers ceased to be a problem. Joseph and Thomas Doane with their three sisters, Hetty, Polly, and Betty, went up to Canada. There, with the war and its passions behind them, they settled down and became responsible citizens.

James Fitzgerald of Chester County (the model for the character of Sandy Flash in Bayard Taylor's *The Story of Kennett*) was a blacksmith, tall and of enormous strength. During the Revolution he joined Pennsylvania's army and went with the "flying camp" to New York. There, for some minor infraction of the rules, he received a touch of the lash. Enraged, he deserted and went home. Being recognized, he was captured and jailed. Released on condition that he join the Continental army, he duly re-enlisted. Again he deserted and went home, triggering the same cycle: recognition, capture, escape. This time, brooding on his punishment, he joined Howe's army and served with the British at Brandywine and Philadelphia.

When the British left Philadelphia, the home-loving Fitzgerald deserted once more and returned to Chester County, but without relinquishing his new allegiance. He became the chum of a Tory named Mordecai Dougherty, with whom he adopted a hiding place at Hand's Pass on the Brandywine. With this as their headquarters the two conducted a campaign of attrition against the United States, concentrating their efforts in their home neighborhood.

Pennsylvania folklore has taken Fitzgerald to its heart. In prose and verse he is the hero of picturesque, unsordid adventures. Like Br'er Rabbit, he usually outwitted his pursuers. He was, it appears, a great humorist, specializing in irony. If we may credit the stories that celebrate his merits, he did not avoid danger but liked to meet it halfway and turn the tables on those who were after him.

They say that at one time he met two tax collectors, both of them armed and on his trail. Unrecognized, he walked some distance down the road with them, enjoying a conversation during the course of which he discovered their intent. One of them, Captain McGowan, wore his hair in a queue. This foppish fashion irritated the worthy blacksmith, who had other grounds as well for disliking McGowan, having overheard him in a tavern boast of what he would do to Fitzgerald if he ever caught him. Choosing the dramatic moment, the blacksmith turned on his companions, disarmed them, and told them who he was. He took McGowan's watch, sword, and pistols, cut off his queue, tied him to a tree, and gave him a flogging. On the captain's complaint, however, that the stolen watch was an heirloom, Fitzgerald returned it to its owner and set him free.

The exploit has been embalmed in verse by an anonymous rhymester with democratic tastes in both haircut and prosody:

> Some he did rob, then let them go free,
> Bold Captain MacGowan he tied to a tree.
> Some he did whip, and some he did spare,
> He caught Captain MacGowan and cut off his hair.

A public meeting was called one day at a tavern on the West Chester Road, according to *The New Doane Book* (published by the Bucks County Historical Society in 1952). Its intent was to concert measures for the capture of Captain Fitzgerald. There the adventurous blacksmith presented himself, disguised and unarmed. Hearing a militia officer boast of how he could take "Captain Fitz" if he could but lay eyes on him, Fitzgerald slipped a candlestick unperceived into his coat pocket and approached the brash captain. Drawing him aside, he said that if he would withdraw with him to a private room, he would tell him where and when he could see the outlaw.

The militia captain entered the room with him. Fitzgerald locked the door, leveled the candlestick (stilll in his pocket) menacingly at the officer, and said quietly, "Young man, I am Captain Fitz, whom you wished to see. I'll trouble you for your watch and what money you have about you."

Fitzgerald took the young man's silk handkerchief out of his pocket and tied his hands.

"Now, sir," he said, unlocking the door, "you may go back to your friends and tell them you have seen what you wanted of Captain Fitz."

As villain-heroes the Doane Brothers were popular, and Fitzgerald even more so, but the best loved of all Pennsylvania's out-

laws was David Lewis of the Lewis and Connelly team. Lewis was
of a slightly later vintage than Fitzgerald and the Doane Brothers,
but he belongs to the same quixotic type and should appear in
their company.

Lewis and Connelly deserve the thanks of the banking community, for in Centre County they revolutionized the saving
habits of the people. Where formerly farmers had kept their
money in a sock, Lewis and Connelly taught them the wisdom of
banking it.

For years these two haunted the Drover's Road (formerly
known as the Great Shamokin Indian Path), which crossed the
mountains between Milesburg and Clearfield by way of Snowshoe and Moshannon. One tale in the Lewis and Connelly
cycle—that of the poor widow and the wicked sheriff—has
been repeated in the folklore of nearly every admired outlaw in
America. Robert H. Lucas of Clearfield heard it from his grandfather, whose farm (graced with an orchard which Johnny Apple-
seed planted on his way to the West) lay on the old path between
Milesburg and Snowshoe.

A poor widow who had a farm among these mountains was
about to be evicted. The sheriff himself held the mortgage and
intended to foreclose. Lewis and Connelly, hearing of her trouble, determined to protect her. Calling on her the evening before
the sheriff's intended visit, they gave her sufficient money to pay
off the mortgage and instructed her solemnly to get a receipt.
When the sheriff arrived, she paid the money and took his
acknowledgment. The sheriff, returning, was met by Lewis and
Connelly, who relieved him of his money and so repaid themselves for their trouble.

Lewis was the star of the team. Stories of his dashing career
proliferated after his death and his character soon assumed its
present heroic mold. He is remembered by the folk as tall, handsome, well-mannered, and strong but gentle. He was equally at
home (and equally prehensile) at the card table and on the
road. Crimes of violence he abhorred; it was his pride that neither
he nor his associates committed them. He admired and respected
courage. When he ambushed a certain Mr. McKean of Newville
who was returning from church through the woods one Sunday
morning, he was so struck by the man's poise and politeness that
he let him go unmolested.

He dressed like a gentleman and rode a good horse. Ambling down the highway one day, he was overtaken by a posse on horseback.

"Have you seen a horseman go by?" they asked. "It's Robber Lewis."

He replied that no one had passed him, expressed an interest in the pursuit, and asked if he might join them. They all dashed off together. After a few miles most of the horses gave out, and the chase was called off.

As the posse turned to go home, the stranger lifted his hat and bade them good-by. "I trust," he said, "you did not find Robber Lewis such bad company," and was off like a shot.

One evening in the Bald Eagle Valley a Pennsylvania Dutchman, traveling alone with a good deal of cash in his pocket, found the falling shadows brought uncomfortable thoughts of Robber Lewis and the unwisdom of being caught by night in this peculiar haunt. He was glad to see a light shining from the window of a cottage, and he stopped to ask if he might have shelter for the night. He was made welcome, and the host pulled up a chair for him at a table where the cards were in play. Whisky passing, his tongue became loosened, and he was soon telling of his relief at finding shelter in the Lewis and Connelly country, especially considering what he carried in his pocket.

The evening passed pleasantly, he slept soundly, and he rose next morning refreshed and with pockets unlightened. As he said good-by to his handsome host, the latter wished him a safe journey.

"You may tell your friends," said he, "that you passed a quiet night with Robber Lewis."

Like Captain Fitz, Lewis was often captured but never long confined. By one trick or another he escaped. At the scene of his last capture in 1820 he was shot in the arm. Taken to the prison at Bellefonte, he was told that his wound had developed gangrene. A doctor informed him his only chance for life was to have the arm amputated. But life without his good right arm had no appeal for Robber Lewis. He declined the operation and died a few days later, July 30, 1820. His daughter was long a respected resident of Harrisburg, the capital city.

17 *Some Pennsylvania Utopias*

Man must experiment. Without change and novelty, his mind decays. Freedom to experiment (and to make mistakes) is therefore one of the marks of a healthy society. That is why the United States has reason to congratulate itself on having produced more than a hundred utopian experiments of some size, even though most of them failed.

Some failed because they were not rooted in human nature; others, because they contained the flaw of some single fanatical extreme. They went against nature. There is point in the old Iroquois proverb attributed to Deganawidah: "When you fill your kettle with water from the stream, *dip with the current.*"

Herein is seen the clarity of William Penn's vision. He organized a free society in which man's natural bent for experimentation was encouraged, but under safe conditions. It was the virtue of so diversified a population as Pennsylvania's that, if any experiment reached dangerous proportions, it would be counterbalanced by other movements tending in a different direction. The consequent tempering of extremes in the life of the Commonwealth has been one of her most healthy characteristics.

The mystic experience, stirred by the Great Awakening, produced among the early German and Swiss immigrants in Pennsylvania many beautiful, if extravagant, religious experiments. "Pennsylvania," writes Gordon Alderfer, "turned out to be the real proving ground of the mystical tradition." Something of the spirit that produced these early experiments survives among the Pennsylvania Dutch plain sects. Among such people as the Amish, for instance, the effort has been made to restore the purity of early Christian living, as they understand their Bible's definition of it. At the same time, the strong "in-group" feeling that separates the "saved" from the rest of the world, and the ruthless punishment of erring members by "avoidance" are reminders of the danger of fanaticism even in the gentlest of causes.

William Penn was a reformer who "dipped with the current." He had learned about human nature on land and sea, in royal courts and county jails. He knew that religious emotion, unless intelligently anchored in the second commandment of Jesus, "Love thy neighbor as thyself," can be inquisitorial and cruel, as had been demonstrated in England and Europe by the persecution of heretics and in New England by the witch-hunting and Quaker-hunting of a theocratic government. He felt strongly about this and often wrote accordingly:

"To be Furious in Religion is to be *Irreligiously* Religious."

"Some Folks think they may *Scold, Rail, Hate, Rob,* and *Kill* too; so it be *for God's sake.*"

"It is as great Presumption to *send our Passions upon God's Errands,* as it is to *palliate them with God's name.*"

Penn sought to avoid religious persecution in his own province, not only by separating church from state, but also by encouraging religious divergences in the hope that the froth of fanaticism might exhaust itself within small groups of enthusiasts. Pennsylvania was thus saved from the more dangerous effects of religious hysteria by the same sort of principle as is at work in the "melting pot" or even the federal union of the states. The principle was expressed by Franklin D. Roosevelt in these words: "The beauty of our state-federal system is that the people can experiment. If it has fatal consequences in one place, it has little effect upon the rest of the country. If a new, apparently fanatical program works well, it will be copied. If it doesn't, you won't hear of it again."

Throughout Pennsylvania's political life, from William Penn to John Dickinson and from President Buchanan to the present day, the Commonwealth has exhibited a spirit of compromise rather than the all-or-nothing ardor of a Patrick Henry. The state has at the same time shown a steady progress toward better living for all her people; and the amenities of life have not long been denied any one part of her population because of extremist claims to dominance made by another, whether on grounds of religion, race, or income.

When Penn arrived in 1682, experimentation was in the air. Penn himself was the product of a movement for reform then sweeping the British Isles, a movement of which Pennsylvania was to be the finest fruit. Though the Proprietor was capable of enthusiasm, he had a well-balanced mind. He was bold, unconventional, but not erratic. He was self-critical, and he was generous in accepting other people's ideas to supplement his own. He was blessed with the ability to distinguish between the essential and the unessential—a gift vital to the religious enthusiast if his work is to endure.

Unfortunately, many of the men who were inspired to taste the freedom promised them in Pennsylvania were of smaller stature, and their experiments, though always interesting and often sound in principle, slipped out of orbit because of some obsession with unessential detail. Such, for instance, were the New Mooners, who believed prayer to be more efficacious during the early phases of the moon. Such also were the Solitary of Ephrata, who believed that marriage is "the penitentiary of carnal man."

Of all the religious utopias born in Pennsylvania, two have drawn most attention to themselves. One was the Cloister of the Seventh-Day German Baptists at Ephrata, some of whose buildings are preserved by the Commonwealth under the administration of the Pennsylvania Historical and Museum Commission. They are among the best extant examples of early German architecture in America. Standing under the slopes of Zion's Hill, they are a memorial to one of the most thorough experiments in applied mysticism this continent has ever seen. The other was the Harmony Society. The solid brick buildings of Old Economy, located near Pittsburgh, are preserved by the state as a memorial to the Harmony Society's attempt to realize the mystic tradition in an industrialized society.

The cloistered community of Ephrata was founded in 1735 by Conrad Beissel (1690-1768), a man of sincere piety but with a touch of paranoia, who has been described as not unlike what Adolf Hitler might have become if he had followed a religious vocation. Beissel was a devout Christian whose sensitive mind and fervid imagination had been inflamed in Germany by the preaching of the Pietists and by the mystical books of Jacob Böhme. Persecution in his home country and then the spectacle of denominational quarrels in Pennsylvania (where "confusions" gave churchgoers opportunity to release the Old Adam without incurring consciousness of sin) fastened upon his mind a belief that communion with God was to be found only in retirement from the world.

Beissel made impassioned converts and persuaded them to burn the religious books used in the Lutheran and Reformed churches. At Ephrata he was inspired for a time to live as a hermit, reigning alone, without subjects—"the Narcissus of Conestoga," as Professor Walter C. Klein calls him. A later revelation caused him to set up a cloistered community. There, with his Brethren and Sisters, he fasted, grew a long beard, and went on missionary journeys among the prolific Pennsylvania Dutch population, preaching the superior blessedness of celibacy. Wives deserted their husbands, as did Frau Christopher Saur (thereby assuring for Beissel's movement a very bad press); and husbands deserted their wives, as did for a time Conrad Weiser.

Beissel's Scotch-Irish neighbors at Donegal made many wild charges: that he was a Jesuit missionary from Mexico sent to break up Pennsylvania Protestantism; that he was a magician; that he was a whoremonger. There was, in truth, during his creative years no more evil or sickness in him than a hypertrophy of the ego might create. He was an over-intense but earnest seeker after Divine Reality, who trusted his strange intuitions too implicitly.

He sometimes preached with his eyes closed, opening them at length to find that his ramblings had emptied the meeting hall. It is said that he sang a forty-three stanza hymn of his own composition. He allowed his imagination to turn the steep dormer windows of the Brothers House at Ephrata into "magic casements opening on the foam" of theosophical and Rosicrucian speculation. Truly, as the author (probably Peter Miller) of the *Chronicon Ephratense* wrote, "God made use of him to manifest forth the wonders of eternity."

In a world-wide reaction against cold rationalism, the fame of Ephrata spread far. To the community came seekers for the light, not only from Pennsylvania, but also from Europe. Some of them, like Conrad Weiser and Peter Miller of the neighboring Tulpehocken community, sought escape from the storm of religious controversy that was the backwash of the Great Awakening.

Others, like the Eckerling brothers, sought a place in which to exploit the refinements of a romantic and religious aestheticism. Under the Eckerlings, who crept into places of authority, such practices as the wearing of a tonsure, the "Baptism of the Dead" (by proxy), the ringing of midnight bells, and the marching of torchlight processions to the accompaniment of the strangely beautiful Ephrata music seemed to corroborate the worst suspicions of the stern Donegal Presbyterians.

Despite all these extravagances, Ephrata was productive of much good. The community sustained itself, or very nearly, by its own labors. It had its own farms, mills, and flocks. Gifts from friendly outsiders made possible for the inmates an ambitious program of music, printing, and book decoration. A German printing press, one of the most famous in the colonies, was set up about 1745. Today the products of that press—including the *Martyrs' Mirror,* a German translation of *Pilgrim's Progress,* hymnbooks, and other books of devotion—are among the most precious examples of early American publications. Religious poetry was written and sung. A school was established—one of the first Sunday schools in the United States. The composition of music was cultivated. Today at Ephrata a choir, gowned in white, renders that music (with a little adaptation) in the *Saal* at concerts that recall the midnight ceremonies of two hundred years ago.

The brotherhood gave their neighbors help in raising barns and in harvesting crops. However, coupled with this self-sacrificing concern for the wants of others was the cultivation of self-sacrifice for its own sake. The members sought peace for their souls through mortification of the flesh. They slept on narrow planks eighteen inches wide with only wooden blocks for pillows. They broke their rest with midnight services that never lasted less than two hours and sometimes ran on till dawn.

"I know men here," wrote Conrad Weiser, "who more than once have fasted for seven days and nights and from one year's end to another have not had one full meal, have allowed themselves only 3 or 4 hours sleep at most in the 24."

Some of the most mystically inclined discovered a way, they thought, of attaining the modest "immortality" of 5557 years. The method was for the candidates to retire during the full moon in the month of May to the top story of the building known as

Zion and to shut themselves up there for forty days and forty nights without sleep, drinking only rain water that had fallen during May and eating nothing but bread crusts. They were required to partake of a few drops of a potent elixir and a few grains of the *materia prima,* which would first destroy teeth and flesh but afterwards, if the partaker were successful, restore them. At the end of this probation one might attain communion with the seven Archangels: Anaël, Michaël, Raphaël, Gabriël, Uriël, Zobadiël, Anachiël. After that one might hope to win the seal of the Sacred Pentagon containing the Ineffable Name.

Some pilgrims were lured by this moonshine to attempt to climb the heavenly steep toward the magic number 5557. One brother is said to have gone so far along the way that he lost his reason and had to be flogged back to sanity. The graves at Ephrata bear unhappy witness to the steepness of the ascent.

But one should not laugh. As a protest against the bitter denominationalism of the time their movement was useful, and as an experiment in holy living it was salutary. The very extravagance of the experiment demonstrated man's unconquerable desire for something in life beyond "getting and spending." At the same time it showed how easily religious emotion can lose itself in the occult, and it exposed the futility of dipping against the current.

During the eighteenth century there were many other small religious bodies in Pennsylvania practicing the communal life as part of their faith (holding all things in common, which they took to be the teaching of Jesus). In the nineteenth century, though similar communities continued to be born, the emphasis changed from a purely spiritual to an economic experiment. The story of the Harmony Society will serve to illustrate what has been called the secularization of utopia.

Johann Georg Rapp (1757-1847) of Iptingen, Württemberg, inspired by the mystical writings of Jacob Böhme, Swedenborg, and the German Pietists, confident also that it was God's light within him that taught him to defy the discipline of the established Lutheran Church, put himself at the head of a group of separatist farmers and mechanics. When harassment by the local Church authorities became unbearable, George Rapp crossed the ocean to spy out the land in America. He found the spot he was looking for at what is now Harmony, Pennsylvania, in the forest beside Connoquenessing Creek, near the site of

Washington's "Murdering Town." There, twenty-five miles north of Pittsburgh, Rapp bought about three thousand acres and sent for his adherents in Germany.

His purpose was to organize a community where men might live the Christian life in productive labor. The goal was salvation, not through mortification of the flesh (though abstemiousness was practiced), but by the discipline of manual labor. They manufactured goods first for their own self-sufficiency and then for their neighbors' benefit. There was no proselytizing. The force of example, it was thought, would be sufficient to bring in a succession of younger recruits to assure the community's survival.

Father Rapp—tall, bearded, cheerful, and talkative—inspired trust in his simple followers. He was practical and he was positive. He was sure he had discovered the secret of Christian living. "Work is worship," wrote Carlyle in the same spirit a little later. Rapp gathered mechanics of all kinds around him. Under his leadership they produced what was necessary to keep up with, or a little ahead of, the times. As soon as he was able, he brought in the best modern machinery and experimented to make it better. The Rappites manufactured one of the first steamboats on the Ohio River.

On February 15, 1805, the Harmony Society was founded with the signing of the Articles of Agreement, in which the signers gave all their property to George Rapp and Associates for the common benefit of the Society and agreed to work diligently without pay. In return they were promised full support for themselves and their families, in sickness and in health. Rapp was elected head of the Society, and a young business genius, Frederick Reichert (whom George Rapp adopted as his son and who thereafter was known as Frederick Rapp), was elected industrial superintendent.

"What George Rapp lacked . . . in executive ability," wrote John S. Duss, a later Harmonist, "Frederick made up in the organization and maintenance of a perfectly coördinated economy."

Though the early days of land-clearing meant labor with empty stomachs, within a few months the Society had made itself into a smooth-running machine, and it was soon a pace-setter in the industrial world west of the Appalachians. By 1806 the community numbered about seven hundred, the larger part of whom were laborers. If it had been otherwise, they could not have built the town so well and so rapidly.

During the first year they cleared 150 acres; during the second, almost four hundred more. The first year saw a grist mill and nearly fifty log houses erected; the second, a large barn, a hotel, a sawmill, an oil mill, a tannery, and a brick storehouse. In their second year the Rappites raised all the grain they needed for themselves, sold the surplus (six hundred bushels), and manufactured three thousand gallons of whisky—not for themselves (they used it sparingly) but for their hard-drinking western neighbors. In five years they had bought and paid for nearly seven thousand acres of land, cleared two thousand acres, and built three villages besides the town of Harmony. The latter, as reported by their historian John S. Duss, had 150 houses, mostly of brick, a store, "two brick buildings for textile manufacturing, another for dyeing, a woolen factory, a spacious brick meeting-house, a four-story granary, two distilleries, two flour mills, two fulling mills, an oil mill, hempmill, brewery, blacksmith shop, nail factory, brickyard, potash boiler," besides four large barns, a number of stables, and a large brick warehouse on the Ohio.

The mainspring of Rapp's faith was the belief that the Second Coming of Christ was at hand. Earnestly his followers prepared for it by their industry, humility, love of their neighbors, and self-sacrifice. In pursuit of the latter virtue they came in time to give up tobacco, and they entered into a grave re-evaluation of the married state. It was an article of their faith that the fall of man lay not in the temptation of Eve but in her creation. The division of man into sexes was a sign of his shame. In a wave of religious revival that swept the community in 1807 it was decided to give up marriage. Thereafter no more marriages were contracted at Harmony, and no children were born there. Those who were already married renounced the marriage bed. Husbands and wives did not necessarily separate. They continued to live together, but only as brothers and sisters. There was no spying, no gossip, no slander. In all honesty and love these Harmonists prepared for the coming of their Lord.

Their daily routine was strict but not as severe as that of the Solitary at Ephrata. They arose at five or six o'clock in the morning and retired at nine. Nearly everyone took part in some form of manual labor, which Rapp believed was best for body and soul. The day's work was broken by five meals: a light breakfast between six and seven, lunch at nine, dinner at twelve, *Vesper Brodt* (perhaps with wine) at three, and supper between six and seven.

As an industrial experiment the success at Harmony was almost overwhelming. Surplus goods were manufactured at such a rate and of such superior quality that the demand for them was soon greater than could be supplied under the handicap of inland transportation (they were not on a navigable river). They had outgrown their locality.

Accordingly, in 1814 the Harmony Society made a fifteen-day journey in flatboats down the Ohio and up the Wabash some seventy miles to establish the town of New Harmony, Indiana, where they hoped to enjoy the commercial advantage of steam navigation. The change proved less beneficial than they had expected, partly because of the jealousy of their new neighbors and partly because the western market developed more slowly than they had anticipated. In 1824-1825 they sold their property to Robert Owen and moved back into Pennsylvania, building their own steamboat, the *William Penn,* to help in the removal. About eighteen miles below Pittsburgh at which is now Ambridge (near the site of the Indian Logstown) they built a town which they called Economy and entered their golden age.

It was a beautiful, spick-and-span German town, Economy, as may still be seen by visitors to this gem among the state's historical properties. The streets were wide; the brick pavements were neat; the houses were solid but unpretentious. Bands of green ran like ribbons down both sides of the street, for it was a rule that trellised vines should be grown between the bottoms of the upper windows and the tops of the lower windows on all houses facing the street. The effect was that of an avenue of Christmas boxes.

A utopian air pervaded even the steam-heated factories. Fresh flowers were placed daily on the machines. The air was filled with music. Men and women sang at their work during the day and again in relaxation during the evening. The Duke of Saxe-Weimar, who visited Economy in 1826 (the year after it was founded), saw factory girls, after the day's work was done, assemble in one of the factory rooms to sing hymns and folksongs.

Though the name had been changed from Harmony to Economy (recognition of a subtle change in motivation), religion was not neglected. Under George Rapp's guidance the Harmonists—celibate and tobaccoless—continued to make ready for the Lord's coming.

Frederick Rapp's genius for sizing up a commercial market and introducing the latest machinery brought Economy to a peak of industrial success. A large woolen factory, a large cotton factory, a five-story grist and flour mill—these were soon making the town's products famous. Cotton goods, hats, blankets, flannels, flour, plants, fruit trees, and wines, when shipped from Economy, were so successful on the market that competitors began to scream "Monopoly!" The *Allegheny Democrat* even urged the state legislature to dissolve the Society.

It was not, however, the rage of competitors but weakness from within that in the end brought the Harmony Society down. In the first place, the practice of celibacy undermined it. There were no children to grow up and take the place of their elders. The influence of example, in the absence of any proselyting, was less compelling than they had expected. As the original members grew older, few recruits came in from outside to replenish the waning energies of the group. Charles Nordoff, who visited Economy toward the end of the century, found that most of the 110 members were old people.

In the second place, Rapp's faith in the imminence of Christ's coming produced disillusionment among some of the members as the years passed and the skies did not open. It softened up others for the catastrophe that came with the appearance of the bogus "Count Leon."

This lordly rascal—Bernhard Müller, alias Graf Maximilien de Leon—arrived at Economy with a retinue dressed in picturesque Bavarian costumes and announced himself the Lord's Anointed. Jonathan Lenz, who played the French horn in the Harmonists' band that welcomed the troupe, recalled afterwards that the Count "did not come like the Savior humbly riding on an ass, but in a coach-and-four, with epaulets and sword and uniformed courtiers"—forty in number.

Rapp was not taken in as some of the others were. Nevertheless, he was constrained to let the unholy masquerader spend the winter of 1831-1832 at Economy, where he won a considerable following by artfully urging a return to the marriage state and a general loosening of moral standards. When at length

Rapp's loyal followers exposed the Count and drove him out (with the aid of the police), there was a grand secession. Count Leon took with him some of the Society's best young people and $105,000 in compensation for their relinquishment of their claims.

That incident broke the heart of Frederick Rapp, the industrial superintendent. It was not the loss of the money (a great sum for those days, but quickly made up at Economy) that troubled him as much as the sudden vision of what stupidity and malice can do when they join to destroy something beautiful and good. He died on June 24, 1834.

Father Rapp lived on. He lived to hear of Count Leon's establishment of the New Philadelphia Society at Philipsburg (now Monaca) ten miles down the Ohio River. But this brain child of the bogus prophet was soon in financial difficulties. Count Leon tried to get more money out of Economy but failed. Soon he absconded, seeking fresh and more congenial pastures in the West. Of these he was denied long enjoyment, for he died shortly afterwards of cholera.

For a few years more, Father Rapp kept up the courage of the Harmonists. To the end he maintained his belief that he could not die before he had seen his Savior on this earth. He boxed the ears of a boy who expressed doubts. As he lay on his deathbed, his last words were, "If I did not know that the dear Lord meant I should present you all to Him, I should think my last moment had come."

18 *The Moravian Indian Mission*

If William Penn came back today to see what had been happening since he left his province in 1701, the episode most likely to please him would be the Moravian mission to the Delaware and Mahican Indians. It is of special significance today as a bold and intelligent attempt to solve the race problem (then posed between Indians and white people), not by colonialism, *apartheid,* or absorption, but by co-operation. The method used to accomplish this was quite modern—about two hundred years ahead of its time—and not unlike President Kennedy's project of volunteer "peace teams" to go abroad and help people who are a little behind in the mechanics of civilization to catch up with their neighbors.

The Moravian experiment was generous in concept and design, and it was conducted with a vision and daring such as would have appealed to Penn's soldierly heart. More than that, it fulfilled a particular wish he had expressed in a letter to the Indians dated October 18, 1681: "God hath been pleased to make me concerned in your parts of the world, and the King of the country where I live hath given unto me a great province therein; but I desire to enjoy it with your love and consent, that we may always live together as neighbors and friends."

The Moravian Church, known officially as the *Unitas Fratrum* or United Brethren, was born in Bohemia in 1457. Since 1722 it has been called Moravian because in that year, during a time of persecution, some German-speaking members of the Unity from Moravia found refuge on the estate of Count Zinzendorf of Saxony in Germany and under his leadership revived their ancient Church.

Of all the German mystics in Pennsylvania the Moravians were the most level-headed and co-operative. No less devout than the Harmonists and the brotherhood of Ephrata, they were more healthy-minded, less fanatical. They were not beaten by the dry winds of theological controversy which tore so many of Pennsylvania's churches apart in the eighteenth century. The Moravians lived normal but unselfish lives, devoting themselves to others' welfare, material as well as spiritual. Their work among the American Indians was only a fragment of their world-wide missions, but nothing they ever did was more dramatic or more heart-warming. The story of the Delaware mission belongs peculiarly to Pennsylvania, for it chiefly concerned Pennsylvania's Indians and it was conducted in the spirit of William Penn.

The Moravian Indian mission was first established in 1740 among the Mahicans at Shecomeko in the province of New York. It might be said to have begun with the conversion of Wassamapah, a great brute of a man who threatened to kill the first missionary, Christian Henry Rauch. But Rauch possessed the quiet fearlessness that distinguished the Moravians and made them so astonishingly successful in the woods. One evening he went to Wassamapah's cabin and asked if he might spend the night by his fire. The Indian, taken aback at the white man's thus placing himself so unreservedly in his enemy's power, let him sleep—and live. It was a law of hospitality among those people that a man who slept by their fire was thereafter under their protection. Wassamapah became the missionary's guardian and soon also his friend and disciple.

When hostilities between the French and English during King George's War forced the removal of the mission to Pennsylvania, Wassamapah went along. At Bethlehem, where the Moravians had set up their own little utopia (the beautiful architectural remains of which are today being restored), Wassamapah became a noted preacher. His remains rest there now beside those of his white brethren in the old Moravian churchyard.

There at Bethlehem in the Forks of the Delaware (the land enclosed by the Delaware River and the Lehigh) the mission was enlarged by the addition of numbers of the neighboring Delaware Indians—so greatly enlarged that it came to be known as the Delaware, rather than the Mahican, mission. Soon a new town with log houses, streets, gardens, farms, and orchards was established on the Lehigh at the mouth of Mahoning Creek, where Lehighton and Weissport now stand. The Moravians named it Gnadenhütten, meaning "Tents of Grace." A log church stood in the center, and beside it a school, where reading and writing, music, certain trades, and the latest farming methods were taught. The Moravians looked forward to a time when the Indians, without losing pride in their own race, would compete with white men on equal terms in the new way of life to which the continent seemed destined. This was just such a solution to the race problem as William Penn might have hoped to see.

Many Indians at that time, whether Christian or not, looked on this form of coexistence as the best hope for peace between the races. What attracted them to the Moravian method was the understanding of Indian values which the Moravians brought to the problem. There was no condescension, no attempt to make white men of them. The Moravians understood the Indians' point of view, which was once expressed thus by a Mohawk, Julius Cook: "We must learn to think like white men, but we must keep the best of our own traditions, for if we do not we shall die inside."

It took all but superhuman courage to keep the experiment alive in the face of repeated disasters. King George's War, and the suspicions it evoked, caused the mission's removal from New York. In 1755, during the French and Indian War, Gnadenhütten was destroyed (like its namesake in Ohio twenty-seven years later), and the missionaries there were killed by enemy Indians from Nescopeck on the Susquehanna. At the war's end other mission towns—Wechquetank and Meniolagomeka—were established in the mountains north of Nazareth. During Pontiac's War, however, the Paxton Boys made known their intent to kill the Moravian Indians at those places (as they subsequently massacred the defenseless Conestoga Indians during the Christmas season of 1763), and only a quick removal to Philadelphia saved them.

In 1765 the mission was moved to Wyalusing on the North Branch of the Susquehanna. The forest was cleared and the model Indian town Friedenshütten (Tents of Peace) soon became famous. White men and Indians came from miles round to see it. There was nothing else like it in all the colonies. A few years later another mission was established by David Zeisberger, foremost of the missionaries, at Goschgoschink (West Hickory) on the upper Allegheny. These missions were so successful that the Great Council of the Delawares, bent on reconstituting their nation in the Muskingum country of present Ohio, invited the Moravians to bring all their converts west and set up model Indian towns where the great Indian world of Delawares, Shawnees, Wyandots, Iroquois and others could plainly see for themselves how this experiment in Christian brotherhood was really working.

After much debate the Moravians accepted the invitation. A contingent of some two hundred Indians with their cattle and other possessions took the trail across the mountains from the North Branch of the Susquehanna to the West Branch, and thence by way of Bald Eagle's Nest (Milesburg), Snowshoe, Moshannon, Chinklacamoose (Clearfield), and Punxsutawney to the Allegheny River at Kittanning and the Beaver River at Kuskuskies (New Castle). After a short stop they moved on to the Tuscarawas Branch of the Muskingum, where the Great Council had set aside some thirty miles of river flats for them. There, near the present New Philadelphia, they built a town for the Delawares, naming it Schönbrunn or "Beautiful Spring," and a few miles away another for the Mahicans. This latter they named Gnadenhütten after the lost town on the Lehigh.

Great chiefs of the Delawares joined them: Glickhican, Echpalawehund, and White Eyes. The whole Indian world was stirred. So nearly successful was this experiment in healthy race relations that during the Revolutionary War, American commissioners proposed in a conference with the Indians at Pittsburgh in September, 1778, that there be added to the original "Thirteen Fires" a fourteenth Indian state headed by the Delawares.

But the dream came to an end on March 8, 1782, when a body of Pennsylvania and Virginia militia, pursuing an enemy war party which had murdered settlers, came upon friendly Moravian Indians working in the fields at Gnadenhütten and in a spasm of race hatred killed and scalped ninety of them, mostly women and children. Among the slain were chiefs Glickhican and Echpalawehund.

The mission did not die. Some of the Christian Indians, it is true, broke their vows and went to war to avenge the death of their kin. One of these was Anton, who had recently saved the life of James O'Hara (Pittsburgh's first industrialist) but who now had lost his wife and all his children in the massacre at Gnadenhütten. But others remained to carry on the mission work loyally, though the spirit was never again the same. For years the mission was constantly on the move. Fear of white men hung over it like a poisonous cloud.

The non-Christian Indian world, which had been watching the mission with much hope, now turned away in revulsion. In a nearby Shawnee village there was a boy in his teens named Tecumseh who grew up to lead a movement to solve the race problem by driving the white men back across the mountains.

After the disaster at Gnadenhütten the governments of the United States, Great Britain, and Pennsylvania did their best to make amends for what had happened. They all granted lands to the Moravians—on the Muskingum, on the Thames River in Canada, and in Pennsylvania's French Creek region—on which to continue their humanitarian experiment. The Pennsylvania Assembly gave them two tracts in the Erie Triangle, one on French Creek near what is now Union City, the other on Conneaut Creek at the Ohio border. But the Indians were afraid, in the face of incoming settlers, to make use of these gifts, and the lands were at length sold for white settlement.

In the modern city of Gnadenhütten, Ohio, there is a public park where you may see the mound that covers the remains of the Indian martyrs of 1782. Beside it stands a monument with this inscription: HERE TRIUMPHED IN DEATH NINETY CHRISTIAN INDIANS.

"In great attempts," wrote Longinus, "it is glorious even to fail."

19 *The Growth of Political Parties*

Pennsylvania had endorsed the federal Constitution, believing that the surrender of her sovereignty served both the national interests and those of her own citizens; but the adjustment to her new situation could not be accomplished without friction. Many Pennsylvanians resented the state's acceptance of a subordinate role.

Resentment was intensified by the absence of established channels of protest. There were no organized political parties through which local complaints could be aired and made effective. Critics of party government today are forgetful of the fact that organized parties, with all their faults, provide a necessary means of public expression, a catharsis of the body politic. If they sometimes stimulate animosities, they more often make these same animosities less dangerous by giving them an outlet.

In the last decade of the eighteenth century and the first decades of the nineteenth, there were no organizations parallel to our modern political parties. There were only "climates of opinion." For some years after the adoption of the federal Constitution, Pennsylvania's political divisions were in the main a reflection of national divisions. On the one hand were the Federalists, who believed in a strong national government and distrusted the common man. Their adherents were what today would be called conservatives. George Washington, although he abhorred "faction," might have been said to live in the Federalist climate, as did also Alexander Hamilton and John Adams. On the other side were the Anti-Federalists. The word originally connoted opposition to the federal Constitution; but as time passed and fears of a strong government grew less, what distinguished the Anti-Federalists from their opponents was a greater trust in the common man and a greater concern for his welfare. In general this was what is known today as the liberal outlook. Those living in this "climate," disliking the term Anti-Federalist, preferred to call themselves Republicans. The term has nothing to do with the modern Republican party. The original Republicans came to call themselves Democratic Republicans and at last simply Democrats, as they are known today. The modern Republican party was not born until the time of David Wilmot, a Pennsylvanian, when the shadow of the coming Civil War lay upon the nation.

In 1790 there was no party organization. It took a decade of evolution to transform the welter of "plotting and conniving" (to borrow a phrase from Harry Marlin Tinkcom's *The Republicans and Federalists in Pennsylvania 1790-1801*) into anything comparable to the disciplined parties familiar to Americans today. In Pennsylvania's election of 1792 the names of General Peter Muhlenberg (who leaned toward the Anti-Federalists) and his brother Frederick Muhlenberg (who leaned toward the Federalists) were placed on both party tickets at the same time. But the impact of national issues, and especially of Federalist policies, on local prejudices eventually consolidated opposition in Pennsylvania and forced the organization of a strong Republican (i.e., Democratic) party. The change in political climate was strongly emphasized by the contrast between the election of the nonpartisan Governor Thomas Mifflin in 1790 and the election of the strongly Republican Thomas McKean in 1799.

The year 1794 provided the catalyst that precipitated an organized Republican party. That was the year of the Whisky Rebellion, the climax of the controversy over the Erie Triangle, and the furor inspired by Jay's Treaty.

Ever since the French and Indian War and Pontiac's War, western Pennsylvania had entertained a fear of Philadelphia. In January, 1791, Alexander Hamilton aggravated this fear and created bitter controversy by obtaining adoption of the excise tax on whisky. To many people in western Pennsylvania this appeared nothing less than an attack on that section's economic life. Whisky, at that time, was "western money." It is easy to see why. To transport grain from western fields over the mountains to markets in the east was too expensive to be profitable. But when the grain was turned into whisky, it became an important article of commerce. Whisky even came to be reckoned a medium of exchange in western Pennsylvania. Field workers were not infrequently paid their wages in whisky rather than in cash. It was a scandal among the Moravian Indians in the west that when they hired themselves out to white men for so much a day at harvest time, they were often paid, against their will, in whisky—a commodity strictly forbidden in their towns.

To protest the excise tax, accordingly, public meetings were held, attended by some of the ablest men in the western counties. On August 21, 1792, Albert Gallatin attended a meeting at Pittsburgh in which a resolution was adopted condemning the excise tax law as endangering civil rights and threatening to ruin western Pennsylvania.

Attempts to enforce the national excise law roused violent opposition. When an excise inspector in Allegheny County served writs on certain defaulters who had failed to register their stills —writs requiring them to attend a federal court in Philadelphia (a journey that took three times as long as it takes today to travel by train from Pittsburgh to San Francisco)—a mob of armed men attacked and burned his house. A meeting to discuss resistance was held at Braddock's Field, and afterwards thousands who were opposed to the excise law marched through Pittsburgh.

The federal government, intent upon preserving its authority, directed a reluctant Pennsylvania to call up the militia. On October 4 George Washington at Carlisle reviewed troops from Pennsylvania and New Jersey. Troops from Maryland and Virginia held rendezvous at Cumberland, Maryland. Some fifteen thousand men marched into western Pennsylvania. They met no opposition. After a stay of four days at Parkinson's Ferry on the Monongahela, during which they rounded up a number of suspects, they returned to Philadelphia. Two of the suspects were condemned to death but pardoned by Washington. The members from the four western counties (Westmoreland, Fayette, Washington, and Allegheny) were expelled from the Pennsylvania House of Representatives. Western Pennsylvania was temporarily disfranchised.

The futility of armed resistance against the federal government had thus been demonstrated. It had also been shown that changes in the law could be made only through the Congress of the United States. At the same time it had been made apparent that to accomplish such changes there had to be a permanent organization, a disciplined political party, to apply constant pressure upon Congress.

Another popular grievance which suggested the need of a strong party organization was provided by the Erie Triangle and the dispute over surveying the town of Erie in 1794. The Triangle, containing over two hundred thousand acres and providing a good harbor on Lake Erie, was at one time claimed by both New York and Massachusetts. To settle the controversy, the United States bought it from both of them. Pennsylvania, anxious for an outlet on the Great Lakes, proceeded to buy it from the Iroquois Indians in 1789 and from the United States in 1792. The Indian purchase was questioned. Although payment had been made to certain Indians, Red Jacket and others claimed that the recipients of the money were not responsible chiefs with authority to sell.

The difficulty was further complicated by international tensions deriving from the war for the Northwest Territory. Encroachments by white people on Indian lands west of the Ohio River (the international boundary recognized by the Fort Stanwix Treaty of 1768) kept the border in a turmoil. Indian reprisals against river boats and settlers brought General Harmar into the Indian country in 1790. He was repulsed. In 1791 General St. Clair and the bulk of the American army were all but annihilated by Little Turtle and his Miami Confederates. Two years later Anthony Wayne was sent west with another army to try to settle the matter of the western boundary once and for all. It was felt he could handle the Miami Confederates if they received no further Indian support, but it was known that the Iroquois were debating whether or not to join them. Cornplanter, speaking for the Seneca women, urged his people to stay quiet, but other voices were raised in Iroquois councils demanding war.

In the spring of 1794 Anthony Wayne and the Miami Confederates faced each other in the field. If the Iroquois came in now at Wayne's back, anything might happen. When at Fort Franklin on May 1, 1794, a white man murdered a friendly

Indian of the Delaware nation (which the Iroquois regarded as under their protection), it was feared that this might be the spark to set off the dreaded Iroquois war. The federal government accordingly stepped in. General Knox, Secretary of War, wrote to Pennsylvania's Governor Thomas Mifflin requesting him to call off the proposed survey for a town at Presque Isle because of "the high probability of an immediate rupture with the Six Nations . . . encreased by the recent murder of one of their people."

Pennsylvania, not fully understanding the situation, took offense at the federal government's interference in what they regarded as an internal matter. She did, however, call off the survey.

The Iroquois remained neutral, thanks in large part to Cornplanter (to whose memory Pennsylvania and the United States owe a profound debt). Anthony Wayne's victory over the Miami Confederates at Fallen Timbers, near the Falls of the Maumee, on August 20, 1794, removed the threat at his and Pennsylvania's back. But along with gratitude for this outcome Pennsylvania nursed a grievance against the federal government, and this helped to focus local political sentiment.

More important to the crystallizing of political parties in Pennsylvania than either the Whisky Rebellion or the Erie Triangle dispute was the excitement over Jay's Treaty, which was signed in London, November 19, 1794. Ratification of the treaty by the American Senate set off such a wave of Toryphobia that it became a question whether the treaty could be put into effect. In the federal House of Representatives a resolution authorizing the necessary appropriations ran into passionate opposition. The House resolved itself into a committee of the whole, with Frederick Augustus Muhlenberg (who had been speaker in the First and Third Congress) in the chair. After a heated debate, the committee divided evenly, forty-nine to forty-nine, and responsibility for the national decision was left to the chairman. "After some little hesitation," as the *Gazette of the United States* reported on April 30, 1796, he cast his vote for the appropriation.

It was a patriotic and a brave action. It gave the country the peaceful breathing space she so desperately needed, but it ended Frederick Muhlenberg's political career (he was never again elected to Congress) and it nearly ended his life. He was murderously attacked and stabbed by his brother-in-law, Bernard Schaeffer, younger brother of the John Schaeffer whose attempt to make a fool of Benjamin Franklin, it will be recalled, had earned him some years of repose in the Grand Châtelet prison in Paris.

Frederick Muhlenberg's grandson, Dr. William Augustus Muhlenberg of St. Johnland, Long Island, used to say that the former speaker of the House of Representatives offset his political loss by family gain, and he told this story to prove it. Frederick's son Henry was in love with Mary Sheaff, daughter of a Philadelphia merchant who was a Federalist and strongly in favor of Jay's Treaty. Aware of Frederick's crucial position in the event of a tie in the House, Mr. Shaeff is reported to have delivered an ultimatum: "If you do not give us [the Federalists] your vote, your son shall not have my Polly." Fortunately love and duty (as Frederick Muhlenberg understood them) did not clash, and so duty did not, as in the popular rhyme, "go to smash." Instead, as Dr. Muhlenberg used to end his tale, "The vote went the right way, peace was restored, and here I am."

Many other incidents, such as Fries's Rebellion (against the "window tax"), served to augment the tide of popular resentment in Pennsylvania against Federalist policies and to consolidate her dominant party, the Republican (i.e., Democratic). Feeling ran dangerously high. "Conflicting ideas and provocative events had combined," writes Dr. Tinkcom, "to engender intense partisan rivalry and bitter hatreds that have seldom been equalled in the State's history."

The election in 1799 of Thomas McKean as governor—with the help of Peter Muhlenberg—showed how public opinion had become predominantly Republican in Pennsylvania. But by this time opinion within the Republican party itself was changing. Formerly opposed to the Constitution of the United States, Republicans were now the Constitution's most loyal defenders. The turmoil that arose out of the presidential election of 1801 provided an occasion to test this new loyalty.

The vote in the Electoral College that year was a tie: seventy-three votes for Thomas Jefferson and seventy-three for Aaron Burr. To break the tie, the election for President was referred to the House, which balloted state by state. For a decision it was necessary that the winner should have the votes of nine out of the sixteen states. On the first ballot Jefferson had eight, Burr six, and two states were divided. The second ballot was the same— eight, six, two—and so were the third, fourth, fifth, and on down to the nineteenth, when, at midnight, the balloting closed. Peter Muhlenberg of Pennsylvania voted steadily for Thomas Jefferson. Next day voting continued through the twenty-eighth ballot, never varying from the tally: eight, six, two. Nerves were at the breaking point. Members slept in the committee rooms and, when the call came to vote, appeared in their nightcaps.

When the Federalists proposed the passage of a law declaring the election null and void and leaving the appointment of a President to the predominantly Federalist House, Jefferson said to James Monroe that, if such a law were passed, the middle states would arm. It was rumored in Federalist circles that the Republicans in Philadelphia had actually seized the public arms. At the same time in Republican circles it was rumored that the Federalists were plotting to burn the Constitution at the point of the bayonet and that seventy thousand Massachusetts militia were "ready to support an usurper."

Governor McKean of Pennsylvania consulted with Peter Muhlenberg about steps to save the Constitution. It was arranged that, in case the proposed law was passed, Major General Peter Muhlenberg should march the Pennsylvania militia on the national capital (then in Philadelphia) and depose the usurping government.

Balloting continued for six days, with the threat of civil war hanging over the Electors. At last on February 17, on the thirty-sixth ballot, the tie was broken when ten states voted for Thomas Jefferson.

That year, 1801, was the high-water mark of the Republican party in Pennsylvania. The Federalist party disintegrated. The Republicans, on the other hand, were welded together by great issues and high emotions and strengthened in their sinews by a well-organized machine.

Success carried with it the seeds of its own destruction, however. The Republican party, in the absence of a strong opposition—something to combat—nearly foundered in a sea of petty personal squabbles. The War of 1812 saved it for a time. The conflict with Britain won approval and even popularity among many Republicans whose Anglophobia was easily aroused. Then as the war dragged on with too much evidence of inefficiency, interest began to die. A spurt of enthusiasm occasioned by news of Perry's victory on Lake Erie ("We have met the enemy and they are ours") and of Harrison's victory in the Battle of the Thames at Moraviantown (where the Moravian Indians had been unmolested for a generation) helped the Republicans win the election of 1813. But the 1813-1814 session of the legislature was, as Dr. S. W. Higginbotham describes it in *The Keystone of the Democratic Arch: Pennsylvania Politics 1800-1816,* "devoted principally to politics, logrolling for special interests, and a legislative raid on the public purse" (the members raised their own salaries).

The war had split the United States apart, and the campaign against Canada was going badly. New England openly opposed "Mr. Madison's War." The interruption of commerce was injuring the American economy. The dissolution in 1811 of the Bank of the United States (which Robert Morris had founded at Philadelphia in 1781) increased the difficulty of financing military adventures, and the ending of the Napoleonic Wars in Europe released British troops for a more active campaign in America. The new capital on the Potomac was threatened. Over seven thousand Pennsylvania militiamen assembled in York, intending to march to Washington's defense. But they were too late. Washington was burned in reprisal for the burning of the Canadian town of Dover across the lake from Erie. Philadelphia expected to be next. The city girded itself for defense. A fund of half a million dollars was raised by the city and its suburbs. Volunteers even began to rush up fortifications.

The heart of the nation, however, was not in the war. Factional disputes undermined the war effort. Venality and personal jealousies proved stronger than patriotism in a somewhat dubious cause. The same disintegrating influences finally ruined the Republican party. In the election of 1814 it suffered heavy losses, and in 1815, following the Treaty of Ghent, which the United States ratified on February 17, 1815, the party was rejected by the electorate.

With the coming of peace and the decline of the export trade which the Napoleonic Wars had artificially stimulated, merchants' minds turned from abroad to the domestic market and the application of capital to American manufactures. Pennsylvania, it was realized, had the makings of a great industrial community. She had coal and she had iron. All she needed was an adequate transportation system to bring the two together and get the resulting product across her vast mountain ranges to the seaboard market waiting for it.

20 *Breaking the Mountain Barrier*

Nature played a curious trick on Pennsylvania. She placed in her rocks a fabulous wealth of iron, coal, and oil and provided a great ocean port at Philadelphia for the distribution of those riches among the markets of the world. But between the port and her inland treasure houses she placed gigantic obstacles: great rivers flowing in the wrong direction and range after range of what the Indians called the Endless Mountains, standing athwart the travelways like the ramparts of medieval castles.

Of the three great rivers of Pennsylvania only the Delaware touches the port of Philadelphia. The Susquehanna, which flows into Chesapeake Bay, finds a convenient port at Baltimore. The Ohio-Allegheny joins the Mississippi to reach salt water at New Orleans. To capture and hold the trade of the Susquehanna and Allegheny valleys for the port of Philadelphia has from the start been the prerequisite for Pennsylvania's commercial eminence.

William Penn saw the economic necessity of making a con-

venient water connection between the Delaware and Susquehanna rivers. It should be, he thought, by way of the Schuylkill
River, Tulpehocken Creek, and Swatara Creek (which enters the
Susquehanna at what is now Middletown). The far-sighted Penn
was more than a hundred years ahead of his time. A waterway
by just such a route as he proposed was completed when the
Union Canal was opened in 1827. Meanwhile other methods
of meeting the problem of transportation had been attempted.

When the Indians traveled, they sometimes used rivers and
sometimes trails. The Susquehannocks brought canoe loads of
goods from their villages near Lancaster to Dutch or Swedish
trading posts by ascending Conestoga Creek in Lancaster
County, portaging to French Creek in Chester County, and de-
scending the latter creek to the Schuylkill. But canoe travel was
not so easy in Pennsylvania as it was in Canada or New England.
The canoe birch did not grow here. Indians had to use either
dugouts or clumsy vessels made of elm bark or another bark too
heavy for portaging. Canoe travelers in Pennsylvania, unless they
imported the frail birchbark canoes from the north country, had
to make new canoes at the end of every long portage. And there
were plenty of such "carries" over the heights of land between
stream heads, as for instance the portage from Sinnemahoning
Creek near the present Emporium Junction to the Allegheny
River at Canoe Place near Port Allegheny. Such portaging was
necessary because Pennsylvania's rivers did not penetrate all
parts of the region as did the rivers in New England. As a
result the principal means of transportation among the Indians
of Pennsylvania was not by river but by trail.

The Indians had developed an efficient system of paths: long-
range highways, for instance, from a number of points on the
Delaware to corresponding points on the Susquehanna, and from
the Susquehanna by way of the Raystown Path, the Frankstown
Path, the Great Shamokin Path, or the Forbidden Path to the
Allegheny River. The elaborate system even included alternate
routes for wet seasons or dry, for war parties or peace embassies.
For about a hundred years after the first trading posts had been
set up in Pennsylvania, white men were content to use the Indian
paths, except for short journeys between towns in the lower
Delaware Valley. For moccasined men and women the Indian
paths were adequate.

But when, influenced by the initiative of investors like James Logan and adventurers like George Croghan, the Indian trade became big business and large trains of pack horses regularly crossed the mountains to the plains beyond, the rerouting of travelways began. Some mountain short cuts suitable for un-burdened warriors were too steep for pack horses with two-hundred pound loads, and longer routes by way of side hills had to be found. It often happened that soft ground which safely bore moccasined feet became so broken and churned up by horses' hooves that it was difficult for man or horse to get through. New routes over higher, firmer ground were necessary. After a heavy storm some trails became so cluttered with windfall (over and under which a man on foot could climb or crawl) that the pack train could not pass and new ways had to be found.

So the Indian paths, turning into bridle paths, underwent changes of route here and there. The wagon roads, when they came, though in general they followed the bridle paths, made further changes, sometimes to afford a wider passage between the trees, sometimes to avoid a narrow cliff path, sometimes to run down off the ridge to new settlements in the valley. Until recent times few of Pennsylvania's high roads have been more than adaptations of old Indian paths.

The Swedes traveled by water between their small settlements along the Delaware, and the Dutch clustered about their river trading posts. Even after the arrival of William Penn the widen-ing of trails into roads came but slowly. In 1700 the Assembly of Pennsylvania, taking cognizance of the problem, authorized the governor and Council to lay out roads. But it was not until 1706, when the Queen's Path was completed from Philadelphia to Chester, and 1711, when the Old York Road was established on an Indian trail that ran from Philadelphia through New Hope to New York, that the era of public road-building began.

Like spokes from the hub of a wheel, roads spread out from Philadelphia north, west, south, and east. Besides those already mentioned, early roads were opened to Whitemarsh, North Wales, and Skippack, and up the Schuylkill Valley toward Norristown. In 1722 a road was opened to Doylestown and Easton.

But the greatest early success in road-building was with the Conestoga Road. At one time it followed the Great Minquas

Path, which ran from the site of Philadelphia to the Susquehannock fort on the Susquehanna River near Columbia by way of what is now West Chester, the Gap, Strasburg, and Rockhill. Later it was rerouted in a more northerly direction by way of Compass, White Horse, and Lancaster.

By 1733, when this road was completed, it had drawn Lancaster and Philadelphia together and become of great importance to the economic life of the Commonwealth. Lancaster, the earliest inland town of considerable size in the English colonies, was close to the southward-flowing Susquehanna. The Conestoga Road was expected to bring the products of the Susquehanna Valley to the port of Philadelphia.

But these expectations were not fulfilled. The huge oak-framed Conestoga wagons—deep bedded to keep their loads from shifting on the hills—tore the road to pieces. A little rain reduced it to a quagmire. Six horses (the normal complement for a Conestoga wagon, though eight were sometimes used) could drag only a little over two thousand pounds from Lancaster to Philadelphia. As the hinterland developed, this road, the main channel by which inland products reached their chief market, became choked. Baltimore, Philadelphia's perpetual rival, reaped the benefit.

It was fear of Baltimore that inspired Philadelphia, through a private company, to build the Lancaster Turnpike (chartered in 1792, completed in 1795) and so to initiate the era of the American "pike." Philadelphia was resolved not to lose the trade of the Susquehanna Valley, especially at a time when the great surge of population into the West had begun. The first macadam road in the United States was built from Philadelphia to Lancaster and soon extended to Columbia. On this new and astoundingly successful road the Conestoga wagons were able to carry double their previous load.

For the next hundred years there was a race between the various Atlantic seaports to capture and hold the trade of the growing West. The port of New York had a great advantage over her rivals in that her waterways, the Hudson and Mohawk rivers, both navigable, pierced the Appalachian mountain barrier by way of the Mohawk Gateway and so provided a comparatively easy route to the Great Lakes and the plains. The success of the Lancaster Turnpike taught Pennsylvania the value of good roads, and she entered a period of turnpike-building that in a few years revolutionized her transportation. By 1832, when the turnpike boom reached its peak, 220 road construction companies had been chartered and 3,000 miles of turnpike built or planned for.

But as the competition for trade with the West increased, so did the demand for cheaper transportation. To carry four or five thousand pounds of goods between Lancaster and Philadelphia (as the turnpike now permitted the Conestoga wagon to do) was still expensive, involving as it did wagon upkeep and several days' food for a driver and six horses. William Penn's dream of an artificial waterway to meet the province's transportation difficulties was recalled.

George Washington and many other dreamers about the future of America had seen the need of a waterway to connect the eastern seaboard with the country beyond the Alleghenies. To meet this need, New York State utilized the Mohawk Gateway in building the Erie Canal, which was opened in 1825—a date that heralded the downfall of Philadelphia as the nation's first port.

Meanwhile Pennsylvania had set a number of canal projects in motion. The first, the Conewago Canal, was opened below York Haven in 1797 in order to carry boats round the rocky rapids known as the Conewago Falls on the Susquehanna River. The Schuylkill Navigation Company, spurred by the discovery of anthracite coal, was opened from Philadelphia as far as Pottstown in 1824, and all the way to Port Carbon (108 miles) in 1825. When the Union Canal was opened in 1827, connecting Delaware and Susquehanna navigation by way of the Schuylkill River, Tulpehocken Creek, and Swatara Creek, much of the Susquehanna Valley trade was drawn away from Baltimore.

By this time Philadelphia recognized New York as her most serious rival, but her reply to the Erie Canal was some time in the making. Meanwhile she concerned herself with a number of local problems, chief among which was that of getting her unique store of anthracite coal to market. In 1829 the Lehigh Canal was opened to Mauch Chunk, and it was extended soon to White Haven.

An attempt was made by means of the Delaware and Hudson

Canal to tap the Wyoming coal fields by bringing the coal to Honesdale on the Lackawaxen and then on down to the Delaware River. The great obstacle was the gigantic bulk of Moosic Mountain. How could they lift barges from Carbondale across that barrier to Honesdale?

The answer to the question was an inclined railroad. Its rails were made of hemlock wood reinforced with wrought-iron straps. Two locomotives were brought over from England, and one of them, the "Stourbridge Lion," was the first to run on rails in the United States. On August 8, 1829, it steamed over the fifteen-mile stretch from Honesdale to Carbondale and then returned. Horatio Alden, who drove the "Lion" over Moosic Mountain, had never driven a locomotive before and he never drove one again, but his position in the history of railroading in the United States is as solid as the mountain itself. The hemlock rails were found to be too light to stand the Lion's weight, a fact that gave impetus to the building of lighter railroad engines in this country.

Pennsylvania, discouraged by her mountainous terrain, did not immediately follow up the "Stourbridge Lion's" achievement. She left to South Carolina the honor of conducting the first successful railroad operation in North America (1830). She did, however, produce one of the first locomotives built in the United States. That was Mathias W. Baldwin's "Old Ironsides." On November 23, 1832, "Old Ironsides" replaced the horses which for five months past had been pulling the train of cars—open, bowl-shaped, each with a driver perched high in front—to and from Philadelphia on the Germantown Railroad. So successful was this steam engine on the Germantown line that in 1833 the state legislature chartered the Philadelphia and Reading Railroad to tap the anthracite fields in the Schuylkill Valley region.

The problem of Pittsburgh and the West now occupied the Commonwealth's attention. How was Philadelphia to keep Pittsburgh's growing trade in the family? The construction of paved highways across the mountains was no permanent solution. The cost of that long haul over many steep ranges—Laurel Hill, Allegheny Mountain, Sideling Hill, Tuscarora Mountain, and the Kittatinny Mountain, to mention only the most formidable —was too high to keep Pittsburgh and the extensive area for which it was a funnel in any degree of bondage to Philadelphia. But the success of the Union Canal pointed the way to larger schemes, and their fulfillment was to have a profound effect on the development not only of Pennsylvania but of the whole United States of America.

The "Stourbridge Lion" had accomplished one thing of great importance to Pennsylvania. It had shown a way to overcome the chief obstacle to moving boat cargoes without transfer from Pittsburgh to Philadelphia. The dream of a through-state canal had long inspired the merchants of both towns, and water routes were chartered by way of the Juniata and Conemaugh rivers to within thirty-six miles of each other. Only the interposing ridge of the Allegheny Mountain broke the connection. A commission appointed by the Pennsylvania Legislature proposed a "leading uninterrupted canal" from Pittsburgh to the wharves at Philadelphia, and a start was made on this, the Pennsylvania Canal, in 1826. Five years later a plan proposed by Moncure Robinson (the father of railroad engineering in Pennsylvania) for the building of a railroad to carry boats and passengers over the mountain from the Juniata Division at Hollidaysburg to the Western Division at Johnstown was adopted. By 1834 the Allegheny Portage Railroad was completed.

For its day it was an amazing engineering achievement. The canal itself overcame an elevation of 2,102 feet above Philadelphia and 1,691 feet above Pittsburgh. From the canal basin at Hollidaysburg the Portage Railroad ascended 1,398 feet. Between Columbia on the Susquehanna River and Hollidaysburg on the Juniata there were eighteen lift locks; between Pittsburgh and Johnstown, sixty-six. A mile-long towing bridge took boats across the Susquehanna, and aqueducts took them across the Juniata and Allegheny. As for the Portage Railroad, a total of eleven miles of great cables—hemp ropes three and a half inches in diameter—drew the boats and cars on iron rails up five planes on each side of the mountain. Stone arch bridges carried the railroad over the Beaver Dam Branch of the Juniata at Hollidaysburg and over the Little Conemaugh eight miles east of Johnstown. Approaching the latter city a tunnel was built, nine hundred feet long. All in all it was a presage of the railroad epic that in another quarter of a century was to cross the Rocky Mountains and span the continent.

It was on the Portage Railroad that John Augustus Roebling, the German-born engineer who is best remembered for the

Brooklyn Bridge, made his reputation as a manufacturer of wire ropes. On the Portage Railroad one day he saw two men crushed to death when the hemp rope on one of the inclines broke. One of his wire ropes, four hundred feet long, was subsequently tested on plane No. 3. This proving successful, in 1844 his 2,295-foot wire rope was used for the 180-foot elevation of plane No. 10. Next year he made his first big coup with the suspended aqueduct which carried the Pennsylvania Canal over the Allegheny River. He went on to complete suspension bridges over the Monongahela at Pittsburgh, at Niagara, and over the Ohio at Cincinnati. Death came to him while he was constructing the Brooklyn Bridge, which his son afterwards completed.

Charles Dickens' narrative of a journey over the Portage Railroad is one of the most attractive passages in his *American Notes:*

It was very pretty travelling thus, at a rapid pace along the heights of the mountain in a keen wind, to look down into a valley full of light and softness; catching glimpses, through the tree-tops, of scattered cabins; children running to the doors; dogs bursting out to bark, whom we could see without hearing; terrified pigs scampering homewards; families sitting out in their rude gardens; cows gazing upward with a stupid indifference; men in their shirt-sleeves looking on at their unfinished houses, planning out tomorrow's work; and we riding onward, high above them, like a whirlwind.

But the mountains west of Hollidaysburg where the Portage Railroad surmounted the Allegheny Front were also the scene of the Pennsylvania Canal's demise. A little to the north, where the old Indian path to Kittanning started up the mountain (the place is now known as Kittanning Point), the Pennsylvania Railroad tackled and overcame the same obstacle by means of the awesomely beautiful Horseshoe Curve. This, the miracle of Kittanning Point, was one of the great moments in Pennsylvania history, marking the entrance to a new era in transportation. Today the traveler from Philadelphia to Pittsburgh by rail may see, as the train begins its long, winding crawl from limb to limb of the Allegheny Mountain, a dirt road passing beneath the tracks through a small viaduct, marking the course of the old Kittanning Path.

In 1857 the government of the Commonwealth sold the main line of the Pennsylvania Canal (Philadelphia to Pittsburgh) to the competing railroad. It is ironical that it should have been the railroad that killed the canal, since it was the canal that had given birth to the railroad. The Columbia Railroad (out of which grew the Pennsylvania Railroad) had been built as a canal link, connecting the Delaware and Susquehanna waterways by a shorter route than the Union Canal could provide. In a few years this short railroad was earning more than all the rest of Pennsylvania's "State Works" (the public canals), and it pointed the way to a revolution in transportation.

The canals were not immediately discarded. Some of them continued to carry freight until well into the twentieth century. The last of them, the Lehigh Canal, carried coal until the 1920's. They had served their purpose. By providing cheap transportation for coal, iron, and other products, they had drawn distant and isolated parts of the state together. They had developed industry and commerce. More than that, by introducing and encouraging the railroads, they had helped to accomplish a momentous change in the whole country's economy and to achieve a measure of national unity unthinkable in the days when the six-horse Conestoga wagon carrying freight over the Santa Fe Trail and the lighter "prairie schooner" were the chief means of transcontinental travel. In this, as in other fields, Pennsylvania sowed good seed for the nation.

21 *A Game without Rules*

Democratic government in New England grew out of the town meeting. In Pennsylvania it sprang nearly full-grown from the head of William Penn. By his First Frame of Government he established the principle of responsible government. In successive frames and in the final Charter of Privileges he fortified democracy with devices recommended by experience to make it work better. So it was that by the time of the Revolution, Pennsylvania already had a long tradition of democracy to guide her—democracy unencumbered by theocracy, patroonship, or slavery. That is not to say that Pennsylvania was a paragon. Grass-roots politics can be no more elevated than the state of public education, and public education in Pennsylvania was for long "under wraps."

The temptation to regard Penn's Holy Experiment as a failure becomes almost irresistible to anyone who looks at Pennsylvania politics during the first half of the nineteenth century. In place of the practical idealism of William Penn and John Dickinson personal ambition was the motive and slander the weapon in the new political warfare. Pennsylvania, with her all but universal (male) franchise, exhibited the weaknesses as well as the strengths of what has been called a "natural" (i.e., untrained) democracy. Some good men, but no great men, were elevated to the governorship, and the general tone of political debate was petty and abusive.

Nevertheless, Penn's experiment had not been a failure. The laws still ruled, however small in stature were most of the men who administered them. There was no tyranny and in consequence no revolution. Life was secure. Pennsylvania's chief in-

172

dustry, farming, was productive; manufactures were increasing; and some great improvements were achieved in transportation, public finance, and education. Changes were made in the constitution to rid it of certain weaknesses which time had disclosed. And the end of the period saw a new wave of the same practical idealism which had distinguished the adolescent years of Pennsylvania's democracy. During the fretful period which saw petty meanness in politics, malpractice in local banking, the hysteria of Anti-Masonry, and mob action in the so-called Buckshot War, Pennsylvania had demonstrated that the structure of her constitution was sound and that her people, by and large, were capable of responsible government: that, in a word, her ship of state could survive both storm and calm.

It was during this period, too, that sectionalism in Pennsylvania showed itself a benefit to the state. The menace of bloc-voting on racial, occupational, or geographical lines was averted by the fact that these lines intersected. The farmers' vote (farmers in 1820 made up the great bulk of the population) was broken up between east and west as well as among English, Scotch-Irish, and German. The German vote was broken up between east and west. The Pennsylvania Germans were clannish, but as both the major parties usually selected a Pennsylvania German for governor, the German vote was divided. The Pennsylvania Germans have almost had a monopoly of the governorships of Pennsylvania, but not of state officials.

If any one group tended to dominate the political scene, it was the Scotch-Irish, who began to assert their leadership about 1820. Combative but genial, clannish but adventurous, they were born for political leadership in a democratic community. Their Church, with its elective officers, trained them in democratic procedure. Governor Martin D. Brumbaugh called Pennsylvania a "Scotch-Irish government." Though tenacious fighters, the Scotch-Irish were imaginative, companionable, and blessed with ability to project themselves and understand other people's needs and wishes. They did not vote blindly as a bloc. Pittsburgh (their capital in Pennsylvania) as often as not found itself at logger-heads—as during the Whisky Rebellion—with neighboring Scotch-Irish counties.

One of the oddest and least amiable episodes in Pennsylvania history was the rise of Anti-Masonry. This popular hysteria has been likened, not ineptly, to the witch-hunting frenzy of New England two centuries earlier. The fires of Anti-Masonry were ignited by the unresolved mystery of William Morgan's disappearance from western New York in 1826. Morgan, a former Mason, had published a hostile book purporting to reveal Masonic secrets. Word went round that murder was an accepted Masonic policy to prevent such disclosures and that evil-doers, when brought to trial in certain courts, escaped conviction if they gave the masonic sign. Pennsylvania-German Pietists hated Freemasonry because of its oath-taking ritual. The Scotch-Irish hated it because it seemed to savor of aristocracy and especially because the Grand Lodge of Philadelphia had a habit of opposing the more radical "back county boys." The movement took form as a political party.

Upon the Freemasons, Thaddeus Stevens (the best and worst of men) called down from heaven bolts of classical oratory. Freemasonry, he declared in 1831, was a "bloody god," and its adherents were Neroes and Caligulas. It "corrupts the fountain of justice; stays the arm of the law; stops the regular action of government; binds the mind in darkness." It was the enemy of religion, morality, and liberty. The Masons should be cut off from "all communion with the holy and the good." Of all the figures in Pennsylvania history Thaddeus Stevens has least in common with Little Lord Fauntleroy.

Anti-Masonry reached its peak of strength in 1835 when, as the result of a split in Democratic ranks, it elected its candidate, Joseph Ritner, to the governorship. Three years later it died, unlamented, of its own emptiness. By 1838 its adherents came to recognize that they had been victims of what is, according to G. K. Chesterton, the most terrible of all known things: nonsense.

Under the Constitution of 1790, eight governors of Pennsylvania passed across the scene: Thomas Mifflin (nonpartisan), 1790-1799; Thomas McKean (Democratic Republican), 1799-1808; Simon Snyder (Democratic Republican), 1808-1817; William Findlay (Democratic Republican), 1817-1820; Joseph Hiester (Democratic Republican), 1820-1823; John Andrew Schultz (Democratic Republican), 1823-1829; George Wolf (Democratic Republican), 1829-1835; Joseph Ritner (Anti-Mason), 1835-1839. They were not particularly brilliant men, and yet, considering the population with which they had to deal, they were a little better than adequate, as the career of George Wolf will show.

There was nothing spectacular or romantic about this lawyer from Easton who filled the governor's chair for two terms, 1829-1832 and 1832-1835. He was a Pennsylvania German, honest, industrious, meticulous in his work, not overly ambitious, without profundity, and certainly not a dreamer. Yet the most important achievement in this half-century of Pennsylvania's political history was accomplished by this unimaginative man. He had sanity. He knew the taste of nonsense and rejected it. He had, moreover, complete tenacity of purpose when he felt that principle was at stake.

So it was that with the help of the inspired maverick, Thaddeus Stevens, George Wolf introduced to Pennsylvania a statewide system of free public schools. It was a small enough beginning, as the law stood, but he had opened the door. He had broken the jinx of a superstition that book-learning is an enemy of religion. Opposition to taxation for education came principally from the German counties, where the plain sects were slow to see that in the long run neither religion nor political freedom were likely to survive in the absence of an informed and perceptive citizenry.

It is a truism (which every generation has to learn afresh) that "Knowledge is power." William Penn understood this. In the Preface to his First Frame of Government he wrote: "That, therefore, which makes a good constitution must keep it viz., men of wisdom and virtue, qualities that, because they descend not with worldly inheritance, must be carefully propagated by a virtuous education of youth."

The earliest attempts at education in Pennsylvania were provided by church schools. The Quakers led, with schools that were free to the poor of all faiths, that enrolled girls as well as boys, and that even employed women teachers. Olive Songhurst, who in 1702 taught in the Quaker School in Philadelphia, is said to have been the first woman schoolteacher in this country.

The Constitution of 1776 called for the establishment of schools in all the counties, teachers' salaries to be paid by the public, "that the poor may be taught gratis." But though lip service was paid to public education in 1776 and again in the Constitution of 1790, Pennsylvania found herself during the first quarter of the nineteenth century lagging behind all the northern states in free public education.

There were several reasons for this. The plain sects among the Pennsylvania Dutch had a fear of education. When James P. Wickersham, Pennsylvania's superintendent of schools, began his educational reforms in the latter part of the nineteenth century, he had first to prepare the way with public addresses in which he endeavored to convince his hearers that learning was not a device of the devil but actually, as he said, "God appointed."

Others among the German-speaking citizens feared the breakdown of their language and culture if a common school system were established. Some farmers feared a widening of their children's horizons lest it make them dissatisfied with farm life. Some of the more well-to-do citizens, who had the means to provide private education for their own children, lacked faith in the common man and hesitated to put power into his hands through the education of his children.

On the other hand, the more liberal element among business and professional men believed, as did Thomas Jefferson, that education was the cornerstone of democracy. In 1827 the Pennsylvania Society for the Promotion of Public Schools was organized, and it led the fight for an improved school system. It found eager support among the Quakers, the Scotch-Irish, and the Moravians. So it was that when George Wolf in 1832 was elected for his second term, he staked his career on the passage of a new school law. With the help of Thaddeus Stevens in the Assembly, he succeeded in getting the legislation passed.

The Free School Act of 1834 divided the state into school districts, authorized (but with local option) the levying of local taxes for school support, and provided a state fund that might be drawn upon by those school districts that levied school taxes. A system of school inspection was also instituted. This was the foundation of Pennsylvania's present school law.

The prime weakness of the Free School Act was that it did not require the children to attend. Until the passage of the first compulsory attendance law (March 10, 1911) education was at the discretion of parents and children. Even parents who recognized the importance of education for their children failed to understand the necessity of continuous attendance. Chores at home and weather abroad cut down the attendance; and most country schools were kept open for only a few months in the year, closing by the end of March. Mr. Evans, superintendent of schools for Lancaster County, complained in 1862 that the school year was over before the boys got properly settled into their classes. As late as the 1860's four months a year was as long as Pennsylvania's schools were required by law to remain open.

Teachers' salaries were abysmally low. Henry Moyer, a skilled teacher at Rockridge School (near present Hershey) a hundred years ago, began his career at eighteen or twenty dollars a month. Equipment was scanty and crude in the one-room country schools: desks and benches, a pot-bellied stove, some framed mottoes on the walls, and under the mottoes pegs for the pupils' coats. Blackboards were exactly what the name suggests: boards painted black and hung on a nail. The library at Harmony School (near Five Points in Lancaster County), when Milton Hershey attended it, consisted of one book: a broken-backed and dismembered *Webster's Dictionary*.

Immediately after the passage of the Free School Act there came such a fierce popular movement for its repeal that the legislature was all but stampeded. The Senate in fact gave way, and the House was preparing to scuttle into the Dark Ages for safety, when Thaddeus Stevens rose to his noblest act of statesmanship and defended the governor's educational policies with an eloquence that defeated the repeal motion. The controversy lost Governor Wolf his hoped-for third term as governor; but, to his everlasting credit, the Free School Act remained on the statute books. Such school districts as had approved it benefited from it at once, and it has remained the basis of Pennsylvania's school law ever since.

The Constitution of 1790 survived for forty-eight years, which was long enough to disclose certain weaknesses, not so much in its principle as in its mechanical detail. The governor, under its terms, controlled too much patronage, his appointments reaching into nearly every corner of the Commonwealth's life. He appointed the attorney general, the auditor general, the surveyor general, all judges, all justices of the peace, all notaries public, all sheriffs, all coroners, and all clerks of the court. He even appointed licensed auctioneers, prison wardens, and a host of superintendents and inspectors all over Pennsylvania. Such immense areas of patronage drew widespread hostilities upon the state's chief executive. Governor Joseph Hiester in 1820 requested the Assembly to take the load off his back. But opposition to change came from office-holders and their friends and from large conservative groups in the state, chief among which were the Pennsylvania Dutch. These groups were strong enough to stem the growing public demand for a new constitution.

At last, however, in 1837 a constitutional convention was assembled. The resulting Constitution of 1838 introduced many reforms. Judges were to be appointed for limited terms and their appointment was to be subject to confirmation by the Senate. Justices of the peace, clerks of the court, and other local officials were to be elected by the people. The governor's tenure was to be limited to two terms. Still more important was the provision made for amending the constitution without the necessity of calling a convention. Passage of a proposed amendment by two successive legislatures and its ratification by the people at the polls was all that was now required. The strengthening of the elective principle in this constitution and the easing of the process of amendment became evident in 1851, when an amendment was passed making state judges elective.

Pennsylvania during the first half of the nineteenth century went her democratic way, advancing the standard of living, but not producing any great political leaders. It has been noted by Charles McCool Snyder in *The Jackson Heritage* that until near the middle of the century no Pennsylvanian "played a prominent role in a presidential administration."

22 *The Underground Railroad*

Hide the outcast; betray not him that wandereth.

—Isa. 16:3

There is no more piquant—nor at first consideration more puzzling—episode in the history of Pennsylvania than that of the Underground Railroad: piquant, because of the colorful, even fantastic, incidents that occurred in the clash between the rights of property and the rights of man; puzzling, because the Underground Railroad was in large part operated by law-abiding Quakers in defiance of the Fugitive Slave Law.

The puzzle is soon resolved. The Quakers (especially those of the liberal wing, followers of Elias Hicks) inherited a long tradition of opposition to slavery. They held a stubborn belief that the right to "life, liberty, and the pursuit of happiness" is really "unalienable," and they rejected man-made laws that sought to take it away. They believed, as President Kennedy said in his 1961 Inaugural Address, "that the rights of man came, not from men's generosity, but from God."

William Wright, a Quaker of York Springs, Pennsylvania, who measured the Fugitive Slave Law of 1850 against that principle, came to this conclusion: "I . . . consider the Fugitive Slave Law no law in that it contravenes the law of God." The Negroes of Boston in 1850 put the same thought even more pointedly when they announced: "God willed us free; men willed us slaves. . . . God's will be done." Devout Hicksite Quakers, heeding the promise of Isaiah "to undo the heavy burden and let the oppressed go free," gave precedence to the law of God when it conflicted with the law of man and proceeded to set His people free.

There is nothing new about this doctrine of the higher law, nor

179

is it today outworn. "Men of Athens," said Socrates at his trial in 399 B.C., "I honor and love you; but I shall obey God rather than you." The Nuremberg trials of Nazi war criminals in 1945-1946 were an attempt to establish the same principle in the modern world: that it is criminal—under no matter whose command—to obey orders that contravene the basic rights of man. The United Nations Organization was formed to give sanction to that principle.

Slavery never found much root in Pennsylvania. The first recorded American protest against slavery came from some early German Quakers of Germantown. It is true that by the middle of the eighteenth century there were some eight thousand slaves in Pennsylvania; but as early as 1754 the Quakers officially condemned slavery and in the next year barred from Meeting those who practiced it. In 1780 the Commonwealth passed an act for the gradual abolition of slavery within its bounds. No child thereafter should be born a slave in Pennsylvania. The Quakers, who took the lead in this, enjoyed the quiet backing of the Pennsylvania Dutch.

There is no good history of the Underground Railroad. Its operations, being illegal, were necessarily kept secret; and historians, in the absence of official documents, have fought shy of the subject. The best sources of information are the reminiscences of refugee slaves or of those who helped them to escape. The best collection of these was made by a Philadelphia Negro, William Still, who in 1872 published *The Underground Rail Road. A Record of Facts, Authentic Narratives, Letters, &c. . . . By William Still, For many years connected with the Anti-Slavery Office in Philadelphia, and chairman of the Acting Vigilance Committee of the Philadelphia Branch of the Underground Rail Road*. On the title page is a line from Deuteronomy 23:15: "Thou shalt not deliver unto his master the servant that has escaped from his master unto thee."

It may be, as some historians say, that the influence of the Underground Railroad on American history has been exaggerated. Certainly the number of slaves who escaped was not large enough to make any serious drain on Southern economy. It has been estimated that about two thousand slaves escaped every year between 1830 and 1860, which was slight indeed when compared with the millions of slaves in the South and their increase by about fifty or sixty thousand a year. Nevertheless, the presence of runaway slaves in the North and the stories that circulated of their escape with the aid of Underground Railroad personnel kept the public alive to the issue involved and so helped to develop sentiment for abolition.

North of the border of Canada, in which country the greater part of the escapees sought refuge, the Underground Railroad had another kind of influence, scarcely noticed at the time. It helped the development of a Canadian national consciousness. Children in Ontario's Niagara Peninsula listened eagerly to escape stories told by many Negro gardeners and handymen. Parents and children read copies of a yellow-backed edition of *Uncle Tom's Cabin* showing a picture of Eliza crossing the ice with this legend under it: "Canada the land of liberty though not a republic." Such things stirred a patriotic pride which bore fruit in the establishment of the Confederation of Canada in 1867.

A tap on the window at night set in motion the wheels of the Underground. Fugitives were hidden in barns, mills, mine holes, carried in wagons behind bales and boxes, and stowed away behind barrels in canal boats.

Elijah Pennypacker at Corner Stores in Lancaster County had one of the best stations on the road. If women and children were in the party that came to him, he used to drive them from the barn in his light Dearborn wagon while the men walked down the road by themselves. If he suspected slave-hunters to be around, his wife sat in the front room with a neighbor, sewing and keeping an eye on the road.

The fact that there were many escape routes confused pursuers. Several routes converged at Columbia, one coming up from Havre de Grace and Peach Bottom, another from Hanover and York. Many free Negroes had long since settled at Columbia, an early Quaker community, and refugee slaves found there a temporary hiding place as well as a door to freedom. It was at Columbia that a disgusted slave-owner remarked, "There must be an underground railroad out of this place," and straightway the institution had a name.

Some fugitives followed the Shenandoah and Cumberland valleys to Harrisburg, whence they fanned out to stations north and east. Williamsport had a station. So had Canton and Towanda.

A Mohawk Indian, Daniel Hughes (who had been born at Canisteo, formerly known as Passigachkunk, on the Forbidden Path), was an agent on the Underground, taking passengers by unaccustomed ways—old Indian paths—over the mountains and up the Susquehanna Valley to Oswego, New York.

An agent lived near the village of Estella in Sullivan County, where the old Genesee Road (the Towanda Indian Path) wound its way among the mountains. He busied himself so discreetly with the escape traffic that not even his family knew he was involved until one day his movements aroused suspicion and his son asked him what he was doing.

"Hunting lost sheep," he replied.

Western Pennsylvania had a large share of abolitionists. The city of Erie was an important escape port. From Quaker settlements in Center and Clearfield counties a branch of the Underground ran through the towns of Indiana and Brookville. The latter was made famous by the exploits of three abolitionists who worked there as a team. Two Negroes (as reported by the Venango Historical Society in their news sheet of June, 1961) working on the French Creek Canal at Franklin were arrested on August 11, 1834, and handed over to the slave-hunters. On their way through Brookville with their quarry the slave-owners had the Negroes put in the county jail for safekeeping overnight. The fact was known to the three abolitionists: Arad Pearsall, the jailer; Elijah Heath, a county judge; and James Steadman, the county treasurer.

In the jail that housed the Negroes there was residing at that time a master of the arts of abstraction, Butler B. Amos, doing six months' time for larceny. Equipped, as he happened to find himself that evening, with a file and an auger, he used the one to cut the Negroes' chains and the other to bore holes round the lock in the jail-house door and so draw it out. To give the Negroes a good head start, Judge Elijah Heath had the two slave-hunters (in good Pennsylvania Blue-Law fashion) arrested for traveling on Sunday.

In Clearfield County today they tell a story (as reported by Dudley Tonkin in *My Partner, the River: The White Pine Story on the Susquehanna*) of a good Methodist Robin Hood, George Atcheson, who had a sawmill on the West Branch. He built himself a frame mansion with a secret room where he could hide

seven or eight runaway slaves, and he employed gunmen to protect them when slave-hunters rode up in the wake of blood-
hounds:

It was the duty of the men with the long barreled muzzle loading
rifles to cause the dogs to suddenly decide to make Clearfield County
their eternal homes. After some of these men had lost their most
prized dogs, they began to pick up their hounds and carry them on
the horse in front of the saddle. This did not help the situation either,
for officers of the law or the hound dogs. Atcheson's sharp shooters
have been known to have killed the dog in the arms of a posse rider
on his horse.

Philadelphia, home of American Quakerism, was an important
center for the Underground, being the terminus of a line from
Wilmington, Delaware. Of the Philadelphia arrivals none was
more dramatic than that of Henry "Box" Brown, who came by
way of Adams' Express. He had been nailed and hooped up by
a friend, James A. Smith, in a box three feet long, two feet wide,
and two feet, eight inches deep. For nourishment on the twenty-
six-hour journey he had with him a few small biscuits and a
bladder of water. He had also a large gimlet to let in air. The
box, addressed to a shoe dealer—William E. Johnson, Arch
Street, Philadelphia—was marked THIS SIDE UP WITH CARE, but
the expressmen were careless, and for miles Brown traveled on
his head.

A member of the Vigilance Committee in Philadelphia was
alerted, and a son-in-law of James and Lucretia Mott arranged
(with the help of a five-dollar gold piece) to have an Irish ex-
press-driver deliver the box quickly to the antislavery office. What
happened when the box was opened is described by William Still,
who was there:

The witnesses will never forget that moment. Saw and hatchet
quickly had the five hickory hoops cut and the lid off, and the
marvellous resurrection of Brown ensued. Rising up in his box, he
reached out his hand, saying, "How do you do, gentlemen?" The little
assemblage hardly knew what to think or do at the moment. He was
about as wet as if he had come out of the Delaware. Very soon he
remarked that, before leaving Richmond he had selected for his
arrival-hymn (if he lived) the Psalm beginning with these words:
"I waited patiently for the Lord, and He heard my prayer." And most

touchingly did he sing the psalm, much to his own relief, as well as to the delight of his small audience.

Box Brown spent a few days at the home of the Motts and afterwards with William Still. Then he went on to Boston. His friend in Richmond, James A. Smith, did not fare so well. He tried to send two other slaves to freedom by the same method, but they were caught. Smith, as reported in the New York *Tribune,* was arrested and served eight years in prison.

Gallant Boston was a mecca for escaping slaves. Like Henry Box Brown, Ellen Craft and her husband made their way from Philadelphia to Boston and there enjoyed one of the strangest triumphs in the history of the Underground Railroad.

Ellen Craft had a fair enough skin to pass as white. She planned, accordingly, to escape in the guise of a young gentleman attended by a faithful slave (her husband). Lacking a gentleman's beard, she swathed her face as if it were swollen with toothache. Since "Master" was traveling as a gentleman and must register at first-class hotels, it was necessary to have a plausible excuse for his inability to write his name. She put her right arm in a sling. She wore green spectacles and, lest her voice betray her, pretended to be deaf, the darky attendant explaining volubly his master's sad disabilities.

As a picture of slave loyalty to an ailing master the masquerade touched the best in Southern chivalry, and all went well until the Crafts reached the border state of Maryland. At the railroad station in Baltimore the ticket agent refused to sell the servant a ticket, informing them that the law required bond for all Negroes applying for tickets to go north. William Craft put on his best act, explaining his master's predicament: he was hastening to Philadelphia for medical treatment and uncertain whether he could live long enough to reach that city alive; delay would be fatal. The ticket agent let them through. Once in Philadelphia, toothache, blindness, deafness, the broken arm, and general debility—all silently stole away.

After a time the couple went to Boston. Thither the slave-catchers trailed them, invoking the Fugitive Slave Law for their arrest and return to bondage. But the Bostonians were too much for them. When Hughes and Knight ("two prowling villains," as William Lloyd Garrison's *Old Liberator* described them) got warrants for the fugitives' arrest, no officer could be found to serve them. Instead, Hughes and Knight themselves were arrested on the charge of slandering William Craft. They were released on bail of $10,000. Twice again they were arrested on the charge of conspiracy to kidnap William Craft, "a peaceable citizen of Massachusetts," and released on bail of $10,000 each time—total, $30,000.

It was in connection with this case, which gave much satisfaction to the improper Bostonians, that the Negroes of Boston, assembled in Belknap Street Church, passed the resolution quoted earlier: "God willed us free; men willed us slaves. We will as God wills. God's will be done."

In view of the notoriety they had received and the danger to which this exposed them, it was thought best to send William and Ellen Craft to England for safety. After the Civil War these "chattels personal" returned to the United States and bought a plantation in Georgia.

The little town of Christiana, Pennsylvania, being on the Underground Railroad between Columbia and Philadelphia, was the center of a considerable Negro population. On Thursday, September 11, 1851, slave-hunters were detected approaching that town and a word of warning was circulated. When Edward Gorsuch, a slave-owner, with his son, his nephew, and a party from Maryland approached the home of William Parker about dawn in pursuit of two runaway slaves, the slave-catchers found themselves unwelcome.

The Marylanders forced entry into Parker's house but, when trying to fight their way to the second floor where the family had retired, they found themselves resolutely blocked. From an upper window Parker's wife blew a dinner horn as a signal to the neighborhood, and a crowd of colored men arrived, armed with guns, clubs, axes, and corn-cutters.

An angry parley ensued, lasting for an hour and a half. At the end of that time one of the Negroes attempted to come out of the house and was warned back. Persisting, he brushed against Edward Gorsuch as he passed. Gorsuch fired his revolver. At that signal the Negroes let go with everything they had. Gorsuch was killed, his son wounded, and the rest of the slavers fled.

And he that stealeth a man, and selleth him, or if he be found in his hand, he shall surely be put to death.—Isa. 21:16

The Christiana "riots," as the events were called, made a big splash in the news. Most of the newspapers, fearing the breakdown of law, were hostile to the Negroes in this affair. A United States marshal, A. E. Roberts, arrived at Christiana with forty-five United States Marines, a posse of about forty police, and a body of special constables. Twenty-five Negroes and three white men were arrested and put in Moyamensing Prison in Philadelphia. William Parker escaped and got safely to Canada. When the case came up for trial, it was discovered that two of the Negro prisoners known to be runaway slaves had also escaped. The U. S. marshal was suspected of having obeyed the higher law.

But there were still plenty of victims to be sacrificed on the altar of legalized inhumanity. Forty persons in all were indicted for treason in the Christiana affair. Thaddeus Stevens, one of the most justly hated men in American history, nevertheless had a few stars in his crown, and this was one of them. He threw a brilliant spotlight on the issue involved, freedom versus slavery, and not only won acquittal for all the defendants but also managed to produce a reversal of popular opinion. Out of that trial came one of the greatest single victories of the Underground Railroad. Professional slave-hunters were discouraged from pushing their trade too far, and the public in the North was awakened to the pressing need of a solution for the whole problem.

Edward Gorsuch, though the cause which his death advanced was not of his own choosing, did not die in vain. While the accused were in Moyamensing Prison, John Greenleaf Whittier wrote:

> God's ways seem dark, but soon or late
> They touch the shining hills of day.

23 *Abraham Lincoln in Pennsylvania*

Early in the morning of February 22, 1861, Abraham Lincoln on his way to the city of Washington for his inauguration raised a flag of thirty-four stars over Independence Hall.

"I am filled with deep emotion," he said, "at finding myself standing here, in this place, where were collected together the wisdom, the patriotism, the devotion to principle, from which sprang the institutions under which we live."

It was a brave action he had taken in attending these ceremonies on Washington's Birthday. The evening before, he had learned (through Allan Pinkerton's men) of a plot to murder him on his way through Baltimore on the night of February 23. He had been urgently advised to leave Philadelphia at once and pass through Baltimore on the night of the 21st. But he declined. He knew how important it was, in view of the impending crisis with the South, to keep the good will of Pennsylvania; and that, he believed, could best be done by keeping his word and attending the ceremonies arranged in his honor at Philadelphia and Harrisburg.

As he raised the flag at Independence Hall, he spoke these pointed words:

I have often inquired of myself what great principle or idea it was that kept this Confederacy so long together. . . . It was that which gave promise that in due time the weight would be lifted from the shoulders of all men. . . . Now, my friends, can this country be saved upon that basis? If it can, I will consider myself one of the happiest men in the world, if I can help to save it . . . . But if this country cannot be saved without giving up that principle . . . I would rather be assassinated upon this spot than surrender it.

He took the train to Harrisburg, and that afternoon at the State Capitol he spoke briefly to the House and Senate, which were met in joint session. He thanked them for the promise of military assistance should emergency arise, but expressed the hope that the use of troops would never be necessary. He also expressed regret that at Independence Hall that morning he had not been able, as he said, "to harmonize and give shape to the feelings that had been really the feelings of my whole life." It was to take two years of maturing in the grief of civil war before the final shaping came to him at Gettysburg.

Instead of spending the night at the Jones House in Harrisburg, where he had registered, or at Governor Curtin's residence, to which he had been invited, he waited at the hotel till dark, changed his tall hat for a less familiar one, and drove to the outskirts of the city to catch a special train for Philadelphia. In that city he met Allan Pinkerton; and with him and Colonel W. H. Lamon he boarded a sleeper on the 11:00 P.M. train for Baltimore. At Baltimore, horses were attached to his car and it was switched to the Baltimore and Ohio tracks. Another train carried it on to Washington without incident.

When six weeks later—three days after the firing on Fort Sumter on April 12, 1861—Lincoln called for seventy-five thousand volunteers, the Pennsylvania Assembly unanimously pledged its resources "in men and money." Where the Commonwealth stood on the issue of secession could hardly have been doubted. She had been host to the Constitutional Convention of 1787; and when the time came for the signing of the Constitution, she and her daughter Delaware were alone among the states in giving the Constitution their entire support. Of the thirty-nine signatures, thirteen were contributed by Pennsylvania and Delaware.

Nor could there have been any doubt about where Pennsylvania stood on the question of slavery. Not only did she move with the times, slavery being now alien to the conscience of most of the Western world, but she moved in accordance with her own long tradition in support of human rights. The first recorded protest against slavery had been made by German Quakers at Germantown in 1688. The Pennsylvania Society for the Abolition of Slavery had been founded in 1775. From the days of Anthony Benezet, who had established an evening school for colored people in Philadelphia in 1773 and had induced the Assembly in 1780 to pass a law (the first in America) for the gradual abolition of slavery, the Commonwealth had been in sympathy with what George Mason of Virginia said at the Constitutional Convention, August 22, 1787: "Slavery discourages arts & manufactures. The poor despise labor when performed by slaves. . . . They [slaves] produce the most pernicious effect on manners. Every master of slaves is born a petty tyrant. They bring the judgment of Heaven on a Country."

Also directed against slavery was the more recent career of David Wilmot. He was author of "Wilmot's Proviso," an amendment to the "Two Million Bill" for appropriating money to aid President Polk in his plans to annex New Mexico and California. The amendment contained these words: "Provided, That, as an express and fundamental condition to the acquisition of any territory from the Republic of Mexico . . . neither slavery nor involuntary servitude shall ever exist in any part of said territory." Wilmot's Proviso was blocked in the Senate, but as Governor James H. Duff has written, "Wilmot's action had projected the problem of slavery extension into the forefront of all the problems before the nation."

Stating, "I will cheerfully stand by any organization established for the advancement of these principles," Wilmot took a seat among the Free Soil Democrats in the Thirty-first Congress. In furtherance of the same ideas he became in 1855 one of the prime organizers of a new party, the Republican party, and next year, when its first national convention was held, he was chairman of the platform committee and chiefly responsible for the plank opposing the extension of slavery into free territory. He hoped that this would be a means, he said, of "restoring the action of the Federal Government to the principles of Washington and Jefferson."

In the election of 1856 Wilmot opposed Buchanan. In 1857 he ran for the office of governor of Pennsylvania. He knew he could not win, but he hoped the fight would build the Republican party into something of which the people could be proud. It is believed he played a decisive part in the 1860 nomination of

Lincoln. The Harrisburg *Telegraph* called him "the Gibraltar of Republicanism."

David Wilmot sacrificed himself for a principle. In fighting uncompromisingly for the rights of man and the abolition of slavery, he offended some of the politicians, who took pains to crush him. James Buchanan, on the other hand, sought for compromise, in the belief that he could thus save the party and the nation from disunion. Buchanan reached the Presidency (the only Pennsylvanian who has done so), but he did not obtain the objectives at which his career was aimed. With the election of Lincoln the veil of compromise was torn aside and the stark issues of slavery and separation confronted the nation. Wilmot lived to see the principles to which he had devoted himself prevail. Under his nominee, Lincoln, the nation was rededicated to the proposition that all men are created equal.

In the election of 1860 Lincoln would have been defeated if Pennsylvania had not been for him. But it was not only a humanitarian impulse that drew the Commonwealth to him. While in rural Pennsylvania slavery was the major issue, in the cities protection for growing industries was considered of primary importance. The People's Party (as Republicans called themselves in the East) electioneered for free men but against free trade. It was the conjunction of the party hostile to slavery with such of the Democrats as were hostile to free trade that gave the Republicans their chance. When a few months before the election the Democrats split into two parties over the slavery issue and ran two candidates, the Republicans were given a winning hand.

Long before the Civil War, Pennsylvania had developed a strong feeling for United States nationality. The Commonwealth was no longer a mere local granary. Her manufactures had grown, and her markets extended throughout the whole country. Her sons had emigrated into the Shenandoah Valley of Virginia, into Ohio, and into the far West.

Therefore the firing on Fort Sumter roused Pennsylvanians to defend not an abstract principle but their country—*la patrie*. Three days after Lincoln's call Pennsylvania's five companies, the famous First Defenders (the first, by one day, from any state to reach Washington), were in the nation's capital. They included the Ringgold Light Artillery of Reading (which has been called "the first of the First"), the Logan Guards of Lewistown, the Washington Artillery and the National Light Infantry of Pottsville, and the Allen Rifles of Allentown. Within two weeks of the call, Pennsylvania had enough volunteers to fill not just her quota of fourteen regiments of 780 men each but twenty-five regiments. By the end of the year, Pennsylvania had over a hundred thousand men in service. By the end of the war, she had contributed over a quarter of a million men. The figure 283,000, which is sometimes given, fails to take into account re-enlistments and overlappings of the services.

There was, of course, some division of opinion among her citizens, but the state as a whole, under the aggressive leadership of Governor Curtin, became the keystone of the Union. She had the men and the industries, good transportation facilities, and a strategic position. Harrisburg, the capital, was at the head of the Cumberland Valley, the main travel route between the North and the South. Pennsylvania contributed to the Union army many of its military leaders, such as McClellan (severely criticized by the North, but described by Robert E. Lee as the best of his opponents), the imperturbable Meade, and the brilliant Reynolds, who died in the act of committing the Army of the Potomac to the Battle of Gettysburg—as if with foreknowledge of the outcome.

Pennsylvania, the Quaker State, is apt to think modestly of herself in the military sphere. The fact is that she was the pivot on which the Union cause turned. This was not only because she had the men and materials but also because it was in Pennsylvania that the South's chief hope of winning the war rested. To understand this, it is necessary to recall that General Lee, when he declined the proffered command of the Union forces, did so only from a sense of patriotic duty to Virginia, not from any assurance that the Confederacy could win. He believed, as the war took shape in the field and in the factory, that a merely defensive policy, such as Jefferson Davis favored, could only lead to defeat. The South's one chance of success in Lee's opinion was to take the war to the enemy and by some bold stroke win a decisive victory—one that would encourage the peace movement in the North and win European allies for the Confederacy. Jefferson Davis was opposed to this policy, but in June, 1863, Lee was given an opportunity to try it.

There were rich spoils in Pennsylvania: Philadelphia, Pittsburgh, and more immediately Harrisburg, chief center for the North's communications with the South and for the transport of military supplies to the Army of the Potomac protecting Washington. That army held an almost impregnable position in the capital city's outskirts. If it could be drawn from its base and pounced upon, the war might be ended.

"Lee's object in 1863, as in the previous year," writes Winston Churchill in *The Great Democracies,* "was to force the army of the Potomac to fight under conditions in which defeat would spell annihilation. In this he saw the sole hope of winning Southern independence."

A threat to Harrisburg, the key to Pennsylvania's railroad, canal, and highway systems, coupled with a threat to Philadelphia—the state's chief manufacturing center and source of munitions, ships, and railroad engines—might do the trick. So, after Chancellorsville (May 2-4), the Army of Northern Virginia, at the peak of its morale, crossed the Potomac on the war's greatest gamble.

General Richard S. Ewell's 2nd Confederate Corps was in the van. It was planned that he should occupy Carlisle and then split his forces, one part to move on Harrisburg while the other, under Jubal Early, captured York and Wrightsville. From Wrightsville, Early was to cross the Susquehanna bridge to Columbia, and thence move north to cut Harrisburg's connections with Philadelphia.

When Lee struck north into Pennsylvania, the state was almost totally unprepared to defend herself. A hideous apathy paralyzed her citizens. To Lincoln's call for fifty thousand Pennsylvania volunteers—an appeal that was seconded by Governor Curtin's proclamations—there was almost no response. Pennsylvania had contributed well to the Army of the Potomac, but her martial ardor was in a decline of which Lee now hoped to take advantage.

The War Department tried to meet the emergency by creating two new military departments: the Department of the Monongahela under Major General William T. H. Brooks with headquarters at Pittsburgh, and the Department of the Susquehanna under Major General Darius N. Couch with headquarters at Chambersburg. But as late as June 20, five days after the Confederates had crossed the Pennsylvania border, General Couch reported that except for a demoralized remnant of the Winchester garrison, which Ewell had captured on June 14 and 15, only 56 officers and 742 men were present for duty. Meanwhile the Secretary of War had appealed to New York for help in Pennsylvania's extremity. Governor Horatio Seymour at once despatched eight or ten thousand men from New York City's regiments.

A few days later Pennsylvania woke to the emergency, and some nine thousand men joined General Couch's forces. Philadelphia, Pittsburgh, and Harrisburg all began to prepare their own defenses. At the time Pennsylvania was turning out eighty per cent of the North's war equipment, of which the greater part was produced in Philadelphia and Pittsburgh. Under the command of Major General Napoleon J. T. Duna, Philadelphia hired day laborers to pile up earthworks in the city's approaches. At the Fort Pitt Works, Pittsburgh was building ships for the war on the Mississippi. Men were withdrawn from the building of the *Manayunk* with its fifteen-inch guns and the *Umpqua* with its twelve-inch guns (ancestors of the modern super-dreadnoughts) to build rifle pits and forts on the hills around the city. Harrisburg set its citizens to digging trenches in its environs.

It was soon evident that Lee's first objective was the bridges across the Susquehanna at Harrisburg and Columbia. To protect the span at Harrisburg, General Couch constructed Fort Washington, a system of earthworks on the high ground west of the river. To protect the Columbia-Wrightsville bridge, General Couch despatched Colonel Jacob G. Frick with the 27th Emergency Regiment. This body, with the aid of some 250 men from the garrison at York, held back Jubal Early's Confederates for about an hour and then retreated across the bridge. Preparations had been made to blow up the fourth of the bridge's twenty-eight spans. The explosion, when it came, left the bridge intact, but Frick at once set it on fire. In a few minutes its fiery skeleton provided what the York *Gazette* described as a magnificent scene:

The moon was bright, and the blue clouds afforded the best contrast possible to the red glare of the conflagration. The light in the heavens must have been seen for miles. Some of the timbers as they fell into the stream seemed to form themselves into rafts, which floated down like infernal boats of the region pictured by Dante.

One part of Lee's plan—to cross the Susquehanna at Columbia—had been defeated, but the threat to Harrisburg remained. Mechanicsburg, seven miles to the west, surrendered. On June

28, Couch reported, "By night the rebels will have possession up to my defenses on the river."

That was the most anxious day that Harrisburg has ever known, but it was also the day that brought her relief. On the 28th Lee at Cashtown (between Chambersburg and Gettysburg) learned that Union forces under Hooker had crossed the Potomac in his rear. The same day, though Lee did not learn of it till later, George Meade, a Pennsylvanian, replaced Hooker in command of the Army of the Potomac. Lee, whose principle it was to combine bold strategy with defensive tactics, ordered Ewell (after his failure to cross the Wrightsville-Columbia bridge) to fall back and join him at Cashtown.

On July 1, Major General W. F. ("Baldy") Smith, field commander west of the Susquehanna, occupied Carlisle with two thousand of Pennsylvania's emergency troops. The same evening he received a summons to surrender from General Fitz Lee of "Jeb" Stuart's cavalry division, which had ridden over from York. Baldy Smith declined to surrender. A hundred and thirty-four shells were fired into the town before midnight, when Stuart, who for some days past had lost touch with Lee, learned of the Confederate concentration at Gettysburg and hastened to join his chief.

There is a measure of truth in the statement that the Battle of Gettysburg was an accident—that Meade and Lee had not planned to fight there but happened to collide and could not disengage themselves. It was, however, the place, not the collision, that was unlooked for. Neither Lee nor Meade had picked this particular spot, Gettysburg, for battle; but each commander at the time was groping for the other, and when they met each meant to fight. So it was that when the Union "mounted infantry" ran into a Confederate brigade marching to Gettysburg to pick up some boots, both Lee and Meade exploited the contact.

The boldness of Lee's strategy is well known, but it is sometimes forgotten that Meade, too, could show initiative. In accepting his appointment to command the Army of the Potomac, Meade had written to the high command in Washington to say that his plans were, "if the enemy is checked in his attempt to cross the Susquehanna, or if he turns towards Baltimore, to give him battle." On June 30, Meade sent these instructions to his officers: "The Commanding General requests that, previous to the engagement soon expected with the enemy, corps and all other commanding officers address their troops, explaining to them briefly the immense issues involved in the struggle."

That same evening General John Buford's Union cavalry met Pettigrew's brigade of Heth's Confederate division west of Gettysburg. Buford was the first to see the importance of Gettysburg as a place of battle. He sent word to General Reynolds, who commanded a wing of the Army of the Potomac. Reynolds received the message about midnight, brought up the First Corps, agreed with Buford's estimate of the situation, and sent for Howard's Eleventh Corps. While personally supervising the placing of units in McPherson's Woods, Reynolds was shot and killed by a sniper. The North remembers him with gratitude, for he died in the act of committing the Army of the Potomac to what was to be the turning point of the war.

The early morning of July 1, 1863, opened to both commanders a plenitude of military opportunities. Almost everywhere about them was good terrain for maneuver: a network of roads, plenty of open fields, patches of woods, small hills. Lee, by his threat to Harrisburg and Philadelphia, had succeeded in his first objective—to draw the Army of the Potomac from its base at Washington. An engagement near Gettysburg would keep the Union forces well east of the range of mountains that concealed and guarded his own long line of communications in Cumberland Valley. A Confederate victory at this important road junction would give Lee a favorable approach either to Baltimore and Washington or to Harrisburg and Philadelphia. In case of a Confederate failure, Lee's line of retreat would be protected by the mountains.

On the Union side the necessity of stopping Lee in order to save Northern morale was almost as great as Lee's need of a smashing victory to save the South from suffocation.

The position occupied by Union troops on first contact was not good for much except to get their grappling hooks into the enemy. But when in the afternoon they were driven from Seminary Ridge and south through the streets of Gettysburg, they occupied Culp's Hill, Cemetery Hill, and Cemetery Ridge. General Winfield Scott Hancock is reported to have said that afternoon, "I think this the strongest position by nature upon which to fight a battle that I ever saw."

A diagram of this defensive position shows an inverted *J*, the famous "fish hook," of which Culp's Hill and Cemetery Hill formed the hook while Cemetery Ridge formed the shank. Behind the Union lines, inside the hook, there was excellent ground for maneuver, and the defending army had the advantage of interior lines.

It was unquestionably a good position, and Meade knew how to use it. Lee, when he heard that Meade was to be his opponent in this campaign, is reported to have said of him, "He will commit no blunder on my front, and if I make one he will make haste to take advantage of it."

The three-day battle has been fought over so often in print that it would be tedious to tread the same ground here: with Ewell on the first day all but capturing Culp's Hill at the northern end of the Union line; with Longstreet on the second day driving Sickles out of the Peach Orchard and almost capturing Little Roundtop, from which he could have dominated the Union lines; with Picket and "the flower of old Virginia" on the third day breaking against the center of the Union line, reaching the guns only to be thrown back in final defeat.

In the Pennsylvania State Museum at Harrisburg is a vast canvas by Peter Frederick Rothermel, picturing the moment when Picket's charge recoiled from the Union wall. General Meade stands in the left corner waving his hat. As Dr. Edwin B. Coddington reminds us in "Rothermel's Painting of the Battle of Gettysburg" (*Pennsylvania History,* January, 1960), a slightly different version of the incident was given by Frank A. Haskell, who was present and saw Meade's son, not the commanding general, wave his hat. On receiving news that the enemy had turned, Meade's face lighted up and, as Haskell describes the incident, he said, " 'Thank God.' Then his right hand moved as if it would have caught off his hat and waved it; but this gesture he suppressed, and instead he waved his hand, and said 'Hurrah.' The son, with more youth in his blood and less rank upon his shoulders, snatched off his cap, and roared out his three 'Hurrahs' right heartily. The General then surveyed the field, some minutes, in silence."

There was a very different scene on Seminary Ridge. "Lee met and rallied the retreating soldiers," wrote Robert Conquest in the March, 1958, issue of *History Today,* "in a manner the English colonel [Freemantle, who was there] describes as 'perfectly sublime.' [Said Lee to his men] 'It is I who have lost this fight, and you must help me out of it the best way you can.'"

Though defeated, the Southern soldier never lost his spirit. Aware of this, Meade moved cautiously in pursuit of the retreating enemy; but after being trapped for six days by flood on the Potomac River, the Southern forces managed to get across and escape. Nevertheless, after the Union victories at Gettysburg on July 3 and Vicksburg on July 4, the South had no prospect of ultimate victory.

Besides the Gettysburg campaign, Confederates made two other incursions into Pennsylvania, both reaching as far as Chambersburg. On October 10, 1862, General J. E. B. ("Jeb") Stuart, having ridden round McClellan's army, stopped at Chambersburg. His cavalry seized supplies, burned a military storehouse, and collected more than a thousand horses from the neighborhood.

Two years later, at 5:30 A.M., July 30, 1864, General McCausland entered Chambersburg. He presented the town with an ultimatum: either to pay one hundred thousand dollars in gold (five hundred thousand in greenbacks) or to see the town burned to ashes. The town council, having previously removed all money from the banks to a safe place and all horses and cattle to the hills, refused to pay lest by so doing they prolong the war. It was a brave action. At nine o'clock McCausland gave orders to destroy the town. Colonel William E. Peters of the 21st Virginia Cavalry protested but was placed under arrest. The town was put to the flames, and two-thirds of the inhabitants lost their homes. Bricks from the rubble left by that fire now pave the walks about some of the best houses in the proud old town.

Various reasons have been suggested for McCausland's severity. Undoubtedly the South needed money, and McCausland may have felt himself obliged to make good his promise to destroy the town if it defied him. It is more likely, however, that the flames were in reprisal for the recent burning by Union soldiers of Virginia houses. It may also be that John Brown's having been in Chambersburg when planning his raid on Harper's Ferry had something to do with the ordering of this unhappy conflagration.

It will be remembered that Abraham Lincoln, when he was at Harrisburg on February 22, 1861, voiced regret that he had not that day managed to express adequately the feelings which the sight of Independence Hall stirred into life. It was the natural poet in Lincoln speaking. He had the gift of fusing thought and feeling into words that were like sudden flashes of light in a dark room, and he was unhappy when the flash did not come. It came at last in the cemetery at Gettysburg on November 19, 1863, in what John Hay in his diary called "half a dozen words of consecration."

When David Wills, commissioner from Pennsylvania, invited Lincoln as Chief Executive "to set apart these grounds to their sacred use by a few appropriate remarks," he touched the key to Lincoln's heart and his religion. Lincoln was not a churchman, but he fervently obeyed the second commandment of Jesus ("Thou shalt love thy neighbor as thyself"), which provides the Christian interpretation of the first ("Thou shalt love the Lord thy God"). The opportunity Lincoln had missed at the flag-raising at Independence Hall was given him at the Gettysburg cemetery.

The President's "remarks" were not the improvisations of a busy executive. The tradition that his only preparation was the jotting down of a few random thoughts on scattered sheets of paper is in error. He brought to Gettysburg the day before the ceremony a nearly completed first draft. That evening he asked Wills to tell him exactly what part he was to take in the ceremony, then conferred with William Henry Seward, and afterwards sat down by himself to revise and complete his first draft. Next morning after breakfast he worked for an hour on the speech again. It was this second draft that he held in his hand while speaking in the afternoon.

Though the Gettysburg Address reads like a testament of faith, there is an anxious note in it. The war was still raging, and no one could say with certainty what the end would be. In his reiterated appeal for dedication on the part of his hearers, he still speaks to an embattled Free World.

24 *The Industrial Revolution*

In *Pennsylvania the Keystone State,* Dr. S. K. Stevens challenges New England's claim and declares the Commonwealth to be "the birthplace of the industrial revolution in America." Here the factory system made the sharpest early inroads into home manufactures, and here the resulting labor movement fought its most crucial battles. At Philadelphia in 1775 was organized the first joint stock company for textiles in America: the United Company of Philadelphia for Promoting Manufactures, headed by a Quaker, Samuel Wetherill.

Wetherill's later association with Tench Coxe in a new company known as the Pennsylvania Society for the Encouragement of Manufactures and the Useful Arts produced a rapid advance in textile manufacturing in the United States. Tench Coxe was a man of vision, urging a nation-wide system of manufactures to relieve the country of its dependence on Europe. As early as 1787 —the year of the Constitutional Convention, when a true sense of nationality was yet to come among the several united states— he published "An Enquiry into the Principles on Which a Commercial System for the United States of America Should Be Founded."

In Pennsylvania the happy conjunction of coal, iron ore, and limestone (for fluxing the impurities from the ore) made it inevitable, in view of Pennsylvania's manpower and her organizing skill, that she should be the greatest steel-producing state in the Union. Her vast resources of coal, and especially her virtual monopoly in this country of anthracite production, gave her a lead in the application of steam power to manufactures. It was the introduction of steam power that caused the death of home industries and the birth of the factory system with its gigantic machinery, its large staffs of employees, and its outlay of capital to maintain all this.

Since the days of the fabled Wayland Smith, iron manufacture has been an object of mystery and respect; but it was the discovery of anthracite that gave the industry its title of nobility. The adoption of anthracite coal as a fuel in place of charcoal removed the iron foundry's need of a neighboring forest to provide fuel and so encouraged the removal of the industry to the city. With this change came another: the rise of the giant corporation engaged in many businesses subsidiary to its main activity. There was the Brady's Bend Iron Company, for instance, which owned ore mines and coal mines and produced both raw iron and finished products such as iron rails.

The nineteenth century saw a wide variety of major industries in Pennsylvania, but iron and steel, of which machinery for most of the other industries is made, have really been the key to the Industrial Revolution here.

In 1776 Pennsylvania was primarily a farming community. Ninety per cent of her people lived on farms or in communities with a population of less than ten thousand people. The Commonwealth led all the English colonies in agricultural production. It was only to be expected that among her earliest manufactures milling—the production of flour and other grain products—should be foremost. By 1820 the milling of flour and meal had become the most valuable, in terms of dollar returns, of all her industries, and flour was her most important export. Many other Pennsylvania industries were based on agriculture, such as the tanning and making of leather goods, the manufacture of woolen clothing, and distilling. This last was a convenient way (as illustrated by the Whisky Rebellion) of turning the grain of isolated farms into a merchantable commodity. Governor Keith in 1722 erected a malt house at what is now known as Graeme Park, in order, as he said, to help the farmers during a time of depression to dispose of their grain. All these were home industries, requiring small capital.

The iron industry was different. From the beginning it required more capital and a larger, tighter organization. Perhaps that is why the industry was slow in developing in democratic Pennsylvania. Neither the Dutch nor the Swedes are known to have had iron works in this area, unless the tradition be accepted that iron was worked at Tinicum during Governor Printz's time. William Penn had planned to establish iron works, but nothing came of it. It was not until 1716 that Thomas Rutter erected the first bloomery forge on Manatawny Creek in Berks County. In 1718 Samuel Nutt, Sr., established the Coventry Iron Works on French Creek in Chester County.

With the discovery of these and other small pockets of iron in the Schuylkill River drainage area a new and picturesque element —the iron community—was added to Pennsylvania's already rich mixture of occupations and races and religions.

The ironmaster lived in a handsome stone house overlooking the furnace and the workmen's cottages. He was rich, according to the standards of the time, and he had to be, for the undertaking demanded heavy initial expenditure and the maintenance of a large work force. Since charcoal was the fuel to be used, he had to have a large tract of forest land, thousands of acres in extent, to assure him a good supply of wood. This meant isolation from well-settled areas. The community, in consequence, had to be self-sufficient. There had to be wood-cutters and charcoal-burners, miners to bring up the ore and pick-and-shovel men to quarry the limestone which was to flux it. There had to be iron-workers to tend the furnace and teamsters to take the pig iron and iron bars to flatboats on the Schuylkill for transportation to Philadelphia. There had to be farmers to feed the community, a storekeeper, overseers, managers, and bookkeepers.

It is often said that the typical iron plantation in Pennsylvania was like a Virginia tobacco plantation. There is a measure of truth in that, but the comparison must not be carried too far. The iron community, it is true, was self-contained. The workmen, some of whom were indentured servants, bought their household necessities at the company store. Most of the men, however, were independent. They could come and go as they pleased. On pay day there often remained a substantial credit after all deductions for purchases had been made.

In 1820 Rutter erected the Colebrookdale Furnace on Ironstone Creek, a tributary of the Manatawny, which flows into the Schuylkill at Pottstown. Thereafter the industry spread rapidly north and west of Philadelphia. In 1727 Anthony Morris and Company established the Durham Iron Works far up the Delaware River near Easton.

The most important and dramatic development came with Peter Grubb's discovery in 1732 of the three green hills of ore— Big Hill, Middle Hill, and Grassy Hill—at what came to be known as the Cornwall Mine, which was for many years the greatest source of iron ore in America. In 1734 Grubb bought land here, and in 1742 he set up the Cornwall Furnace, built against a hillside, as was then the custom, so that the charcoal, ore, and limestone could be dropped in from the top in order to make loading easy for the teamsters. He named it Cornwall after the county in England where his father had been born. Miners were brought over from Wales—a fact attested today by the typically Welsh village of Cornwall still seen at the foot of the South Mountains, its neat rows of stone houses almost touched by cars sweeping by on U.S. 322, known locally as the Horseshoe Pike. The forests of the South Mountains assured a plentiful supply of wood for charcoal.

During the Revolutionary War, the Cornwall Mine provided the American armies with cannon and shells. It has been estimated that between 1740, when it began production, and the year 1908 no less than twenty million tons of ore were brought out. Only recently has it been realized that the supply may be exhausted within measurable time. The mine still employs some two hundred men and delivers annually about half a million tons. It is believed that it still has reserves of another twenty million.

The open pit of the Cornwall Mine—that immense abyss which remains one of the wonders of Pennsylvania—is no longer in use. But underneath the whole length of it there is now a tunnel (not for sightseers) with openings cut in the sides—like doors or windows—through which falls the crumbling ore moved by pressure from the weight of rock above.

By the time John Huber in 1750 erected Elizabeth Furnace (a property later acquired by "Baron" Stiegel of Stiegel glass fame) near Brickerville in Lancaster County, Pennsylvania was leading all colonies in iron production.

The Revolution gave an impetus, as all later wars have done, to the iron industry in Pennsylvania and helped its westward march. The Nanticoke Bloomery was established on Nanticoke Creek in Luzerne County in 1778. The Carlisle Rolling and Slitting Mills near Carlisle in Cumberland County appeared in 1782. W. Chambers and Brothers established the Mount Pleasant

Iron Works in Path Valley in 1783. By 1785 the Bedford or Cromwell Furnace had been erected in Huntingdon County.

With the erection in 1789-1790 of the Alliance (Jacobs Creek) Furnace in Fayette County the iron industry approached the Pittsburgh area, which is today considered to be its natural home. Pittsburgh, indeed, was to nourish Pennsylvania's first giant industry and give the Commonwealth leadership in America's Industrial Revolution.

Meanwhile, the charcoal-fed iron furnaces in the Schuylkill, Lehigh, and Susquehanna valleys were starving to death as the forests that supplied them with fuel became exhausted. For a time the iron industry of southeastern Pennsylvania seemed to be in a decline. It recovered, however, when the use of anthracite in blast furnaces was developed. Canals made the hard coal available at reasonable cost. As a consequence, many of the old charcoal furnaces were rehabilitated and adapted to the use of anthracite, and larger furnaces were built to make the fullest possible use of this better fuel.

A great revival of the iron industry in the older part of Pennsylvania then began. Blast furnaces came again into full operation, and the demand for local iron ore produced the greatest mining boom the region had ever seen. Over a hundred small iron mines were operating, and the Cornwall Mine was producing more than ever before.

Soon, however, with the increasing use of ore imported from the Lake Superior area and of coke from the vast beds of bituminous coal in western Pennsylvania, the Pittsburgh district grew so prodigiously that the iron industry began to center there. In the end, most of the small anthracite furnaces in eastern Pennsylvania were abandoned, and the iron industry in the east declined. Today it has risen again with the Bethlehem Steel Company's blast furnaces, open-hearth furnaces, rolling mills, and by-product coke ovens. This gigantic plant spreads along the shore of the Lehigh River at Bethlehem and also the Susquehanna River at Steelton, a suburb of Harrisburg. There are smaller (but still gigantic) plants at Lebanon and Coatesville. The huge plant now being developed near Morgantown is Bethlehem Steel's bid for the future.

Andrew Carnegie was, of course, only one of many men who profited from the rapid development of the steel industry during the latter part of the nineteenth century. But his career aptly illustrates the changes in American industry during his lifetime.

Carnegie's spectacular rise from a bobbin boy in a cotton factory to the man whom J. Pierpont Morgan congratulated as the richest in the world had an appropriate setting in Pittsburgh's tumultuous medley of hills, cliffs, and river cuttings.

Born in Scotland, Andrew Carnegie came to America with his father, a weaver whose home industry had been destroyed by the factory system. After his experience as a bobbin boy at Allegheny City, Pennsylvania, Andrew became a telegraph clerk and later a district superintendent of the Pennsylvania Railroad. His first investment was $217.50 worth of stock in the Woodruff Palace Car Company, which was later absorbed by Pullman.

His introduction to the iron industry came through his interest in the railroad. His imagination was caught by the spectacle of the expanding rail system of the country. He saw the waste and inefficiency of the wooden railroad bridges that spanned Pennsylvania's rivers, and he organized the Keystone Bridge Company to replace the short-lived, inflammable wooden structures with durable iron. The success of Keystone not only was profitable to the Pennsylvania Railroad but also gave an impetus to transportation all over the country. Keystone's iron bridge, placed in 1865 across the Missouri River at Kansas City, gave to that town of high bluffs and deep ravines, which only a generation before had been a French trading post, the key to its spectacular rise as a commercial metropolis. Within a few years no less than eighteen railroads were serving it. The Keystone Bridge joining Omaha, Nebraska, with Council Bluffs, Iowa, was the link that bound this country together in a vast transcontinental railroad system.

Carnegie did not only sell rails and build railroad bridges. He helped to finance the Union Pacific. He was consulted by the Vanderbilt interests about tunnels through the Allegheny Mountains in Pennsylvania for the projected Southern Pacific Railroad—the tunnels that are now used by the Pennsylvania Turnpike. "Carnegie Beams" were used in many of the country's most prized constructions—the Statue of Liberty, the Brooklyn Bridge, and the Eads Bridge across the Mississippi at St. Louis.

When plans were being laid for the Philadelphia Centennial in 1876, Andrew Carnegie persuaded the committee to construct the main exhibition building not of wood but of iron and steel. It was not the first time iron and steel had been used in building construction, but their use in such a prominent place and at such a time gave them the best possible advertisement in the architectural world.

Great changes have come about in the iron and steel industry since 1860. In that year the United States produced nearly a million tons of pig iron but only eleven thousand tons of steel. Consequently, sheer steel and crucible steel, excellent for weapons and for the best tools of all kinds, were expensive to make. Then just before the Civil War, Sir Henry Bessemer in England and William Kelly (a Philadelphian by birth) in Kentucky invented a process of blowing cold air through molten iron. Carnegie brought the Bessemer steel process to Pennsylvania, and soon the night in Pittsburgh's environs was enlivened with bursts of the changing red, violet, orange, and white lights that a Bessemer in full blow shot into the sky.

After 1866, when the conflicting claims of the Kelly and Bessemer interests were adjusted, the industry in America began to manufacture steel in a large way. Further changes—especially the open-hearth method, which was slower but more efficient—improved the product and decreased the cost of production until steel became the foundation of modern industry—"king," as Carnegie called it, of the machine age.

Just as John D. Rockefeller organized the developing oil industry, so Andrew Carnegie organized steel. In 1892 Carnegie consolidated the Keystone Bridge Company, the Edgar Thomson Steel Works, the Homestead Steel Works, the Duquesne Steel Works, the Beaver Falls Mills, the Union Mills, and the Lucy Furnace into the Carnegie Steel Company with a capital of $25,000,000. By 1900 the company's capital stock was $160,-000,000.

When in 1901 Andrew Carnegie decided to retire and devote himself to philanthropy, a giant merger of ten companies including Carnegie Steel was financed by the elder J. Pierpont Morgan and named the United States Steel Corporation. The merged companies owned 149 steel plants, 1,000 miles of railroad, 112 Great Lakes vessels, and vast ore, coal, and limestone lands. The new corporation had a total capitalization of $867,550,394. The authorized capital was $1,404,000,000, half of which was watered stock; but in a few years, as the corporation gathered in more and more subsidiaries and increased its business, its assets turned out to be greater than the capitalization.

Though Carnegie's career reflects the changes taking place in American and world economy, he was not in any way a revolutionary. He was a practical man with a zest for bettering the things he found immediately at hand. His enormous financial success was due not to any deliberate and far-reaching campaign to change the American economic order but to an alertness in seizing the opportunities that the traditional economy (expanding with the nation) put in his way. He was aware of this, and throughout his life it colored his attitude toward wealth. He often said he did not know how he came to make so much money. He felt there was something a little shameful about being a multimillionaire, and he regarded his philanthropies as restoring to society the wealth which society had bestowed on him.

Today the country's greatest concentration of steel is in the Pittsburgh area, which includes many Monongahela, Beaver, Allegheny, and Ohio river towns and extends westward to Youngstown, Ohio. "Of all the steel-producing states," writes Arthur C. Bining in *Pennsylvania's Iron and Steel Industry,* "Pennsylvania still remains the leader with a rated steel capacity of more than one quarter of the whole."

25 *Dusky Diamonds*

Down in a coal mine, underneath the ground,
Where a gleam of sunshine never can be found;
Digging dusky diamonds all the year around,
Away down in a coal mine, underneath the ground.

—*Pennsylvania Songs and Legends,* George Korson, ed.

The vast coal measures in Pennsylvania have made her the greatest mining state in the Union. The story of her coal—of the struggle to get it and the consequent changes brought about in American society—is one of the most exciting in our national annals.

In Paleozoic times great swamp forests covered the greater part of Pennsylvania. By a lucky chance the same geologic convulsions that turned her swamps into peat beds and coal measures by just the right application of heat and pressure, thrust some of the coal so deeply beneath the earth's surface that millions of years of stream erosion have been unable to reach it and wash it away. So it was that when man first found a use for Pennsylvania's coal, there were some twenty-two billion tons of anthracite and seventy-five billion tons of bituminous coal waiting for him: ninety-seven billion tons of coal looking for a market.

The Chinese had been burning coal for thousands of years, and Europeans had been using it as fuel since the thirteenth century. Coal had been found on Cape Breton Island, Canada, in 1672. In 1701 coal was mined in Virginia. But Pennsylvania's coal lay in the earth until about 1750 before receiving its first public recognition. John Patton's so-called Trader's Map—date unknown, but the first reference to it was in 1753—noted the presence of

"Sea Coal" on the Kiskiminetas River, a tributary of the Allegheny. It was another seventy years before Pennsylvania coal became of commercial importance.

The region's backwardness in the use of coal as fuel is not difficult to understand. The Indians, who were few in numbers there, found all the fuel they needed in the forest. They probably knew of the burning properties of coal but seldom bothered to use it, since dry wood was easier to ignite. According to the *Jesuit Relations* the explorer Pierre Esprit Radisson found the plains Indians, in the absence of firewood, using *charbon de terre*. In eastern Pennsylvania the Indians must have known of the existence of anthracite, for the Susquehanna River and the Lackawanna River, Nanticoke Creek and Ransom's Creek (at Plymouth), have all cut through and exposed veins of coal. The Monongahela Indians are known to have used cannel coal for making figurines and other small ornaments. Indians used finely ground coal as a base for black paint. No evidence, however, has been found that the Indians of Pennsylvania used coal as a fuel.

The use of bituminous coal in any quantities in Pennsylvania was earlier than the use of anthracite. The softer coal was found over a far larger area, underlying about a third of the state. It was easier to get at, and it could be more easily transported on the smoothly flowing Monongahela, Allegheny, and their tributaries. A coal mine opposite Fort Pitt was opened for the garrison in 1760. George Washington visited a coal mine near Connellsville in 1770. The accessibility of the fuel encouraged the early growth of western manufacturing. In 1797 James O'Hara and Isaac Craig of Pittsburgh set up on Coal Hill the first American glassworks to use coal as fuel.

Outlets for soft coal were found in other developing industries, especially where steam engines were used; and since many of these industries were in Pittsburgh, that city soon acquired a reputation for the smoke which soft coal so plentifully emits. Early in the nineteenth century Pennsylvanians began to convert coal into coke for use in iron foundries. So great was the demand that by 1832 Pittsburgh alone was using four hundred tons a day.

Pennsylvania's importance as a coal-producing state rests largely on her possession in the northeastern counties of the largest anthracite region in the world. Anthracite coal burns longer, gives more heat, emits less smoke, and leaves less residue than other coals. It is, however, more difficult to ignite, and so came more slowly into use.

Early settlers are known to have burned anthracite. During the French and Indian War anthracite was used to heat the barracks at Fort Augusta (Sunbury). In 1762 John Jenkins with a party from Connecticut found anthracite coal at what is now Wilkes-Barre and recognized its potential value. During the next year the Susquehanna Company of Connecticut, in its plans for the laying out of the townships in the Wyoming Valley, reserved for the use of the company "all beds or mines of iron ore and coal." Three years later Colonel Francis, who had been to Wyoming, reported to Richard and Thomas Penn the presence of "good lands and much coal" in those hills. Another traveler, David Schopf, reported in 1783 that a bed of brilliant black coal a mile above Wyoming burned without leaving a bad odor.

The use of anthracite in Pennsylvania, however, was sporadic and confined to the backwoods. No one attemped to put it into Philadelphia homes. Although anthracite was more readily available in Philadelphia than western bituminous, it would not burn on an ordinary hearth. Moreover, coal was heavy, and to transport it from Wyoming or Mauch Chunk over mountain trails and down rocky rivers was prohibitively expensive.

Blacksmiths in the Wyoming Valley were glad enough to use coal. As early as 1769 or 1770 the brothers Obadiah and Daniel Gore from Connecticut were using anthracite in their forges. During the Revolutionary War coal from Mill Creek above Wilkes-Barre was taken in Durham boats down the Susquehanna to Harris's Ferry and carted thence to Carlisle to help in the manufacture of firearms. By 1802 Oliver Evans, a Philadelphia inventor, was burning coal in a grate. But it was not until 1808, when Judge Jesse Fell of Wilkes-Barre designed a grate especially for burning anthracite (which needs a good draft from below), that the first serious demand for anthracite arose.

The story of the Smith brothers, Abijah and John, of Wilkes-Barre illustrates the development of popular interest in the new fuel. They brought a load of anthracite coal down the Susquehanna to Columbia in 1807, but were unable to sell it and had to dump it on the ground. A few months later, February 8, 1808, their neighbor, Judge Fell, proved that his grate needed no blast. Abijah and John immediately returned to Columbia with more coal and some of Fell's new grates. The brothers sold their cargo, and the first battle for the market had been won. By 1813 Charles Miner in his newspaper the *Gleaner,* published at Wilkes-Barre, reported that the coal of Wyoming had already become "an article of considerable traffic with the lower counties of Pennsylvania."

But transportation was a major obstacle to the full use of anthracite. Not until the great canal system of Pennsylvania was developed could its use become general. In 1818 the Lehigh Navigation Company was formed and the Lehigh Coal Company began to mine coal. Two years later the two companies were merged into the Lehigh Navigation and Coal Company. In that year, 1820, the first shipment of Lehigh coal—365 tons—from Mauch Chunk began the great coal era. In 1825 the Schuylkill River Canal was opened. Backed by Stephen Girard, who had invested heavily in coal lands, shipments of coal from the region tapped by the canal doubled in amount in five years, then re-doubled, and re-redoubled, going from 6,500 tons to 79,973 tons.

The completion of the North Branch Canal as far as the Nanticoke Dam in 1830 gave further impetus to coal shipments. The first boat, the *Wyoming,* built at Shickshinny, carried ten tons of anthracite down the Susquehanna to Northumberland and Middletown, thence through the Union Canal to the Schuylkill, and so on to Philadelphia. By 1834 the canal had been extended to Wilkes-Barre. In that year the Allegheny Portage Railroad was completed, giving western bituminous a market in Philadelphia.

The railroad history of Pennsylvania is closely linked with that of coal. Two years before the historic Moosic Mountain run of the "Stourbridge Lion," the Mauch Chunk Railroad had been completed by the Lehigh Coal and Navigation Company in order to bring coal down from Summit Hill to barges on the Lehigh River. It was a gravity line, nicknamed the "Donkey Railroad" because, while the loaded cars came down under their own weight, donkeys or mules pulled the empties up again. However, because steam was later introduced at the same place, enthusiasts have sometimes erroneously called the Mauch Chunk the first steam railroad built in America.

When the Philadelphia and Reading Railroad was chartered in 1833, it had an eye on Schuylkill anthracite. The first train reached Mount Carbon, near Pottsville, in the coal regions on

January 1, 1842. The Lehigh Valley Railroad (whose crack express was named the "Black Diamond") opened its service between Easton and Mauch Chunk in 1855. The Lackawanna Railroad (named for the river that runs through Carbondale and Scranton to Pittston on the Susquehanna) gave the Wyoming Valley outlets on both the Atlantic Ocean and (through the Erie Railroad) the Great Lakes, thus completing the emancipation of the coal regions from freight wagons and canal boats.

Since 1800 the relative production of bituminous and anthracite coal in Pennsylvania has fluctuated wildly. Bituminous mines in 1800 produced about 87,000 tons, while anthracite mines in the same year produced only 250. But with the introduction of proper grating and canal transportation, anthracite picked up rapidly and in 1832 pased bituminous in the race, the production figures for that year being: anthracite, 501,951 tons; bituminous, 450,940 tons. By 1900, however, bituminous had leaped ahead again. The figures for that year were: anthracite, 57,367,915 tons; bituminous, 79,842,326 tons. Peak production of anthracite coal came in 1917 with 99,611,811 tons. For bituminous the peak came in 1918 with 178,000,000 tons.

Behind these cold figures stand the warm-blooded men of the mine patches and coal camps: a brave breed, drawn from many nationalities, hardy, independent, proud of their craft, and proud of their bards and minstrels.

> The man in the moon had charge of the light plant,
>   Our cottage walls were not of bricks;
> Young and old enjoyed the night camp
>   On the green at Number Six.

Coal mining, especially in the deep anthracite mines, is one of the most arduous and certainly the most dangerous of all major industries. It is no wonder that Pennsylvania's great body of miners developed qualities of reckless independence. They were strongly prejudiced and difficult to hold together; but when once organized, they had a capacity to take and give punishment surpassed by no other body of workers.

Living conditions in the anthracite mining towns during the second half of the nineteenth century seem now incredible. In that occupation, more clearly perhaps than in any other, were seen the tensions of the Industrial Revolution in Pennsylvania. The disparity between poverty and wealth was at its ugliest. The men worked for long, sunless hours underground, enduring the debilitating effects of foul air and dust, the dangers from falling roof and face, the threat of gas explosions, fire, and flooding. Safety devices were only slowly introduced—such as the Davy lamp, water pumps, ventilating fans, and mine inspection. As late as 1870 there were 221 deaths in one year from accidents in the anthracite mines of Pennsylvania.

Mining villages or "mine patches"—described by Christopher Tunnard and Henry Hope Reed in *American Skyline* as "groups of bleak gray wooden frame houses zigzagging up and down the hilly countryside or nestling grimly in a hollow"—were fit company for the culms of mine waste that turned some of Pennsylvania's most beautiful mountain valleys into visions of hell on earth. Pay in the mines was low. Employment was irregular, depending on the fluctuations of the market. Most of the miners were in debt to their employers. Some companies paid in scrip redeemable only at the company-owned store. Literacy was low, for education was neglected. Tensions between groups of differing national origins were high, for as the years went by, the original miners of Welsh, English, Irish, Scotch, and German extraction were being overwhelmed by imported labor: Slavs, Italians, Poles, Hungarians, and Negroes.

There were, however, other influences tending to pull the miners, of whatever national origin, together and to give the whole community a sense of identity. Among them were the hardships endured, the grievances shared in common, the pride all felt in their mining skills (often passed down from father to son), and last but not least, the circulation by "tramp minstrels" of indigenous mine ballads. It was these last that did as much as anything else to help miners understand John Mitchell's union gospel: "The coal you dig isn't Slavish or Polish or Irish coal; it's coal."

Miners were growing restive under the shadow of the "coal king," who owned not only the mine, the village, the houses, the church, and the school but everything else around them, from the company doctor who brought them into the world to the cemetery that received them at their exit. George Korson, in his chapter on coal miners in *Pennsylvania Songs and Legends,* prints an epitaph from a miner's grave in Hazleton:

Fourty years I worked with pick & drill
Down in the mines against my will
The Coal King's slave, but now it's passed;
Thanks be to God I am free at last.

An explosion had to come, and the Molly Maguires provided it. The Molly Maguires, named after a secret society in Ireland whose members adopted woman's dress as a disguise, was a labor organization established in the 1850's in the anthracite region by members of the Ancient Order of Hibernians. Bad living conditions in the anthracite region gave the Mollies an excuse for violence, and age-old methods of intimidation gave them power for a time to escape punishment. They attacked superintendents, murdered mine bosses, and put the fear of death (with great loss to justice) into judges and police. The excesses of the Mollies turned public sympathy away from the miners' legitimate grievances; and when Franklin B. Gowan, president of the Philadelphia and Reading Railroad (which through its affiliated Coal and Iron Company owned much of the anthracite), set out to smash the Molly Maguires, law-abiding citizens wished him success.

The Pinkerton Detective Agency was called in. It laid long-range plans, in the course of which one of its men, James McParlan, joined the Mollies, reached their inner circle, and at risk of death used his position to protect their victims. Suspected at length, he barely escaped with his life but survived to expose the whole murderous network. His adventures among the Mollies provided Conan Doyle with plot, characters, incidents, and locale (although he changed their names, the towns are recognizable to anyone who knows the mining region) for a Sherlock Holmes novel, *The Valley of Fear*.

The unsavory episode of the Molly Maguires retarded the correction of mining conditions. It took another twenty-five years and the five-month strike of 1902—Johnny Mitchell's strike—to bring the miners' plight to proper study and final adjustment.

26 *Greentop Gold*

When man first arrived in Pennsylvania many thousands of years ago, its land surface was covered with a green forest mantle. It was a mixed forest, for Pennsylvania was midway between the northern and southern forest zones. Toward the south were the hardwoods: white oak, black walnut, locust. In the north the evergreens competed for foothold on the mountainsides with yellow birch, cherry, beech, sugar maple, and the like. In some sectors great stands of white pine and hemlock blotted out the sun.

It has been estimated that about ninety-eight per cent of Pennsylvania's present 45,302 square miles (over 28,000,000 acres) was once covered with forest. Today some 15,000,000 acres—more than half the total area—are still forest, though most of the trees are second growth.

Lumbering in Pennsylvania is as old as its inhabitants. The Indians used saplings to build their long houses and cabins, and larger trunks for the stockades surrounding some of their villages. The Swedes and Finns cut down good-sized trees to make log houses, which became the American pioneer's standard shelter. As early as 1683, William Penn informed the Free Society of Traders that Pennsylvania had plenty of hemlock bark for tanning. It was early recognized that in her great stands of white pine she had the best spar timber in the country if not in the world. Shipmasts of Pennsylvania pine carried sail throughout the seven seas. In the early years of the eighteenth century the British government passed laws protecting American white pine, which was superior to anything of the kind procurable from the Baltic States for the British navy. With prosperity and the coming of clapboard, shingle-roofed houses, there was a demand for boards; and to supply the local markets, sawmills dotted the stream sides. Some of these, being able to operate only when a good rain had raised the creeks on which they depended, were derisively called "thundergust mills."

As an independent industry of considerable size, American lumbering began in Maine. Thence it spread westward as the demand grew and Maine's virgin timber disappeared. For a while New York held primacy, but she yielded to Pennsylvania. This state held her leadership for a considerable time. Besides the wealth of broad-leaved trees on both sides of her Allegheny Mountains, she had in some of her northern counties great forests of white pine and hemlock which, though their darkness at first brought them the epithet "Shades of Death," were hailed as "greentop gold" by later woodsmen.

A turning point in the history of lumbering in Pennsylvania was the formation of the Susquehanna Boom Company and the completion in 1850 of the Williamsport Boom. Other booms on the river, such as those at Jersey Shore and Lock Haven, also served for the collection and sorting of logs, but the seven-mile-long Williamsport Boom was by far the greatest. It made Williamsport the key spot on the river for the lumber industry and for some thirty years the lumber capital of the world.

The Civil War spurred the industry, increasing as it did the demand for oak timber for ships' decks and for docks. During the war years few rafts were run without oak logs. It was necessary to adjust the proportion of oak to pine, for oak is not very buoyant and a raft without sufficient pine to carry it well above water is a hazard to the crew. A raft with too much oak might dive to a depth of five or six feet in going through a chute or over a dam. Dudley Tonkin of Cherry Tree reports that "Most pilots insisted on enough pine to carry the oak above water."

As Pennsylvania's virgin forests diminished, the supremacy of Williamsport declined. Its end was hastened by the disaster of May Day, 1889, when the Wiliamsport Boom broke and turned loose on the river some three hundred million board feet of logs. Chaos reigned on the face of the waters. Most of the logs were ultimately recovered, and temporary mills were erected all along the lower Susquehanna to process them. The disaster nevertheless caused enormous loss. Pennsylvania never recovered first place in the industry.

Statistics tell only part of the story, but they give a quick summary of the industry's growth and decline in Pennsylvania. In 1840 Pennsylvania had 5,389 sawmills, and the product that came out of them was valued at $1,150,220. In 1850, the year the Williamsport Boom was made ready, the number of mills had decreased to 2,894, many small mills having given way to the larger ones. The value of the product in that year, however, had increased to $7,729,058. By 1870 the value had leaped to $28,938,985, and by 1890 it had made a further slight increase to $29,087,970. The rate of growth in Pennsylvania, however, was dropping, while that of western states was increasing. By 1900 there were still over a thousand logging camps in Pennsylvania, but both Wisconsin and Michigan outstripped her in production. By 1940 Pennsylvania ranked only twenty-second among the timber-producing states.

Lumbering in nineteenth-century Pennsylvania was more than an industry. It was a way of life, with its own social system and its own economic order. The melting pot boiled in these woods. Joining the English and Scotch-Irish, who owned most of the wooded lands at the headwaters of the rivers, were New Englanders, who contributed their traditional know-how to the commercial end of the business. To these were added great numbers of French-Canadians, whose experience in the forests of Quebec and northern Ontario had made them experts at building chutes on small streams to carry the logs around falls. They were also adept at floating rafts over rocky low-water passages on the main river by opening dams (built for the purpose) on tributary streams along the way and thus creating "splash floods" to take the logs through.

Lumbering had its own rich and diversified society, and it had a rigid caste system:

Raftmen formed the highest caste [writes Dudley Tonkin], contemptuous of the loggers who provided the "sticks" for "log rafts" of which the pilots were captains. Below the raftmen were the loggers, who themselves were divided into two castes: loggers of white pine (the noblest of Pennsylvania trees), and loggers of hemlock, the bark of which was used for tanning. Under them came the "pulp cutters"—Swedes, Hungarians, and other "outsiders." On the last rung of all were the "chemical timber cutters"—cutters of wood used in the production of wood alcohol, charcoal, and other derivatives. The feeling between castes was often bitter. During the wars waged between raftmen and loggers, the raftmen have been known to drive nails into white pine logs to injure the saws.

The logging camps in winter made the woods ring with ax and saw and kept local teams of oxen and horses in movement hauling supplies or taking out logs to the rafting-in grounds on the river. Penn's Woods will never see again such ample and heartily enjoyed meals as the camp cook and his assistant, the "cookie," provided. A "stomach robber" (poor cook) did not last long, nor one who could not cook for a variety of tastes. At supper in a good camp there was roast ham for the mountain men and codfish for the down-Easters. And there was snitz (dried-apple) pie for every man at every meal.

The camps had their amusements: clog-dancing contests and fighting with no holds barred. Bitten-off ears and gouged-out eyes were the not infrequent penalties of defeat. Mrs. Marie Kathern Nuschke in "Hicks, Fighters, and Clog Dancers" (*Pennsylvania History,* October, 1952) tells how little Emilien Brisbois, the French-Canadian blacksmith, out-danced the champion clog-dancer of his camp and out-fought its 225-pound bully. He knocked the big man down, rolled him in the mud, and danced on his head with steel-plated shoes because the camp giant had called him "toad."

Chest Creek (and the lumber camps on it) was known in those days as "the fightenest creek in the State." "Every old raftsman of fifty or more years ago knew the Chest Creekers," wrote the son of an old-time raftsman to Dudley Tonkin; "you could always spot them, as they usually had an eye gouged out, an ear torn off, or most of their front teeth gone."

But they were good fellows, most of them. "When the fighting era passed," writes Mrs. Nuschke, "most of these same men married sweet, gentle women, raised families, and became model husbands."

The axman's job was exacting. Felling Pennsylvania's white pine was not like cutting down an apple tree. *Pinus strobus* sometimes towered 200 feet. A specimen now standing in Cook Forest reaches 197 feet. These trees were with good reason called the aristocrats of the forest, for their timbers went into masts for sailing ships. For this purpose every "stick" had to be ninety feet long without a break or blemish. Only the best trees, felled by the most skillful woodsmen, could meet those specifications. The largest spar ever cut on the West Branch of the Susquehanna was ninety-three feet long with a bottom diameter of forty-three inches (measured twelve feet from the butt) and a top diameter of thirty-three inches.

Sometimes, when a giant came down, it was made to strike a sturdy log placed about twenty feet from its base—a point where it was unbreakable—so as to ease its fall. Sometimes a good tree was cut to fall into a hemlock grove. The hemlocks were hurt, but that mattered little so long as my lord pine was saved from injury.

A good axman needed skill as much as muscle. It was said of Crawford Sebring that he could select his tree, walk thirty or forty feet away from it, set a stake in the ground, go back to the tree, spit on his hands, and cut down the tree with such precision that in falling it drove the stake into the ground. Folklorists have noted that the most famous of all lumbermen, Paul Bunyan, skipped Pennsylvania in his fabulous career. No doubt he found the competition too keen.

Once the tree was down, it had to be trimmed, cut to length, and got to water. Taking spar timbers to the rafting-in grounds was an exciting and dangerous job. Before the advent of the logging railroads teams of horses were used, or sometimes wooden log slides (iced troughs) snaking through the woods to the creek bank. Coming down a hill, the logs might get out of control and kill horse or man. Sometimes logs leaped from the slide and crushed everything in their way.

Ordinary logs, once delivered to the river and set afloat, were carried down by the current. Crews of loggers with cant hooks walked the banks, ready to push or roll grounded logs free. But with spar timber it was different. These aristocrats were made up into rafts and piloted unscratched to Williamsport or Marietta.

Rafting the huge logs from headwaters to market took profound knowledge of the river *at all levels* on the part of the pilot, and immense courage and muscle—as well as a dash of good luck —on the part of the crew. The river the raftsmen knew was unlike the smooth stream the tourist sees from his vantage point on the road above it. The pilot saw a succession of white-water hazards: rapids and falls, bridges and bends, rocky promontories, snags and reefs, on any one of which he might "stove" his raft and lose all or part of his "sticks." He had to keep a watch also for "widow-makers," broken branches overhanging the stream that could crack a man's skull and sweep him off into the current.

It was a strange world the raftsmen saw about them, not one you can visualize from a map. In the list of 372 rafting points on the West Branch, as listed by Tonkin, some town names occur, but they are scarcely noticed amidst the rocks and bends, guts, gaps, dead waters, and riffles on which the raft pilot had to keep his eye. To name only a few below Kinports Dam and the "Cherry Tree," there were Rocky Bend, Chest Falls, McCrackens Dead Water, Butment Riffles, Big Stepping Stones, Ninety Foot Gap, Moshannon Falls, Salt Lick Landing, Rattlesnake Run, Coalbar in the Channel, Pilot in Riffles ("bad rock," notes Tonkin: "I know because I hit it once and knocked out 16 sticks"), Hollow Rock ("the greatest one-drop falls on the river"), Port Deposit, and so on into Chesapeake Bay.

The lumber industry was a hardy plant, flourishing through the winter in the logging camps, but reserving its most glorious bloom for spring. As the winter waned, teams were busy dragging logs through the woods. Then when the ice and snow melted and the river was full, the world belonged to the raftsmen. Along the logging streams there was general holiday. Schools were "let out." Every schoolboy felt it to be a point of honor to cross the river on logs when the drive was on. For two cents apiece the boys bought steel caulks for their shoes. One for each shoe was enough; three to a shoe was a sign of wealth and pride. School floors rang with them as the boys came back to their classes.

Women sat up all night baking bread and pies for the rafting crews. When word flashed down the West Branch Valley that the river rafts (250 or 300 feet long) had "tied loose" and were on their way, farm work stopped and the river banks were filled with men and women, boys and girls, waiting to cheer the crews as they went by. When the raft "tied-in" at night at such towns as Clearfield and Lock Haven, the citizens crowded to the waterside to give the pilot and "pushing hands" (the men who worked the great sweeps) a proper welcome.

Logging, like mining, had its minstrels. Some of the folk ballads that grew up in Pennsylvania logging camps have attained a national circulation. An excellent selection may be found in George Korson's *Pennsylvania Songs and Legends*. There one will find "The Mainite in Pennsylvania," with the rollicking beginning:

I landed safe in Williamsport, in a lumberman's rendezvous.

There one will find also "The Jolly Lumberman" with both words and music:

Come all you jolly lumbermen and listen to my song,—
I'll tell you all my story—and I won't detain you long.

In another mood there is "The Death of Frank Farrel" and "The Log Jam at Hughey's Rock."

The "Song of the Shanty Boys" is infectious in its rhythm, and one may learn a lot about lumber camps from it:

The choppers and the sawyers, they lay the timber low;
The skidders and the swampers, they haul it to and fro;
Then comes the loaders, just at the break of day,
A-loading up the teams, for the river haste away.

Best loved of all was a gay ballad celebrating the exploits of Joe McCreery of Cherry Tree, famous for breaking a seven-mile log jam at the mouth of Chest Creek and for using a charge of dynamite to clean out some of the worst rock hazards on the river:

You rivermen have surely heard
About the appropriation
That was made to clear our little ditch
And benefit the nation.

That we might run through Chest Falls,
  Nor get the least bit weary,
So they raised the stamps and gave the job
  To Cherry Tree Joe McCreery.

The few old-time raftsmen who remain are not ashamed to
become a little moist round the eyes when the last stanza is heard:

In years to come when no rafts run
  On our dear little river,
And the cheery cry of "Land! Tie up!"
  Is heard no more—forever,
Down Rocky Bend and through Chest Falls,
  On winter nights so eerie,
The phantom raftsmen chase the ghost
  Of Cherry Tree Joe McCreery.

In 1938 the "last raft" (run by Dudley Tonkin to fulfill a wish
of his father Vincent Tonkin, one of the West Branch lumber
kings) was brought down the river by a crew of old raftsmen with
Harry Connor as pilot. When it cracked up at a new railroad
bridge near Muncy with the loss of seven men, including Harry
Connor, a wave of grief swept the valley from Williamsport to
Cherry Tree and wherever else the memory of old rafting days
was still green.

In the municipal park at Cherry Tree in 1955, R. Dudley
Tonkin erected a monument dedicated to the logging fellowship.
His tribute is expressed in the following inscription:

ALL PEOPLE THAT ON EARTH DO DWELL
SPEAK SOFTLY—TREAD LIGHTLY
TO HONOR THE RAFTMEN—THE LOGGERS
THEIR MOTHERS AND WIVES
OF PENN'S WOODS
CARRY ON

R. D. T.   1955

27 *Black Gold*

In the Oil Centennial year—1959—Pennsylvania congratulated herself on having set in motion the great petroleum industry which has revolutionized the modern world. But petroleum was by no means a Pennsylvania discovery. The ancient Egyptians were familiar with it as a lubricant. Pliny mentioned its use in Sicily as both an illuminant and a medicine. The Bible makes frequent mention of petroleum in one form or another: pitch, bitumen, slime. Noah's Ark, it is said, was made waterproof with pitch. In the thirteenth century A.D., Marco Polo, after telling about the high mountain in Armenia on which the Ark was believed to have rested, described "a fountain of oil [at Baku] which discharges so great a quantity as to furnish loading for many camels"—these latter being forerunners of the tank cars and pipelines with which oilmen transport their produce.

The Spaniards found the Incas of Peru and the Aztecs of Mexico using petroleum to caulk their boats. De Soto used Texas petroleum when he caulked his boats with asphalt near the Sabine Pass. On the banks of Oil Creek in northwestern Pennsylvania, Indians used timber-lined pits to collect the oil. As the water and oil seeped into the pits, the oil rose to the top and the Indians skimmed it off with paddles. David Zeisberger, the Moravian missionary who made a daring journey by the Forbidden Path through Seneca country to the headwaters of the Allegheny River, heard of various oil wells in the area. Of one in particular, which some members of his party visited in the vicinity of present Tionesta, he reported on October 7, 1768: "They brought back some oil from the oil-well. . . . The Indians use it externally as a medicine and it would be possible to use it for lighting. . . . The nature of these oil-wells might well be investigated."

A few years later early settlers used what was called Seneca oil (so named because it was used medicinally by the Seneca Indians, whose land this had once been) in a number of ways. For one thing it was a good lubricant. Mixed with flour, it served as axle grease. Applied to the body, it eased sore muscles, just as Vaseline, a derivative of petroleum, does today. Taken internally, it served as a gentle laxative. Sometimes it was used with a wick for lighting, but in this it was not too successful, for it gave off a lot of black smoke and had an offensive odor.

Curiously, it was the decline of whaling that gave petroleum its first commercial boost. Whale oil had been the world's chief lighting fluid, but about the middle of the nineteenth century the whale supply began to dwindle, and inventive minds turned to other sources of illumination.

Seneca oil was already a household remedy in western Pennsylvania—to be rubbed on sore joints or swallowed "to purify the blood"—when hearty Sam Kier, who owned salt wells at Tarentum on the Allegheny River not far above Pittsburgh, began selling half-pint bottles of Kier's Rock Oil at fifty cents apiece: "the most wonderful remedy ever discovered." It could make the lame walk (so his advertisements claimed), strengthen weak nerves, and overcome feelings of depression. As the poet (his advertising man) said:

> The beautiful balm from Nature's secret spring
> The bloom of health and life to man will bring;
> As from her depths this magic liquid flows
> To calm our suffering and assuage our woes.

All this was really designed as a means not to help the public nor primarily to make money but to get rid of a nuisance on his property. His salt wells were being fouled by intrusions of Seneca oil. When he ran it off onto the ground, his neighbors complained. A possible solution of his problem—how to get rid of the stuff— came to him when his doctor prescribed "American Medicinal Oil" (product of a Kentucky well) for his wife's ailments.

Kier saw a chance to make some money out of the dirty stuff. Assuming that Pennsylvania oil had as many medicinal virtues as the Kentucky variety, he bottled the "ugley grease," labeled it "Kier's Petroleum, or Rock Oil Celebrated for its Wonderful Curative Powers. A Natural Remedy," and sold it at fifty cents for half a pint.

He went farther. He had his oil analyzed by a distinguished Philadelphia chemist, James C. Booth, who discovered that by distillation a really good lighting fluid could be made. In 1850 Kier accordingly built a one-barrel still at Pittsburgh and from it produced what he called "Carbon Oil." This he sold at $1.50 a gallon and entered history as the first commercial oil refiner in this country. He had removed most of the smoke from the oil. It remained only to remove the offensive odor, and this a competitor, A. C. Ferris of New York City, accomplished a few years later by means of acid treatment. Soon the demand for the new illuminant was far in excess of the supply.

This was a long way from the present petroleum industry with a world production (according to 1960 figures) of over seven billion barrels of forty-two gallon size. The supply in Kier's day was infinitesimal by today's standards. At that time men used only oil that had *leaked* out of the earth. But in 1853 Dr. Francis Beattie Brewer of Titusville and a local farmer set out to increase the supply by enticing it from the oil spring below the town. They deepened old pits, dug new ones, and skimmed off the oil, producing by this means some eighteen gallons a day. A sample was sent to Dartmouth College, where it was pronounced valuable if it could be produced in quantity. Professor Benjamin Silliman of Yale University confirmed the report and so inspired the creation of the Pennsylvania Rock Oil Company, which brought "Colonel" Drake to the Hall of Fame.

Edwin L. Drake was a young man of New Haven who, after a short career as a steamship clerk on the Great Lakes, express agent for the Boston & Albany Railroad, and conductor on the New York & New Haven Railroad, had been forced by illness into retirement. But he was not beaten. He invested all his savings (two hundred dollars) in stock of the Pennsylvania Rock Oil Company. Feeling somewhat better in health, he became an employee of the company and was sent out to Titusville to make a secret survey of production. For good publicity the mail sent to him there was addressed to "Colonel E. L. Drake," and colonel he has remained ever since.

His report, when he returned to New Haven, caused a scurry of refinancing. A new company was formed, the Seneca Oil Company of Connecticut, and Colonel Drake was made president and general manager at a salary of a thousand dollars a year, with orders to go back to western Pennsylvania and produce oil.

Aside from the tall silk hat and the title of colonel, Drake's appearance suggested nothing out of the ordinary. But there was a spark of the divine fire in him. He was not content to let Pennsylvania oil *trickle* out of the rocks. He made up his mind to *bring* it out. He prepared to bore an oil well, and he produced what Ruth Sheldon Knowles has called the "first well that sought oil and found it."

That was not an easy thing to do for the first time. It took patience, a fund of humor, and iron obstinacy—qualities not always associated with a man in a high hat.

It was many months before Drake succeeded in getting a "borer." He dashed around the country, hiring one man after another; but none of them took him seriously and none of them turned up—none, that is, until in May, 1859, Uncle Billy Smith arrived and began to tap the greasy shore of Oil Creek. The work went slowly. Water seepage was a problem since the well was only 150 feet from the creek and below its level. The walls caved in. Colonel Drake bought from the city of Erie fifty feet of pipe in ten-foot sections, and Uncle Billy worked the drill inside this casing. At thirty-five feet he struck rock. After that, his progress was at the rate of about three feet a day.

Meantime the Seneca Oil Company of Connecticut had lost heart. Colonel Drake was given orders to close up the works, pay off the men, and come back to New Haven. The company had heard enough of "borers" who were hired but did not report for work, of water seepage, cave-ins, and troubles with the piping. The money was gone. They had had enough. But not so Colonel Drake. He borrowed five hundred dollars from a Meadville bank and went ahead.

On the afternoon of Saturday, August 27, 1859, at a depth of sixty-nine feet, the drill entered a crevice in the rock and dropped six inches. It was time to knock off. So Uncle Billy pulled out the drill and went home. The Sabbath was strictly observed, but on that day of rest Billy Smith, who loved his work, could not refrain from at least looking at it. Coming back and putting his eye to the pipe, he saw something inside about five inches from the top, something that caused him to plug the end of a piece of tubing and use it as a dipper.

What he drew up brought a shout from him, and he sent his son Sammy scampering barefoot to find Colonel Drake and tell him the news.

It was on Saturday that the Colonel and Uncle Billy struck oil, but it was not until Sunday, August 28, that the strike was discovered. Hence there is disagreement about the anniversary date.

The pump was set to work, and soon Colonel Drake and Uncle Billy Smith were bringing oil out of the earth at a rate that filled all the pine barrels that had been made ready, all the whisky barrels they could collect, and everything else that would serve to contain the "black gold." Pitchers, jars, wash basins, tubs, were requisitioned. Margaret Smith, whose washtub was pressed into service, complained afterwards that she was never able to get the thing clean again. When the situation was brought under control and enough receptacles were on hand, it was found that the well was producing at the rate of four hundred barrels a day. The yield soon rose to a thousand barrels.

It must be admitted that luck was with Colonel Drake. Ernest C. Miller in *Pennsylvania's Oil Industry* writes, "Drake happened to drill in the only spot in the oil country where he could have found oil at a depth as shallow as 69½ feet." But if it had not been for Colonel Drake's persistence, there would have been no luck; at least we should never have heard of it.

Colonel Drake was just about the only early oilman whom success did not spoil. He was at heart neither an adventurer nor a financier. He was a craftsman. When he had done his job, he did not buy oil lands in the vicinity as everyone else was doing. He had done his work—enticed the dragon out of the rock. Others could wrestle with it. He settled down quietly as a justice of the peace at Titusville, leaving to others the excitement of a game in which a few grew wealthy and many were ruined. Soon Drake's illness, aggravated by his hurrying about the country looking for oil borers and drive-piles and money, caught up with him again, and he returned to the east. He lived in extreme poverty until some of his old friends whose fortunes he had made remembered him, and the Assembly of Pennsylvania voted him a pension of $1,500 a year. He died in 1880. A grateful Commonwealth has named a memorial park at the scene of his triumph near Titusville "Drake Well Park" in his honor.

Meanwhile the oil region had gone mad. Boom towns sprang up: Red-Hot, Reno, Cash-up, Shamburg, and the like. Hundreds of prospectors and contractors moved in to make a fortune, and an army of thieves and confidence men moved in to take it away from them. It seemed for a time that more money was made by swindlers than by legitimate operators. Charles Vernon Culver, confidence man supreme (after whom the Culver Literary Association of Titusville was named), was described by a contemporary Detroit journalist as "of an open, candid expression and genial pleasing manner," and more recently by Hildegard Dolson, author of *The Great Oildorado,* as "the man who sold the moon." The New York *Tribune,* expressing the hope that the oil regions might cease to be the prey of "adventurous and gambling swindlers," reported that Culver, apparently in pursuit of the same reformation, proposed "a gigantic revolution" in the oil trade— which in a short time he accomplished by bankrupting innumerable investors. James Saeger robbed John Benninghoff, who after losing a first fortune in the Culver bank crash, kept in his home a second one amounting to $150,000, give or take a few thousand. Saeger's accomplices were caught, but he himself escaped and rounded out his days as a Texas cattle king. Ben Hogan, who advertised himself, not immodestly, as "the wickedest man in the world," made a fortune from his gambling houses and other establishments.

Small wells were drilled all over the place, with or without legitimate prospects. Those who struck oil found that public demand was not yet great enough to absorb production, yet swindlers pumped dry wells full and sold them to the unwary. Many men were ruined while the boom was on. Thousands were ruined when it broke, among them Henry Hershey, father of Milton Hershey, the chocolate millionaire.

The discovery of the first flowing wells turned the business upside down and wiped out the small pump operators. Most of the pumping wells were abandoned.

The first of the flowing wells, the Funk Well, was discovered in June, 1861. It began with a flow of 250 barrels a day. Everywhere old-timers (conditioned as they were by the ubiquitous swindlers—"exquisite, magnificent, stupendous, brilliantly successful," as a contemporary, William White, described them) suspected it of being a hoax. They sat back and waited for it to run dry. But the well flowed on until Funk had made a fortune.

Then the Empire Well erupted with a daily output of three thousand barrels. Containers could not be made fast enough to hold its product. The owners tried to dam the flow, but the oil could not be bound and went on flowing quietly but inexorably into Oil Creek. It was not until nearly a year later that its flow diminished and it submitted to the harnessing of a pump.

Meanwhile Titusville had grown in ten years (1855-1865) from a lumberman's village of 243 inhabitants to an oil town of 6,000. It had thirteen hotels, several churches, three banks, a lecture hall, and a plank sidewalk, "by courtesy called a street," as one who used it observed.

The Seneca country of Pennsylvania had become an "Oildorado," as Miss Dolson calls it. The greentop gold of the forest was gone, but a forest of derricks had risen in its place, bringing the black gold up out of the earth. New towns appeared and old towns were rejuvenated. In Franklin a blacksmith struck oil in his back yard, and the town went wild.

The most amazing phenomenon of all that mad time was Pithole. Where four log cabins stood in May, 1865, a town was laid out in June. Three months later the city of Pithole had risen like an exhalation from the Pit itself. Pithole had fifty hotels, and every other shop was a saloon. Already it was the wildest spot in Pennsylvania. An oak-plank road connected it with Titusville. *Facilis descensus Averni.*

But Pithole's days were numbered. In February, 1866, a washerwoman using her pump drew up oil instead of water. The same embarrassment of riches hit other water wells. People began to wonder. The rumor got around that pipes were leaking. Then some of the oil wells went dry. The Tremont Hotel went up in flames. So did the Franklin House, the Mead House, and half the town. An ice jam in the creek sent flood waters rampaging through the city. Boats rode down Center Street. Ice crushed the bridges. Panic seized the inhabitants. Evacuation began. Buildings were torn down. Pumps, pipes, and derricks were taken apart and moved to other localities. Business disappeared. The Oil City and Pithole Railroad went bankrupt. The Pithole Post Office, which had been doing a business second only to that of Philadelphia and Pittsburgh, was choked with uncalled-for mail. By 1868 there remained at Pithole a total population of six people, living in two houses.

The two houses are now gone. All that remains of Pithole is the site, which is preserved and kept open to the public by James B. Stevenson of Titusville. Today you may stand on a breezy hillside where the town once sprawled and look about you through the young trees or above them to the blue of distant hills. A brook flows gently through the valley below. Here and there among the trees small street signs are discreet reminders of the crowds that once pressed by. The grass is cut and the underbrush has been cleared away. The former site of Pithole looks like a well-kept park—as indeed it is. Preserved in silence and utter simplicity, it is a most effective monument to the days of Pennsylvania's oil frenzy.

But Pithole was expendable. The derricks removed from it were erected elsewhere. Oil production in the region as a whole soon trebled in volume. In the process a few became rich and many became poor. But that is not the whole story nor, indeed, the heart of any of it. The coming of the Oil Age, to which the failures contributed as well as the successes, has brought undreamed-of benefits to mankind.

In the few years after Drake struck oil the whole business underwent a transformation. Ways were found for overcoming obstacles to transportation and marketing. Railroad tank cars took the place of oil barrels and oxcarts. The key to a successful industry was found to be in the refining. There ensued a war of giants in the business: producers, refiners, and railroad owners.

It was a man from Connecticut who first struck oil in Pennsylvania, but it was a man from Ohio who organized the new industry and commanded its world market. No two men could have been more unlike than Colonel Drake and John D. Rockefeller. They were both energetic and astute, but there the resemblance ended. John D. worked on a world scale; the Colonel was content with his own back yard. Rockefeller was a superb organizer. His penetrating mind mastered the detail, not merely of the oil business, but of a complicated and evolving new economic pattern. He saw into the future, developed his strategy, and in a series of brilliant campaigns conducted with the cool detachment of an army commander won for Standard Oil practical control of the industry in America.

Today most of Pennsylvania's oil derricks have disappeared, but a few stand, gaunt and black, like ramparts after a forest fire. Crude oil is still produced in the Oil Creek territory and in the newer Bradford fields. In 1960 Pennsylvania produced a total of

5,950,523 barrels. She has the third largest refining capacity in the country.

The oil regions have become respectable. Ben Hogan, "the wickedest man in the world," fell in love with a little evangelist in New York, reformed, married, and became an evangelist himself in the oil region. On August 25, 1959, Governor Lawrence of Pennsylvania, pursuant to an Act of Assembly of that date, appointed the late Edwin L. Drake a colonel in the Pennsylvania National Guard.

Oilmen sometimes complain that Pennsylvania, in drawing so much attention to Colonel Drake, has chosen the wrong oilman to honor. It may be answered that after all this *is* Pennsylvania, which with all its wealth and magnificence is still what William Penn wished it to be: a commonwealth where the common man has his due.

28 *The Labor Movement in Pennsylvania*

Pennsylvania is a labor state. She took an early lead in American manufacturing, and she was among the first of the United States to feel the full effects of the factory system. It was to be expected, therefore, that she should take the lead in efforts to remove the workers' disabilities and to dispel the threat to democratic institutions which the Industrial Revolution seemed to entail.

"The Pennsylvania wage earners were the pioneers of the American labor movement," wrote William A. Sullivan in *The Industrial Worker in Pennsylvania, 1800-1840,* and he added that they were among "the first to organize for collective action." Pennsylvania was the birthplace of American trade-unionism. Her workers regarded their fight as a crusade to return true democracy to the Commonwealth.

The change from the agricultural democracy of Thomas Jefferson's day to the nineteenth-century industrial system brought hardships and disruption to American society. A new class of exploited wage-earners arose. Their plight was not the result of malice on the part of any section of the public. It came about through the operation of impersonal economic laws operating without supervision or restraint in a swiftly changing world. The "merchant capitalist," who has been unjustly blamed for what happened, was the product, not the cause, of the system. The merchant fulfilled a vital and beneficial role, that of the middleman who brought producer and consumer together. His function was to buy in the cheapest market and sell in the dearest. By so doing, he helped to extend the market and distribute American manufactures all over the United States, much to the increase of national unity.

Inevitably competition arose among manufacturers who sought to attract the middleman by lowering the prices of their product. That meant for the workers longer hours and lower wages. Mary Beard in *A Short History of the American Labor Movement* observes that after the Revolution the merchant capitalists brought in from Europe cheap manufactured goods, and in consequence the American manufacturer had to cut wages in order to meet the competition. As a result of wage cuts, long hours (twelve or fourteen), and other handicaps to which the factory workers were subject, a feeling of class consciousness rose among them and with it a realization that they must organize if they were to win for themselves any measure of independence and security. So the trade unions were born.

At the outset, the trade-unionists had little conception of the revolution they were engaged in. It took a hundred years to convert any large section of the general public to the opinions of Stephen Simpson (spokesman for the Philadelphia Working Man's party), who claimed that value was created by labor and that it was the inalienable right of all who produced wealth to share in its benefits.

The origin of America's gigantic labor unions has been traced by Sullivan to the printers and shoemakers (cordwainers) of Philadelphia. As early as 1786 the printers of the city, who had provided themselves with a strike fund, used it in support of a strike against their employers. The shoemakers of Philadelphia are credited with the first permanent organization of wage-earners for the purpose of obtaining better pay. The Federal Society of Journeymen Cordwainers of Philadelphia was organized in 1794. In that same year they forced their employers to accept the "closed shops" (in which none but union members were employed); and in 1799 they made what has been called the first attempt in the United States at collective bargaining.

It was soon found that small unions could not survive, and local craft unions in the cities combined into larger central organizations. Again Pennsylvania was in the lead. The first "city central" was the Mechanics' Union of Trade Associations of Philadelphia, founded in 1827.

Opposition to such unions kept pace with their growth. Employers organized and availed themselves of the protection of the common law against "criminal conspiracy." They won cases in court and threw strike organizers into prison.

In an unregulated competitive system the employers undoubtedly had cause for argument. The factory owner who did not get the most out of his employees at the least cost to himself was unlikely to survive in the market. At the same time the workers' condition cried to heaven for redress. Stephen Simpson was not indulging in a flight of rhetoric when he wrote in *The Workingman's Manual* that the law of criminal conspiracies was being used "to strip the man of labor of his earnings, reduce him to a dry crust and a gourd of water."

Textile workers were the hardest hit. The Schuylkill Cotton Factory, which paid an average wage of three dollars a week, threatened in 1834 a twenty-five per cent wage reduction. When Mr. Corlies' Mill in 1839 proposed a twenty per cent reduction in wages, it was pointed out that the handloom weavers there, after deductions for house rent, fuel, light, etc., would have only $1.65 a week left for food and clothing for a family of four or five members. It was a common practice to pay factory workers not oftener than once a month. Imprisonment for debts of less than one dollar were not infrequent in Philadelphia at the time. Matthew Carey reported in 1829 that thousands of seamstresses who sewed shirts for the army could—no matter how hard they worked—earn no more than fifty-eight dollars a year. Thirty-nine dollars of these, he said, went for rent and fuel, leaving a balance of nineteen dollars a year to purchase food and clothing for themselves and their children. After deductions for lodging, an expert seamstress, he calculated, would have nine cents a day for food and other necessaries.

Although a twelve-hour period was considered in most places to be the normal day's work, there were many exceptions. The factory hours at Norristown were reported by the *Public Ledger* in 1839 to be fifteen in the summer months. Sunrise to sunset was the traditional workday in most factories, but the introduction of lamplight extended working hours in winter when twilight came early.

In 1838 it was estimated that a fifth of all factory workers in Pennsylvania were children under twelve years of age. The bad effects on the health of the young employees were soon evident.

Doctors protested. Other evils increased. One employer confessed that only a third of his employees under the age of eighteen could read or write. There was no hope for democracy when such degrading conditions were allowed to prevail.

The law blocked reform. Most businessmen were sure that workers' unions interfered with the economic laws proclaimed by Adam Smith in *The Wealth of Nations*. Even many of the clergy attacked the unions for "criminal conspiracy." The workers realized that there would be no relief unless the laws were changed. They therefore decided they must go into politics and exert direct pressure on the legislatures. Out of the carpenters' strike of 1827 in Philadelphia, to which all the organized workmen of the city gave sympathetic support, came the Mechanics' Union of Trade Associations, which in 1828 proposed the nomination of candidates to represent the working classes both on the city council and in the state legislature. Other cities followed Philadelphia's example. *The Mechanics' Free Press* of Philadelphia, established in 1827-1828, became the first journal in the United States devoted to the interests of the working man.

Most of the early labor organizers had before them these four objectives: the ten-hour day, the restriction of child labor, the abolition of imprisonment for debt, and free public education. The last, free public education, headed the labor reforms demanded in 1829 by the Workingmen's party of Philadelphia.

The immediate effects of direct political action were disappointing. Hoodlums broke up political rallies. Inexperienced union leaders failed to withstand the threats, bribes, and deceptions of their political opponents. The financial panic of 1837 depleted the funds of the unions, and many of them collapsed. The return of prosperity, however, revived them. They increased in strength, gathered experience, and began to win revolutionary victories.

The workingmen's first great triumph was the attainment of agreement on the ten-hour day. Gladys L. Palmer in her *Philadelphia Workers in a Changing Economy* writes, "The Philadelphia General Strike of 1835 saw unskilled coal dock workers, house painters, bricklayers, masons, plasterers, hod carriers, carpenters, blacksmiths, plumbers, leather curriers, cordwainers, printers, auger makers, saddlers, drygoods store clerks, bakers, and city employees uniting in a demand for a ten-hour day." Under the authority of the city corporation the City Council of Philadelphia set the hours for laborers "from six to six during the summer season; allowing one hour for breakfast, and one hour for dinner." By 1840 the ten-hour day had been accepted (in principle at least) throughout the country.

After the Civil War giant unions came into existence. The Miners' and Laborers' Benevolent Asssociation (more commonly known as the Workingman's Benevolent Association) was organized in 1868 by John Siney. He was an Irishman who had worked in the anthracite mines during the Civil War, a time when inflation produced demands for higher wages to meet the increased cost of living and when violence and assassination were used as common weapons in the labor war. The brutality of the Molly Maguires occupied the public mind and prejudiced it against the mining community. The purpose of the W. B. A. was to provide sickness and death benefits for the miners and to build up a reserve for the support of the strikes. It won several strikes against the railroads, which held a monopoly of the anthracite industry, but failing to win the "Long Strike" of 1875, it collapsed.

The most influential labor organization in the country was for many years the Noble Order of the Knights of Labor. It was founded by Uriah S. Stephens and eight other inconspicuous tailors in the hall of the American Hose Company in Philadelphia on December 9, 1869. Stephens, who became the first Grand Master Workman among the Knights when they were nationally organized, gave a tone to the organization which it preserved throughout its life. As a young man he had studied for the Baptist ministry, but his studies had been interrupted by the depression of 1837 and he became apprenticed to a tailor in Philadelphia.

Stephens was the opposite of what the public expects a class-conscious, rabble-rousing agitator to be. He drew his inspiration from his religious vision of the brotherhood of man. "Cultivate friendship among the great brotherhood of toil," he advised; "learn to respect industry in the person of every intelligent worker; unmake the shams of life by deference to the humble but useful craftsman; beget concert of action by conciliation. . . . The work to which this fraternity addresses itself is one of the greatest magnitude ever attempted in the history of the world.

. . . It builds upon the immutable basis of the Fatherhood of God, and the logical principle of the Brotherhood of Man." The Knights had no such spectacular triumphs to their credit as the later miners' strike of 1902, but John Mitchell, the leader of that strike, got his early experience and vision as a member of the Knights of Labor.

When Stephens retired in 1879, shortly after the Knights had become a national organization, he was followed as Grand Master by another Irishman, Terence V. Powderly. Powderly, who was born at Carbondale, Pennsylvania, was a worker in the shops of the Delaware and Western Railroad at Scranton. He was a Roman Catholic. A small, slender, mild-eyed man with a drooping mustache and a hatred of saloons (he was a total abstainer), he was little at home in the rough-and-tumble of labor gatherings, or indeed in social gatherings of any sort. He even refused to speak at Sunday school picnics.

Yet Powderly was a good organizer and he held the affectionate loyalty of the Knights. An idealist rather than an agitator, he thought the workers' cause could best be advanced by education, for he considered the object of the movement was to raise the workers' status (intellectual as well as economic) to equality with that of the governing classes. He called himself an "equalizer." "Our Order has held me in my present position," he once wrote, "because of the reputation I have won in the nation at large by taking high ground on important national questions, yet the trade element in our Order has always kept me busy at the base of the breastworks throwing up earth which they trample down."

Under Powderly the Knights of Labor won a few battles. In 1885 they defeated the tycoon Jay Gould in a strike that began on the Wabash Railroad and spread to the Southwest System and the Union Pacific. As a result, hundreds of thousands of people became members: shopkeepers as well as laborers, farmers as well as industrial workers, women as well as men. Many came in merely out of curiosity. They marched singing:

> Storm the fort, ye Knights of Labor,
>   Battle for your cause;
> Equal rights for every neighbor—
>   Down with Tyrant laws!

But their success was so overwhelming that it suffocated the Holy Order of the Knights of Labor. Feeling their strength in numbers, the Knights began to make extravagant demands, and these resulted in too many strikes. The public, taking fright, had little sympathy with the laborers in the 1886 strike against the Southwest System. This was Jay Gould's opportunity. He gathered his forces: strike-breakers who broke heads, Pinkerton men armed as if they were a military force, and even state troops. The strike failed, and so did many others that followed. The farm element among the workers began to take control. There were disputes, secessions. Powderly was ousted. Membership declined. The Holy Order of the Knights of Labor lay down and died. It had, however, done its work. It had forced public attention upon specific labor problems. It had not provided solutions, but it had awakened the public to issues which a later generation would tackle without panic.

The Federation of Organized Trades and Labor Unions of the United States was organized in 1881 at Pittsburgh. This was the precursor of the American Federation of Labor, which was founded in 1886 at Columbus, Ohio, with Samuel Gompers as president and which survives as the oldest and strongest labor organization in the country.

With the founding of the United Mine Workers of America in 1890, lines were drawn for the head-on clashes destined to change dramatically labor-management relations throughout the country. By this time the labor unions were "in politics" in the best sense. The general public was becoming sufficiently aware of the problem (the conflict between "unalienable rights" and the jungle laws of laissez faire, between what was just and what was legal) to pass judgment on events as they occurred. The democratic process worked, though slowly, for sanity and justice. This fact is illustrated by five labor contests in Pennsylvania: the Tioga lockout of 1853, the Long Strike of 1875, the railroad riots at Pittsburgh in 1877, the Homestead Strike at Carnegie's steel mill in 1892, and John Mitchell's coal strike in 1902.

Up in Tioga County in the vicinity of Blossburg were deposits of semibituminous coal, which was much in demand by the railways and steam factories for its great heating power. Three coal companies—the Blossburg, the Morris Run, and the Fallbrook Coal—owned the land, operated the mines, and controlled the lives of the inhabitants thereabouts. The so-called Tioga system was designed to make strikes impossible. Roads entering the towns were regarded as private, so that persons objectionable to the mining companies could be arrested as trespassers. The houses occupied by the workmen and their families were rented, not sold, and the companies managed to have the state legislature pass a bill which permitted them to evict a tenant with only ten days' notice. The workers were paid once a month in company currency, which was good only in the company stores. Credit in the stores was advanced to the workers between monthly payments. All this, as well as an arbitrary system of fines for misdemeanors (easily taken advantage of by mine superintendents), kept many workers in debt to the company and dependent on it. Under this system there were no labor "difficulties" between 1845 and 1873, but the company built up in that time a vast reservoir of resentment.

In the winter of 1873-1874, the demand for semibituminous coal fell off and the company withheld cash wages, allowing workers credit in the company stores for three months. In November, 1873, as Herbert G. Gutman tells the story in *The Pennsylvania Magazine of History and Biography* (July, 1959), the companies offered the men a month's back pay if they would sign an agreement not to ask for more wages until the following May. The men refused and formed a local union, the Miners' and Laborers' Benevolent Union of Tioga County, to speak for them. The company immediately fired the union leaders. In December all who refused to sever their connection with the union were threatened with eviction from their homes. Since mid-winter had arrived, the men protested that the employers were forcing them "to put on a badge of absolute serfdom." A Fallbrook Coal Company official declared, "We are justified in our proceedings . . . to our consciences and before God and man." The owners believed that cold weather and the business depression would force the men to terms, destroy the union, and save the Tioga system.

They were wrong. The people of the region began to prove that they could exert pressure. The merchants and the farmers of the region showed their sympathy for the miners by lodging them in their own homes and by hiring lawyers to test the eviction proceedings in court. John Siney, after observing the support the citizens of Blossburg had given the union, called it a "city of refuge."

The lockout failed. In March, 1874, the operators recognized the union. The men went back to work.

The Miners' and Laborers' Benevolent Association met its death in the Long Strike, a struggle over wages, which lasted from February to July, 1875. The public, suspicious of the mining community because of the violence of the Molly Maguires, was unsympathetic. As the strike dragged on, the union funds became exhausted and the organization collapsed. The miners, ever a tuneful lot, expressed their feelings in a song by one of their minstrels:

> Well, we've been beaten, beaten all to smash,
> And now, sir, we've begun to feel the lash,
> As wielded by a gigantic corporation,
> Which runs the commonwealth and ruins the nation.
> Our "Union" lamp, friend John* no longer shineth.
> It's gone up where the gentle woodbine twineth.

As the excesses of the Molly Maguires had injured the miners' cause, so the violent strike of 1877 injured the railroad workers' cause. It began in Martinsburg, Virginia, developed into heavy rioting in Baltimore, Maryland, and for a while took on the appearance of a national uprising on behalf of labor. Pennsylvania has reason to look upon this strike as her own, partly because she was the home of the deeply involved Pennsylvania Railroad, and partly because the most violent riots (and also the most fruitful in their unexpected ultimate effect of teaching unions the necessity of self-control) occurred in Pittsburgh.

A cut in the wages of the workers resulted in public sympathy for them. Strikes broke out spontaneously on the Baltimore and Ohio, the Pennsylvania, the New York Central, and the Erie railroads. Soon all the lines east of the Mississippi were affected, and at last the strike wave spread to the great western lines. Unfortunately the strikers got out of hand. There were riots in Baltimore, Pittsburgh, St. Louis, Chicago, and San Francisco. The St. Louis *Republican* called it a "labor revolution."

It was the Pittsburgh riots that caught most attention and determined the public verdict. The strikers stopped trains and seized the railroad's property. Local militia, in sympathy with the strikers, refused to take action against them. When a body of 650 soldiers was sent up from Philadelphia, a battle was fought. The

* John Siney

troops opened fire and then took cover from the mob in the roundhouse and the machine shops. The strikers, armed, laid siege. Freight cars were set afire and run against the roundhouse, which soon became an inferno. The troops fought their way out and escaped across the Allegheny River.

A mob of some four thousand persons with a sprinkling of tramps and hoodlums began an orgy of destruction and theft. The Union Depot was burned. Two roundhouses, 125 locomotives, some 2,000 passenger and freight cars, a grain elevator, and machine shops were destroyed by fire. There came a total breakdown of social restraint. An eyewitness from the Associated Press, quoted in Martin W. Clements' *Centennial History of the Pennsylvania Railroad Company*, wrote:

The scenes occurring on Liberty Street, along the line of which the tracks of the railroad run, simply beggar description. While hundreds were engaged in firing the cars and making certain of the destruction of the valuable buildings at the outer depot, thousands of men, women and children were engaged in pillaging the cars. Men armed with heavy sledges would break open the cars, and then the contents would be thrown out and carried off by those bent on profiting by the reign of terror. The street was almost completely blockaded by persons laboring to carry off the plunder they had gathered together. In hundreds of instances wagons were pressed into service to enable thieves to get away with their goods.

The business world, shocked at the seeming threat of revolution posed by organized labor, redoubled its efforts to overthrow the unions by every means available: personal intimidation, company police, strike-breakers, and the old charge of "criminal conspiracy." The workers, on the other hand, had learned from this temporary breakdown of the social order that the unions must have sufficient authority over their members to prevent strikes from degenerating into anarchy. Labor had demonstrated its awesome strength; it now had to show that it could control itself.

In 1892 the Homestead Strike clearly proved the importance of public opinion in determining the outcome of a strike. At the Homestead steel mill a union known as the Amalgamated Association of Iron, Steel and Tin Workers had in 1889 negotiated a good three-year contract; but at the end of that time the company sought a wage reduction and refused to recognize the union as a bargaining agent. The men went on strike to save their pay and the union. H. C. Frick, the "coke king," who was then executive official of the Carnegie Steel Company, resolved to break the strike and smash the union at the same time. He informed the men that after July 1 the company would be operated as a non-union shop. He would close the mill on July 1 and open it on July 6 with nonunion men. He surrounded the plant with a high board fence, topped it with barbed wire, and pierced it with loopholes. For double assurance that he would be able to open the plant as intended, he secretly arranged to bring in an armed body of Pinkerton men, three hundred strong, on the morning of July 6.

Most of the nonunion men in the mill (the union accounted for only a fifth of the working force) were loyal to the threatened union workers and supported them in what followed. They seized the plant, established control of the town, and posted sentries on the roads and rivers. On the foggy night of July 5-6, the sentry on a bridge over the Monongahela saw two company barges being towed up the river, and he sent a warning to Homestead by telegraph. When the Pinkerton men arrived at the company wharf at 4:00 A.M., they found the strikers waiting for them. A deadly battle ensued between the Pinkerton men in the barges and the workers posted on the bank. Rifle fire was exchanged briskly throughout the greater part of the day. The strikers brought up a small brass cannon to pound the barges. Dynamite bombs were thrown. Oil was poured on the water and set afire. Three Pinkerton men and ten strikers were killed. Many were wounded.

In the end the Pinkerton men surrendered. When they came ashore, they were forced to run a gantlet of infuriated men and women armed with clubs and rocks. After this ordeal, they were allowed to entrain.

The National Guard was sent to restore order. On July 15, Frick opened the Homestead mill. About three-fifths of the old workers lost their jobs.

At first the public, which was beginning to understand something of the issues involved, was sympathetic with the strikers. However, an incident eight days after the opening of the mill shocked the nation and turned Homestead into a disaster for the union cause. On July 23 a Russian-born anarchist shot and stabbed H. C. Frick in his office. The public, blaming the attempted murder on the strikers (though in fact the anarchist had no connection with them), turned against the steel workers and applauded Frick when he ruthlessly went ahead with his plans to crush the union. It surrendered. Forty years later a biographer of Andrew Carnegie wrote that "not a union man has since entered the Carnegie works."

The failure of the steel workers in the Homestead Strike, like that of the miners in their strike of 1875, was due to the public's fear of violence. The miners' recovery came sooner than that of the steel workers, and it came without violence in John Mitchell's strike of 1902.

"Johnny" Mitchell (1870-1919), although his career is well documented, has become an almost legendary hero in the anthracite region. He is loved and revered by the miners and respected by the public at large. He demonstrated the just and democratic way of conducting a strike: avoiding violence and bringing the miners' grievances to the bar of public opinion.

After the failure of the Long Strike in 1875 only sporadic outbreaks in the coal fields reminded Pennsylvanians of the wicked conditions under which the miners had to work. But the organization of the United Mine Workers of America in 1890 brought encouragement and renewed strength to the workers.

The situation in the anthracite region at that time was difficult for a union to handle because, as Foster Rhea Dulles wrote in his *Labor in America,* "The operators were organized in a virtual trust under railroad domination and could hardly have been more opposed to union recognition, while there was such a large element of Poles, Hungarians, Slovaks, Italians and other newly arrived immigrants among the workers that they lacked all cohesive unity."

The United Mine Workers, under the presidency of John A. Mitchell, called a strike in 1900. It resulted in what Dulles called a truce rather than a settlement. Two years later the miners made their demands again. Conditions in the mines were disgraceful. The average earnings of a worker were $300 a year. The work was dangerous (accidents caused 441 deaths in 1901), yet the operators did little about introducing safety devices. The time had come for a showdown, and John Mitchell was the man to organize it. This was indeed John Mitchell's strike, and thousands of miners, both union and nonunion, were proud to be known as "Johnny Mitchell's Men."

John Mitchell was pitted against George F. Baer, president of the Reading Railroad and spokesman for the mine operators. Baer unwisely attributed to Heaven his authority for what he was doing: "The rights and interests of the laboring man will be protected and cared for—not by the labor agitators, but by the Christian men to whom God in His infinite wisdom has given the control of the property interests of this country." The *New York Times* declared these words to verge "very closely upon unconscious blasphemy." The miners pounced upon the missive from which the sentence was taken and enshrined it in their folklore as "the Divine Right letter."

John Mitchell has fared better in the Pennsylvania countryside than his adversary. Every year in the anthracite region they celebrate John Mitchell's Day and as George Korson notes in *Black Rock,* Mitchell makes a brave figure in mining folklore. The blind minstrel John Craig wrote and sang these lines about him:

"I told you," said John Mitchell, "there soon would come a day
When a scale of pauper wages would have to pass away.
I told those operators, too, who ruled the great coal fields
That the miners were in a union, and would hold the winning hand."

John Mitchell knew the mining business from the bottom, having begun to work in Illinois mines when he was twelve years old. He also had broad mental horizons, a religious background, and an inveterate taste for reading. As a boy he attended night school. As a man he read widely for himself. He led the miners in the inconclusive strike of 1900, and led them again in 1902 to a victory so decisive that it introduced a new era in the relations between management and labor.

His methods were in sharp contrast with those of the Molly Maguires. He abhorred violence and deceit, and he urged good faith in all the union's dealings with employers. But there was nothing soft about him. When he requested the 150,000 miners in the anthracite region to walk out, they obeyed him, and they remained loyal to their strike pledge. The folk song "Me Johnny Mitchell Man," which first appeared and circulated widely during the coal strike of 1902, renders their pledge thus:

Me not shcabby fella,
I'm a good union citizen,
I'm Johnny Mitchell man.

The owners refused to negotiate; but the general public was troubled about what they heard of conditions in the mines, and they were sympathetic to many of the miners' proposals. It was a quiet strike, unmarred by terror and destruction. Month after month it continued. The drain on union funds was severe, but a bountiful potato crop enabled the miners to hold out.

In the end President Theodore Roosevelt, who threatened to send in the army to take over the mines, persuaded the owners to submit the dispute to arbitration. J. P. Morgan, the power behind the operators, requested Roosevelt to set up an arbitration commission. The operators refused to accept a labor member on the commission.

Negotiations [wrote Foster Dulles] again hung in the balance until Roosevelt overcame this last obstacle by the appointment of the Grand Chief of the Railway Conductors, not as a labor representative but as "an eminent sociologist"! On October 23, after more than five months in which their lines had held almost without a break, the miners went back to work.

The award, when it came, did not give the miners all they had asked for, but it extended the eight-hour day, raised wages, and increased the authority of the union. In thus bringing first-class citizenship to the miners of Pennsylvania's anthracite region, American labor took a long step forward. In his book *The Susquehanna,* Carl Carmer calls it "perhaps the most significant and farthest-reaching victory in the history of American labor."

29 Return to Democracy

Over the vast expansion of industry that followed the American Civil War hung the specter of a cruel plutocracy. Great wealth, concentrated in a few giant combines, put into the hands of an ever-narrowing circle of men a power capable of destroying democracy, for society had not yet learned how to subdue and tame the furious energies of the Industrial Revolution. Huge business mergers sprang into being, large enough and strong enough to determine without contradiction the conditions under which men should live and work. The financial tycoons who indulged in this royal sport of monopoly were too intent on the game to notice the sufferings of their victims. Being as yet subject to little government restraint, they indulged in abuses (often thoughtlessly or fatalistically) that made a mockery of the Holy Experiment.

To score its points, big business was often tempted to ally itself with unsavory political machines like that of Boies Penrose in Pennsylvania. The "coal and iron police" established a reign of terror among those subject to them. A police force of this kind, privately organized and consisting for the most part of brutal, unscrupulous men, used any means at hand to attain their employers' ends. They served as spies, *agents provocateurs,* and strike-breakers. Above the law, as they felt themselves to be, they sometimes incited demonstrations in order to provide occasion for "teaching the men a lesson" with a modern equivalent of Napoleon's "whiff of grapeshot." Election frauds, managed on so vast a scale that only big money could finance them, denied the common man the political redress that should have been available to him through the elective machinery.

Those were the days of laissez faire, when money was hard and life was cheap. Working hours were long and debilitating for men, women, and children. Even after the eight-hour day was decreed by law in 1868, in iron and steel it remained a dead letter until well on in the twentieth century. Wages were held down to a near-starvation level, and there was gross overcharging in many company stores. It was believed in some management circles that keeping the men in debt tended to keep them steady: a mossy stone does not roll. In 1881 the average annual income for workers in Pennsylvania was $500. As late as 1910 almost a third of the labor force in iron and steel worked twelve hours a day for seven days a week, and half of the men received less than eighteen cents an hour.

Indifference to human life was by no means confined to employers in the heavy industries. Throughout the country and among all classes of people the appalling rate of accidental death in mines and factories was accepted as the unavoidable accompaniment of progress. If the operators and owners were chiefly to be blamed, it was not because they were less sensitive than other men to the inequalities and brutalities of the economic system but because they had it in their power to correct the abuses and declined to, combining instead to prevent the victims of these inhuman conditions from organizing to protect themselves.

It was not only death or permanent injury (without compensation) that men had to fear. A more serious menace to life came from the pollution of the public water supply by careless sewage disposal and by the discharge into Pennsylvania's streams of the waste from tanneries, pulp and paper factories, coal-breakers, coke ovens, and gas works. People bathed in and drank from rivers so foul that fish could not stay alive in them. In 1906 there were over 24,500 cases of typhoid fever in Pennsylvania and about 4,000 deaths.

Those were the days when industry, spurred by the new techniques of mass production, was reorganizing itself (to the ultimate benefit of mankind) under the leadership of a few masterful men of genius. James Truslow Adams in *The Epic of America* characterized the period as "The Age of the Dynosaurs." If few of these Gargantuan entrepreneurs were native to Pennsylvania (Andrew Carnegie was an import and Milton Hershey a Mennonite deviant), it was perhaps because the democratic tradition was so deeply rooted there. In any case, the general spirit of the times was inescapable. Even Milton Hershey, the great decentralizer, in 1929 all but succumbed to the lure of the giant combine, for a price of $50,000,000. It took the stock market crash to break up the establishment of the International Quality Products Corporation, a proposed merger of Hershey Chocolate (which was the kingpin) with Colgate-Palm Olive, Kraft-Phoenix Cheese, and other companies in the field of food preparation. The agreement, signed on the Black Friday that ushered in the stock market crash and the Great Depression, was soon afterward canceled by mutual consent.

The problem with which Pennsylvania along with the rest of the country was then confronted was how to reconcile the democratic ideals of William Penn and Thomas Jefferson with the new economic feudalism. President Theodore Roosevelt demonstrated by his "trust-busting" that he was alive to the problem. While his diagnosis may not have been profound nor his medicines much more than palliatives, nevertheless, as Adams writes, he acted as "the lightning rod to carry off harmlessly the pent-up fury of the storm," and he helped to keep alive the dream of the good life for the ordinary citizen.

It took the shock of realizing that the frontier was closed and that the nation's resources were not illimitable to make the American citizen feel that another problem—that of conservation—was anything but an Old World apparition. In the closing decades of the nineteenth century men began to regard the seizing of Indian lands and their quick exploitation for private profit as not necessarily in accord with the plans of Infinite Wisdom. A movement was started to interpose government between the individual citizen and the corporations in order to secure for the former the advantages, without the disabilities, of the new economic order. In particular it was hoped to preserve for the nation's children the dwindling resources of forests and waters. Under McKinley and Theodore Roosevelt, 172,000,000 acres of forest lands were withdrawn from homestead entry.

From the vested interests there was vigorous opposition to the conservation movement. Before such progessive legislation could be passed in Pennsylvania, it was necessary to bring about certain political reforms. In 1905 a body known as the Pennsylvania

State Police was created to take out of the hands of the hated "coal and iron police" the administration of the law during strikes and other labor disputes. In January, 1906, a special session of the Pennsylvania Legislature was called to consider necessary reforms. In order to prevent, or at least to make more difficult, the commission of frauds at election time, a law was passed requiring the personal registration of voters. The Corrupt Practices Act increased the penalties for stuffing ballot boxes.

On the national scene, it was a Pennsylvanian, Philander C. Knox (born in Brownsville, Pennsylvania), who as Theodore Roosevelt's attorney general pressed the attack on what Roosevelt called "malefactors of great wealth" by bringing suits in federal courts, popularly known as trust-busting. Roosevelt backed the Meat Inspection Act and the Food and Drug Act, and gave enormous prestige to the movement for the conservation of human and natural resources.

Meanwhile Pennsylvania, roused by the typhoid epidemics, was tackling the problem of communicable diseases. In 1905 the state legislature created a Department of Health and gave it control of sewage disposal and the protection of the drinking water. Under the administration of this department annual deaths from typhoid fever dropped from 24,500 to 125 between 1906 and 1933.

In other welfare measures Pennsylvania shared the growing concern of the rest of the nation, intent on eliminating the hazards of the machine age without losing the benefits of mass production. Questions of workmen's compensation, the care of mental patients, and forest conservation became talked about and acted upon. The last problem, forest conservation, was the first to catch the imagination of the public, thus giving to the word *conservation* the practical and romantic appeal that paved the way for conservation in other fields. It was Pennsylvania that led the nation in the movement for forest conservation—an appropriate preëminence, because until the 1870's, Pennsylvania had outdistanced all other states in the value of its lumber products.

As early as 1873 Governor Hartranft of Pennsylvania drew attention to the problem of diminishing forests. At Chicago in 1875 the American Forestry Congress drew the same matter to the attention of the nation. At Philadelphia in 1876 Burnet Landreth of Bucks County, Pennsylvania, advocated academic training in the science of forestry. In 1886 certain citizens organized the Pennsylvania Forestry Association, headed by Dr. Joseph T. Rothrock. Its magazine, *Forest Leaves,* soon spread an interest in forest conservation all over the state. The appointment of a permanent State Foresty Commission in 1893, following publication of an exhaustive report on the Commonwealth's forest resources, marked the public's thorough arousement to the need of conservation. People came to recognize that, as Henry Clepper wrote in *Pennsylvania History* in 1945: "Pennsylvania became a great industrial commonweath through the exploitation of her natural resources. She can only continue to be great through their wise use and preservation."

The state Assembly in 1897 authorized purchase of 40,000 acres of forest lands at the headwaters of the Delaware, Susquehanna, and Allegheny rivers, an acreage that by 1904 had grown to 443,592. In 1903 the legislature provided for a school of forestry, the Pennsylvania State Forest Academy, at Mont Alto; and in 1907 the Pennsylvania State College established a department of forestry.

Meantime protection had also been given to Pennsylvania's wild animals. In the 1890's it was observed that wildlife in Pennsylvania, unprotected against slaughter for sport or commercial use, was approaching extinction. To see what could be done to arrest the process, in 1895 the Board of Game Commissioners was appointed to study methods of protecting wild creatures. The use of hounds in deer hunting was prohibited, "market-hunting" was forbidden, and licensing of hunters began. Best of all were the laws of 1905, which put Pennsylvania ahead of all other states and all nations in wildlife preservation. These laws favored the establishment of refuges where deer and other wild creatures might propagate and raise their young in peace. Two years later restrictions were placed on the hunting of female deer. Special protection was offered the almost extinct black bear.

The name of Gifford Pinchot, governor of Pennsylvania, 1923-1927 and 1931-1935, will always be associated with the story of American conservation. His ambition as a youth had been to study forestry, but there was no college in American that offered such training. He went accordingly to France and studied at the Forest School in Nancy. On his return as "the first American trained in the profession of forestry," he soon made a name for himself in his chosen field. In 1898 he became chief of the United States Division of Forestry. In 1908 President Theodore Roosevelt appointed him head of the National Conservation Commission.

Once in the governor's chair in Pennsylvania, Pinchot attacked the problem of conservation with something of the same vision and energy that had animated William Penn when he established his Holy Experiment. He launched a campaign that restored Pennsylvania to the ranks of the progressive states. Realizing the need for water power for the developing hydro-electric plants, he persuaded the Assembly to establish the Giant Power Survey Board. Its recommendations for control of public utilities were defeated, but Pinchot created a Department of Forests and Waters and with it a new Water and Power Resources Board that, by its authority to pass on water company charters and dams or other river obstructions, gave the state a considerable measure of control of its water resources.

In 1923 Pinchot created the Pennsylvania Sanitary Board, which made surveys of streams and evolved a plan (the nationally known "Pennsylvania Plan") for the classification of streams according to the degree of pollution and the amount of reduction required to make the water safe for public use. He obtained agreements from the tanning industry and others to dispose of waste without endangering the public health. Interstate provisions were made for safeguarding the waters of the Ohio and Delaware rivers.

In his second term of office Pinchot addressed himself to Pennsylvania's transportation problem. The barriers of mountain and river had been well breached by railroads, highways, and great bridges. But the farmers throughout the state were, in the fall and spring, immobilized by muddy roads. Pinchot promised to "get the farmer out of the mud," and he kept his word. Thousands of miles of hard-surface roads gave Pennsylvania's farms excellent transportation in all seasons. They are the so-called Pinchot roads, which still, thirty and more years later, make nearly every inhabited nook and corner of the state accessible.

Governor George Howard Earle, a Democrat, during his term of office (1935-1939) advanced still further the progressive Republican policies of Gifford Pinchot. He succeeded in establishing a new Public Utilities Commission with powers to regulate services and prices. A milk control commission was also created with power to regulate prices and (with a view to protecting the public health) to supervise the production, processing, storage, transportation, and distribution of milk.

In a word, the government of Pennsylvania in recent years has been returned to the people, so that all men may enjoy the benefits of the machine age.

30   *A Glance at the Arts*

The traveler through Pennsylvania's "Dutch Country" today will not hear much German (*Pensylfawnish*) spoken on the streets, and the quaint Dutch-English expressions—such as, "It's making down" (raining), "If the bell don't answer, bump," and "My off is on" (my vacation has started)—are seldom encountered except in linguistic monographs and popular fiction. Nevertheless, the visitor will still find much that is distinctive to delight him.

He will see the sturdy stone houses with bright geraniums in the windows behind which mother and daughter still make gay quilts and hooked or braided rag rugs. Anyone who has attended the annual Dutch Days at Hershey will remember the varied display of handmade quilts lining the walls of the huge Sports Arena. Beside the houses are the magnificently decorated Swiss bank-barns, and stretching beyond them in bands of green, yellow, and brown are rich grainfields and pastures, kept fertile by careful cultivation and the four-year crop rotation which most German farmers adopted nearly two hundred years ago. Everywhere church spires punctuate the landscape.

When the Germans and Swiss first came to Pennsylvania's limestone country and found it to their liking, they erected temporary log houses like those the Swedes and Finns had introduced on the Delaware. A few of these original structures are still standing, some of them in the towns, though their logs are now usually concealed under a sheathing of clapboards. Soon after their arrival most of the Germanic settlers replaced the log houses by others built of local limestone: one-room structures like the Weiser home, still standing in the Conrad Weiser Memorial Park at Womelsdorf, with a low attic to serve as sleeping quarters for the family. An additional room might be added later, as may be seen in the Weiser house; and in time a fine two-story residence might be built close by, again as illustrated in Conrad Weiser Park.

The original stone house built by Weiser about 1730 had a huge fireplace at one end of the room, with a bake oven behind it, that from the outside looks like a fat stone buttress supporting the gable end of the house. Most of the farmhouses were built over a spring, the cellar forming the "springhouse." A door led into the cellar, not from the kitchen-dining-sitting-room above, but from the outside. This arrangement saved the house in winter from the annoyance of a cold, damp air coming up from below whenever the cellar door was opened.

The front door, as a rule, was horizontally divided, so that while the lower section was closed to keep the chickens out, the upper section could be left open to give the housewife a view of the roadway.

Many of these houses, following Swiss and South German custom, had an inscription carved over the doorway, giving not only the name of the first owner and the date of the building but also a *Haus Segen* or "house blessing" such as this:

> Gott gesegne dieses Haus
> Und alles was geht ein und aus.

> God bless this house
> And all that passes in and out.

Inside the house everything was spic and span, as was everything on the threshold and out beyond. To this day in some Pennsylvania Dutch towns housewives wash the sidewalks in front of the house for Sunday. Until a few years ago travelers on the Horseshoe Pike between Downingtown and Hummelstown saw no lights in the houses along the way after eight-thirty or nine o'clock at night, for the families had all gone to bed, knowing they would be up again before sunrise. In some communities housewives, contending for the honor of being first to get the washing out on the line on washday, rose as early as two o'clock in the morning.

The Pennsylvania Dutch enjoy telling stories against themselves (but woe betide the stranger who does it for them). They laugh at their conservatism, their reverence for custom and rule, and tell with gusto the story of the Pennsylvania Dutch sentry at Gettysburg who fell asleep at his post and was caught.

His commanding officer, finding the man frank about his fault but apparently unaware of its seriousness or the probable consequences, demanded, "Have you nothing to say for yourself?"

"No."

"Don't you understand what happens to sentries who fall asleep at their post?"

"No."

"They are taken out and shot at dawn."

"Vell," said the Dutchman, "if dose are de rules—"

Do not misunderstand the Pennsylvania Dutch when they tell you they are so parsimonious that they call the Scotch spendthrift. They watch their pennies, it is true, but they are not mean. If a passer-by in Lebanon, Pennsylvania, finds you parking your car at a five-cent meter marked EXPIRED, he may stop to tell you there is one down the street with twenty minutes to go. In their own way they are the most generous of people. The amazing contribution, for instance, of the Church of the Brethren (Dunkers) to overseas relief in many countries is something to give all Americans cause for pride.

As for their cuisine, neither Gargantua nor Duncan Hines would have risen from their table unsatisfied. While it may not be true, as legend avers, that "seven sweets and seven sours" have a place on every menu, it is certain that quantity vies with quality at every meal. The present writer has sat down to a Pennsylvania Dutch dinner at Shartlesville comprising sixty-two different dishes, many of them main dishes, of which the diner was expected to partake.

After making due allowance for the heaviness of their cooking, Fredric Klees, author of *The Pennsylvania Dutch,* proclaims it "the best in America with the exception of the French creole cooking in the South." From inside knowledge he sings the praises of Berks County apple tart ("the best pie between the Atlantic and Pacific"—a distance he measures by way of the Americas, Australia, Asia, Africa, and Europe), Amish snitz pie (made of apple slices with a seasoning of sugar, cinnamon, cloves, nutmeg, and grated orange rind), snitz un knep or steamed apple dumplings, fried noodles and noodle soup, fasnachts (eaten only on Fasnacht Day or Shrove Tuesday; "the most delectable of the doughnut tribe"), shoofly pie (a molasses miracle cake with piecrust below and crumbs on top, made only with a full-bodied molasses that is unobtainable except in old-fashioned country stores; the only comestible, in Klees's opinion, that outranks nectar and ambrosia), the Moravian bun (regal brother to the potato cake), the Schwenkfelder cake ("yellow with saffron and rich in raisins"), and stuffing potatoes (for turkey, chicken, goose, duck, and guinea hen; made with a liberal admixture of milk, eggs, butter, onions, celery, parsley, salt, and pepper), to say nothing of scrapple, dandelion salad, and Moravian mints to top it all off.

Those who complain of the Pennsylvania Dutch farmers that their barns are bigger than their houses have a twisted sense of proportion. The Swiss bank-barns are indeed gigantic, but not too large for what they have to do, which is to house the horses and cattle with their feed and store the grain. The houses too are big, quite big enough for *their* function, which is to provide good homes for what are by present standards very large families. If the houses were built bigger than the barns, they would loom out on the landscape like suburban apartment buildings.

The bank-barns face south, overlooking sunny barnyards and protecting them from the prevailing northwest winds. They are called "bank-barns" because wherever possible they are built into a bank of rising ground so that the hay wagons may be driven from the back into the upper story. When they are on flat ground, a walled ramp is built behind, running up to the threshing floor. On the south side the upper story projects in a forebay or "overshoot" some eight or ten feet beyond the stone foundations, giving a protected walk along the front, where a series of doors with horizontal divisions opens on the stalls.

Except in the Mennonite sections, where frivolities of this sort are frowned upon, the barns are decorated with colorful designs commonly known as "hex signs": stars with five, six, eight, or more points set in a circle. The design is traced on a red ground in brilliant yellows, blues, greens, whites, and still more reds.

There is much dispute about the meaning and derivation of these signs. According to August C. Mahr (writing in *The Ohio State Archaeological and Historical Quarterly,* 1945), they came originally from a Mediterranean cult of the sun which spread across Europe. In the eighteenth century they were brought to Pennsylvania from Canton Bern in Switzerland. At one time they were used as a protection against witches—a belief in which is more deeply entrenched among the Pennsylvania Dutch than is sometimes admitted. Nowadays it is orthodox to say the barn signs are only for ornament. But who likes to sit at table in the thirteenth chair?

Some Pennsylvania Dutch barns at Linglestown near Harrisburg are adorned with carved gable posts. These, according to Dr. Mahr, "share with the barn symbols an ancient cultic significance and protective magic function. Their probable provenience from the worship of Donar (Thor), the highest god of the Germans south of the Woden-worshiping plains region of Old Saxony, makes it appear that their presumable functions were the protection of the barn against lightning, and the securing of fertility for the cattle kept therein."

Dr. Mahr goes on to observe that the old-fashioned Pennsylvania Dutchman, inheritor of an ancient peasant culture, will deny belief in any such thing *as long as he talks in English.* But talk to him in *Pensylfawnish* and let him speak in this same Middle German dialect, and you will find a different set of beliefs tumbling into the forefront of his mind. As Dr. Mahr explains it, "he cannot extricate himself from the *group belief* which is super-individual."

As this last quotation suggests, there is a dark side to the Pennsylvania Dutch mentality. In certain moods they are hideously fearful, brooding, and menacing. The Dutch are aware of this, and they try to escape it by engaging in tumultuous sallies of merry conversation; by folk singing, love-making, church picnics; or by painting everything in sight at home with the most brilliant colors they can find—especially red.

Frances Lichten in *Folk Art of Rural Pennsylvania* notes that the housewife whitewashes all the fences and goes on to whitewash "the lower parts of the trunks of the fruit trees on the lawn, and even mountain boulders if she is settled in a region where they crop out in the grass. . . . The chairs on the porch will sing out in a well-considered scarlet, and discarded iron kettles, once so important in the fireplace, now used no longer, are given a coat of the same color, are supported on three sticks, and then are set out under the trees on the lawn, to hold a cherished house plant."

The Pennsylvania Dutch *Fraktur* (illuminated writing, now eagerly sought by collectors in the form of *Geburtscheins* or "birth certificates," *Taufscheins* or "baptismal certificates," and *Trauscheins* or "marriage certificates"), is full of brilliantly plumed and petaled birds and flowers. Dower chests in the early days were decorated by itinerant painters with tulips and roses, doves, eagles and lions.

Dr. John Joseph Stoudt in *Pennsylvania Folk Art* asks the question: Why did these people love decoration of this sort? He finds the answer in their religious faith. Their art was not representational but symbolic, and he explains what these symbols meant to them. The rose was a symbol of Christ; the tulip (the word itself being a corruption of the Turkish *tülbend,* meaning "lily") was the Biblical lily, symbol of purity; the dove, symbol of the believing heart seeking Christ; the eagle, symbol of renewal; the pelican (in myth supposed to feed its young with the blood of its own breast), symbol of Christ's atonement; the unicorn, symbol of strength through purity; the lion, symbol of Christian triumph.

It is admirable that the Pennsylvania Dutch so long treasured in their homes these beautiful symbols and that to this day they have preserved so many of their interesting folk customs. Their culture has outlasted that of most of the other early contributors to Pennsylvania's melting pot. This fact is not surprising. Although among the German and Swiss immigrants there were intellectuals who won high honors in science, medicine, and other professions, most of them were of peasant origin and—as the word *peasant* connotes—were rooted deeply in ancient custom. They settled, moreover, in such a large bloc in Lancaster, Berks, Lebanon, and Dauphin counties that they were able to hold on to their cultural traditions for many generations, even in a strange land.

The English and Welsh Quakers who came to Pennsylvania contained a smaller proportion of the peasant class. As for the Scotch-Irish, they had already strayed from their land of origin, Scotland, before they came to Pennsylvania, and once here they scattered over the frontier in a way that soon lost them most of their distinctive culture.

The political and literary traditions of the English and Scotch, however, if not their folk customs, have remained. American children sing English nursery rhymes and read stories about King Arthur and Robin Hood; and their elders in Pennsylvania have been in the forefront of the American movement to develop the tradition of liberty and democratic government which goes back at least as far as Magna Charta and the Battle of Bannockburn. In religion, too, Americans as a whole follow not the German plain-sect tradition of isolation from the world but the English and Scottish tradition of encouraging religion, in the ringing words of Milton, to sally out and see its adversary. In other words, they mingle with the world and try to influence it, not from the sidelines, but from the center of the arena.

English architecture in Pennsylvania, like the German, was traditional but adapted to the circumstances of the New World. The Seventh-Day German Baptists at Ephrata, when they put up the Sisters' House (which is still standing), built it of logs with a clapboard sheathing; but they modeled it on medieval German buildings with high, steep roofs and narrow windows. English public buildings, on the other hand, and many private residences as well, were built at that time in the better-lighted English Georgian style, as in the State House (now Independence Hall) at Philadelphia and the James Logan house (Stenton) at Germantown.

In music and poetry the strongest early influences in Pennsylvania were German. Both at Ephrata (where a narrow offshoot of the Church of the Brethren flourished for a time) and at Bethlehem (whence the broad and healthy culture of the Moravian Church spread its influence), hymn-writing and the composition of religious music were encouraged and vigorously pursued. The language barrier circumscribed the lasting influence of German hymns, and the music of Ephrata is as yet little known beyond the confines of the Cloister, where a local choir has recently revived it. But the original compositions of the early Moravian musicians at Bethlehem are one of the enduring glories of Pennsylvania's culture. Music is still the soul of Moravian Bethlehem, as attested by the annual Bach Festival, devoted to the church and chamber music of Johann Sebastian Bach.

While the art of painting was in its infancy in Pennsylvania, it was nurtured from several overseas cultures: German, Swedish, and English. As time went on, however, Pennsylvania painting, which found its home chiefly in Philadelphia, acquired a distinctive tone from the Society of Friends—a gentle, friendly interest in ordinary people and familiar scenes; a curiosity that it did not lose entirely even in the heyday of the Ashcan school.

Painting as an art developed late in Pennsylvania. Although the Delaware Indians were familiar with the use of pigments (Benjamin West said he was introduced to painting at the age of seven by friendly Indians in the neighborhood of Philadelphia, who showed him how to mix the red and yellow earths for face-painting), their best artistic talent went not into painting but into carving. They carved many small stone ornaments on pipe bowls, amulets, or combs, and they carved wooden dance masks and effigies for the center post in the Big House Ceremony.

The Swedes and Dutch on the Delaware did not have time for the arts, and neither did the English, Welsh, and Germans who first followed them. The earliest known Pennsylvania painting was a portrait of Johannes Kelpius by Dr. Christopher Witt, made about 1705. It was not until 1735, when John Penn commissioned the Swedish Gustavus Hesselius to paint portraits of the Delaware Indians Lapowinsa and Tishcohan, that the art of painting may be said to have come to any maturity in Pennsylvania.

It is in the work of Charles Willson Peale (1741-1827) that the kindly realism which was to be the hallmark of Pennsylvania painting first found its full expression. Peale possessed something of the scientific spirit, eager, questioning, in which Philadelphia has excelled from the days of Benjamin Franklin. It will be remembered that Peale devoted much of his life to his famous museum housed in the American Philosophical Society on Independence Square. But his scientific zeal was mellowed by human sympathy, and when he painted his fellow men, he did so gently —never with satiric pleasure. Something of the same pleasant realism is seen in the work of most later Pennsylvania painters, from his own to-the-canvas-born sons (he named eight of his children after great artists—Rembrandt, Raphaelle, Titian, and the like) to John Neagle ("Pat Lyon at the Forge"), Thomas Eakin ("The Swimming Hole") and on down to our own contemporary Andrew Wyeth.

Edward Hicks, who painted "The Peaceable Kingdom" (the most famous primitive of nineteenth-century America), was a Bucks County coach-painter and sign-painter by trade, a Quaker by conviction (one of the leaders in the separatist movement headed by his cousin, Elias Hicks), and a prophet by temperament. He inveighed against "fine painting" as "one of those trifling insignificant arts" difficult to reconcile with Christianity, but indulged in it himself, as he confessed, because he needed money. He painted over a hundred versions of his widely known "The Peaceable Kingdom."

There was more of the lion than the lamb in his character. A writer in *Presbyterian Life* observes: "Some students of folk art see a remarkable resemblance between the portrait of Hicks painted by his cousin Thomas and all the Peaceable Kingdom lions, which age from painting to painting as Hicks himself grew older. The other animals are ageless."

Pennsylvania painters have fed the stream of art in other regions. Thomas Doughty and Thomas Birch, who devoted their talents to romantic landscape in Pennsylvania, were among the founders of the Hudson River school. William James Glacken of Philadelphia, George Benjamin Luks of Williamsport, and John Sloan of Lock Haven—all of whom began their careers as newspaper illustrators in Philadelphia and had realistic concepts of life—went to New York and became leaders in the "ashcan" revolt against the conventional niceness in art.

Many of Pennsylvania's early artists painted what Charles Willson Peale called "deceptives," that is, *trompe l'oeil* or ultra-realistic still lifes. For instance, Raphaelle Peale's "After the Bath" shows a newly unfolded towel hung as a screen from a length of tape. In Pennsylvania, *trompe l'oeil* painting received its best expression.

As might be expected, Pennsylvania has produced a great deal of genre painting, pictures of ordinary life, often enlivened by a touch of humor, as in John Lewis Krimmel's "Fourth of July in Centre Square."

Among Pennsylvania's women painters, Mary Cassatt and Violet Oakley, though utterly unlike and certainly unattached to anything that could be called a Pennsylvania school, illustrate certain Pennsylvania predilections. Mary Cassatt of Pittsburgh became an expatriate and lived in France, drawing much of her inspiration from the impressionism of Degas; but the people she painted look as if they would be easier to live with than those depicted by her master.

Violet Oakley had a scientific precision of line and firmness in her composition. Her subjects were symbolic, expressing man's aspiration and her unbounded faith in what this troubled world, if it could recapture the spirit of Pennsylvania's founder, might yet make of itself. These qualities may be observed in her murals at the State Capitol in Harrisburg and in her illustrated volume *The Holy Experiment, Our Heritage from William Penn.*

John Kane of Pittsburgh, a miner, millworker, and odd-job man who made his artistic debut in 1927 at the age of sixty-seven, painted the industrial world he saw about him at the Forks of the Ohio. The hard exactness of his representations is mellowed by his skill at discovering beauty in the gnarled bodies of workers and in the broken rock and earth of hills under attack from modern road engineers.

More recently Andrew Wyeth has been expressing with great power the mood of men who live under the shadow of the atomic "mushroom" cloud. His empty roads and desolate landscapes are not cruel, however. They awaken pity for man and a longing for heaven's warm sun again.

Pennsylvania's writers are less easy to characterize briefly than are her painters, but it may be said that Benjamin Franklin, who has been called "a plebeian in an aristocratic age," set something of the same tone in literature that Peale set in painting: a friendly, comfortable, democratic curiosity. Many writers have followed in that vein, sometimes adding the sweetness of a Kate Douglas Wiggin or the wit of a Christopher Morley. But the vein

has not been found to run very deep, and lists of Pennsylvania
authors often go far afield in an effort to find writers who supplement respectability with distinction. Willa Cather, for instance,
is sometimes claimed as a Pennsylvania author because she
taught school for a while in Pittsburgh; Gertrude Stein, because
she was born in Allegheny City; and Walt Whitman, because he
lived just across the river in Camden, New Jersey.

In his novels of contemporary manners John O'Hara of Pottsville specializes in Pennsylvania settings, but he has broken the
Pennsylvania literary code. He is an unreconstructed realist, a
scientific observer who, like Émile Zola, presents without bias
the facts of a world that has lost its horizons and in which people
live without benefit of clergy. The action of his novels is strongly
motivated, but he fails to achieve the tension of great tragedy
because, while he tells nothing but the truth, he tells only half
of it. The people who move his plots have passion in abundance,
but they seldom dream, seldom see the burning bush of a great
cause. They are not troubled; they only get into trouble.

Conrad Richter of Pinegrove, though he also is a strong realist,
is a more sensitive observer of the human condition. There is
less surface glitter in his work and more depth. His characters
are not monolithic, for he understands the divided mind. His
The Light in the Forest presents the clash between two worlds,
the Indian's and the white man's, bringing it to a crisis not so
much in external action as in the mind of a man who is trying to
live by two contrary standards and suddenly finds himself, like
Hamlet, compelled to make a choice. This is dimensional realism, and it contains the seeds of great writing.

31 *Some Pennsylvania Profiles*

I. *MILTON HERSHEY*

Milton S. Hershey, founder of the Hershey Chocolate Corporation and the Milton Hershey School for orphan boys, was distinctively a Pennsylvania product. This does not mean that he was a mere provincial. On the contrary, he was of national importance, both as one of the first Americans to master the techniques of mass production—some years before Henry Ford—and as one of the leaders in the modern movement for the decentralization of industry.

It is not, however, as an economic portent that he best deserves to be remembered but as a representative of a distinctively Pennsylvanian ethos. In him the religion of the Pennsylvania Dutch plain sects was taken out of its local context and injected into the world of big business—with some surprising results.

Milton Hershey came of Swiss Mennonite stock on both his father's and his mother's side. Exactly where in Switzerland his forebears came from is not known. Mr. Hershey, on information supplied by amateur genealogists, thought it was Appenzell, capital of the canton of the same name. But more recent researches by Martin H. Brackbill of Harrisburg trace Milton Hershey's descent from a Christian Hirschi of Schangnau in the Emmenthal, Canton Bern.

There could hardly have been a better place for a chocolate manufacturer's genealogy to begin. Emmenthal is good dairy country, and its people make the most famous of Swiss cheeses, the Emmenthaler, which is as big as a cartwheel and, for all its holes, weighs up to three hundred pounds. Only ten miles of foothills separate Schangnau from Interlaken and the most dazzling sight in the Alps—the Jungfrau, presiding in splendor over the black peaks and white glaciers of the Bernese Oberland.

Christian Hirschi of Schangnau and some seven hundred of his compatriots were expelled from Switzerland in 1672. They were members of a sect known then as the Swiss Brethren, and later as Mennonites or followers of Menno Simons, who had incurred the hostility of the Bernese authorities because, among other things, of their refusal to bear arms. After spending some years in the German Palatinate, Christian Hirschi—Milton's great-great-great-great grandfather—emigrated to Pennsylvania in 1717. With his friend Hans Brubaker he took out a warrant for a thousand acres of land on little Conestoga Creek just west of the present city of Lancaster. The section included the site of President Buchanan's future home, Wheatland.

From this Christian Hirschi the line is unbroken through Bishop Bentz Hershey, a second Christian Hirschi, Isaac Hershey, Jacob Hershey, Henry Hershey, and finally Milton, who was born at the Hershey homestead in Derry Township, Dauphin County, on September 13, 1857. Milton's mother, Veronica (popularly known as Fanny) Hershey, nee Snavely, also traced descent from the first Christian Hirschi, and her line, like her husband's, was strictly Swiss Mennonite. Her own father, Abraham Snavely, was a bishop of the Reformed (or New) Mennonite Church, a body which split off from the parent stem because it found the orthodox Mennonites not strict enough in discipline.

Milton Hershey's astonishing blend of generous daring (as seen in his Cuban venture) and miserly caution (as seen in his mania for turning out office lights) was a gift from his parents. His father, Henry, was a man of infinite zest and unfathomable curiosity, who entered and failed in (by his son's count) seventeen separate careers, including those of farmer, oilman, inventor, journalist, preacher, horticulturist, steel worker, carpenter, and still-life painter. In his old age he was rescued by his millionaire son from near destitution in Colorado where, according to rumors then circulating, he was driving a dump truck, selling secondhand books, and peddling horse powders of his own invention to small farmers in the foothills of the Rockies. His last years were spent in ecstatic content at the Hershey homestead, where his son had prepared a good library for him, filled with his own choice of books on history, religion, nature study, and experimental science.

Milton's mother was a frugal, cautious, but determined little woman whose one great passion in life was to help her unlucky son Milton succeed as his father had not. Her own father, Bishop Abraham Snavely, was blest with great riches, and she found it hard to live with a mate who would rather read a book than earn a meal. One day when the larder was bare she presented an ultimatum to her husband: "If you go on reading books, I will leave you." They separated, and thereafter she had herself listed in the Lancaster city directory as "widow of Henry Hershey," although the "widower" continued to visit her now and then, for at heart they were really very fond of each other.

Fanny Hershey was with her husband at the time he died in the Hershey homestead, and she saw to it that in death the barrier that had separated them should be finally removed. She had workmen take all his books out of the library and burn them in the experimental chocolate-factory furnace. Fifty years later Harry Tinney recalled the scene: "Monroe Hershey hauled the books out in a wheelbarrow. I opened the [furnace] door and slung them in. Monroe went back a couple of times to the house to fetch them out. She stood back a little and watched, but she didn't say anything."

Milton Hershey had very little schooling. Starting at the Derry Church School, where his uncle Elias was teacher, he went to a succession of one-room schools—six in about eight years. By his own estimate he never got beyond the fourth grade. Country schools in those days were open for only a few months in the year, and there was no compulsory attendance law to make it seem wiser to a boy and his parents to spend daylight hours on a school bench rather than out in the fields catching skunks (a sport in which Milt Hershey was malodorously adept) or doing chores about the barn. The result was that his formal education left him with little to show beyond an elementary ability to read and write and a hearty dislike for books.

To the end of Milton's days abstract ideas and scientific reasoning meant little to him. But he had a good memory and what is called an "experiencing" nature. Everything he heard, saw, felt, smelled, or tasted had meaning for him and was remembered. From his father he learned to experiment. From his mother he learned industry and patience. In developing his chocolate formula, he worked on no abstract theories and attempted no scientific short cuts. He used instead the trial-and-error method, inching his way untiringly through failure after failure to a final and triumphant success.

From earliest childhood he had known the taste of failure, and this inoculation saved him from discouragement in his mature years. When he was four or five years old, his parents took him to the oilfields in the neighborhood of Titusville, where his father tried to sell drilling machinery—shortly after the oil boom had ended. When Milton was fourteen years old, his father—who had always wanted to be a writer himself—tried to start the boy in that direction by apprenticing him as printer's devil on a pacifist weekly, the *Waffenlose Waechter* (*Weaponless Watchman*). When one day Milton dropped his hat into the press —thus adding a heady element to the *Watchman*'s potpourri of German and English prose and poetry—the printer and his devil parted.

Next he got a job with Joe Royer of Lancaster, who made candy and ran a restaurant famous for its "ice cream and lemon squares." Joe set the boy to holding horses for his customers and turning the handle of the big ice-cream freezer. He failed in this latter job because he lacked the necessary physical strength. Joe accordingly sent him to the kitchen to help make candy, and there he found his life's work.

After a few years spent tinkering with candy recipes there, Milton resolved to set out on his own. Like his father, he allowed his imagination to shoot skyward, and he began a series of ambitious failures that carried him well into manhood. He started in Philadelphia in 1876, hoping to profit from the crowds in the city attending the Centennial Exhibition. Though the competition was killing, he held on for several years, during which time the family rallied to his side: his mother by cooking and wrapping candies, his father (in his inimitable, dubious way) by inventing a brand of H. H. [Henry Hershey] COUGH DROPS and a patented MEDICATED CANDY CABINET to exhibit them in.

Milton sold candies on the street by day and cooked fresh batches by night, becoming so exhausted that he was known to fall asleep on his feet. In the end he broke down. His creditors refused to carry him further, and the business collapsed.

At the urging of his father (who had followed the mining rush to Colorado), Milton went out to Denver, only to find that his father as usual had missed the boat. The silver mining boom had burst, and Denver was filled with unemployed. Milton somehow got a job with a candy-maker, who taught him how to make caramels with real milk. That recipe turned out to be the key to Hershey's subsequent success.

In Denver, Milton Hershey learned a lot of other things, too. He learned to steel himself against both the threats and the enticements of a world not much talked about by Dauphin County Mennonites. At that time—1882—Soapy Smith (who was to die in Alaska of well-earned gunshot wounds incurred on the Trail of '98) was one of the kings of the underworld, and Baby Doe was one of the queens. The year Hershey was there, Buffalo Bill was robbed of two thousand dollars' worth of jewels.

Bishop Abraham Snavely's grandson carried a revolver in that haunt of wickedness, and he used it on one occasion to get himself out of a jam. He had seen a BOY WANTED sign in a shop window and went in to apply for a job. Finding himself in suspicious company, he tried to leave but found the door locked. Only the sight of Milton's drawn revolver persuaded the boss to let him go. Denver did not fill Milton Hershey's pocket with gold pieces, but it taught him self-reliance and gave him fresh stamina to withstand the failures that lay ahead.

The Hersheys, father and son, went to Chicago. There Henry Hershey got a job as a carpenter, while Milton hired himself out to a candy-maker. They pooled their resources, but when father Hershey put his name to an unlucky friend's note and had to pay, the Hershey balloon was again deflated.

"If you want to make money," said Henry Hershey to his son, "you must do things in a big way."

They went to New Orleans, planning to borrow money, buy machinery, and take the southern market by storm. Finding, however, that the machinery they wanted was made in New York, they decided to save the cost of freight by going themselves to New York, hub of the candy universe, and storming the biggest market of all.

In New York they borrowed money and set up an expensive cough-drop machine. Milton manufactured caramels and H. H. Cough Drops, while his father drove a candy wagon round Manhattan and across the new Brooklyn Bridge. But the candy market was a hard one to break into. A day of reckoning came. Milton's creditors demanded payment. In desperation Milton hired a wagon, filled it with cough drops, and drove round the alleys trying to sell the stuff to small dealers. While he was inside one place dickering with a prospect, some boys threw firecrackers under his horse. Hearing the tumult that erupted on the cobblestones, Milton rushed out, only to see horse and wagon disappearing in a shower of cough drops. After that, he remained in New York only long enough to earn money, by doing odd jobs, for train fare back to Lancaster.

In Lancaster, Milton was icily received by most of his relatives. But being as incorrigibly optimistic as his father, he borrowed money from an aunt, Mattie Snavely, hired a room with a stove, bought some sugar, and started all over again. His mother and Aunt Mattie wrapped candies, while Milton peddled them round the streets—at the wrong end of town—in a pushcart. The pushcart rivalry was really tough. Milton (now about thirty years of age) pushed his luck too far along South Dorwart Street on Cabbage Hill one day and was stoned out.

An English candy importer visiting the United States tasted Milton Hershey's fresh-milk caramels and recognized their superior quality. He gave Hershey a sizable order. Milton realized that his future depended on his ability to fill this order. He had neither the equipment nor the staff to make caramels in the mass, and the banks turned him down when he tried to borrow money on his prospects. One man, however, Mr. Brenneman, cashier of the Lancaster National Bank, became interested. He was not impressed with Milton's establishment, a small noisy room in a building that housed a carriage factory and a carpet-beating concern. On the other hand, Milton Hershey's quiet, confident manner and his complete devotion to his work made the banker believe for the moment in the Horatio Alger type, and he put his personal name to the young man's note.

The candies were made, shipped to England, and paid for. When Milton received the English check, he rushed down to the bank, still in his candy apron, to pay off his note.

Once Milton's luck turned, it turned completely. Thereafter to the end of his life he never ceased to be surprised at the way money makes money. In a very few years he owned a large factory in Lancaster, where he made his Crystal A. Caramels: the aristocratic Lotus, Paradox, and Cocoanut Ices, all made of cream, and the plebeian Icelets, Empires, and Melbas, made of skim milk.

Milton had a sharp eye for the market, anticipating changes before they occurred. Chocolate was then on the horizon. His father had apparently been reading up on the subject and was thinking of going to Brazil to grow cacao trees for an expected boom in chocolate candy and cocoa. Milton caught his father's enthusiasm. Caramels were a passing fad, he thought, but chocolate—"A sweet to eat, a food to drink," as he was one day to advertise it in New York—must be in never-ending demand. He was sure that the first man to exploit fully the immense new market for a popularly priced chocolate would make a gigantic fortune.

At the World's Columbian Exposition at Chicago in 1893 he saw a machine for making chocolate candies, bought it, hired chocolate experts, and set aside a part of his huge factory for experiment. After long tests and many failures he settled on a milk chocolate bar (made with *fresh* milk) as the thing to concentrate on, and he assembled all the instruments of mass production to turn it out at a price everyone could afford. With roasters and hullers and milling machines, agitators and condensing kettles, plow machines, chasers, melangeurs, and longitudes, he made the Hershey Chocolate Bar, next to the Stars and Stripes the most widely known American product in the world of his day.

In 1900 he sold his caramel business for a million dollars. Examining sites for the mammoth chocolate factory he now planned to build, he rejected Baltimore, Yonkers, and Kingston, New York, and selected his own birthplace, Derry Church, Pennsylvania. It was not mere sentiment that dictated the choice but penetrating insight into the future. For one thing, this was good dairy country, and fresh milk was the secret of his success. There was also a good water supply. Best of all, in Derry Township of Dauphin County he had available a dependable labor supply: a countryside inhabited by the industrious, home-loving, Pennsylvania Dutch folk to whom he belonged and who could be trusted to be loyal to their own.

He built his factory in a cornfield and in 1903 laid out the town of Hershey. There, from a rural base, he set out on the course of mass production and national distribution which soon made him a millionaire many times over.

Milton Hershey's philanthropies were not an afterthought. Though he had rejected the theological doctrines of the Reformed Mennonites, the vision of life they had shown him—especially through the example of his mother and his uncle, Bishop Elias Hershey—remained with him to the end. The Golden Rule was his article of faith. He plowed his fabulous millions back into the community around him in many ways: by using his capital in time of depression to erect public buildings, thus giving employment at the time and providing future benefits to his people; by building a great residential school for orphan boys, in which the weaknesses of mass education were avoided by housing the youngsters in small "family" units or farm cottages; by providing amusement parks, golf courses, swimming pools, theaters, and athletic fields as the best means of healthy recreation; by giving financial assistance to all local churches, whatever their denomination; by helping the public schools; by setting up a junior college; by providing a good library and a museum to help keep the community from the mental stagnation that sometimes afflicts the carefree and the prosperous.

The first thing that impresses a visitor in the town of Hershey is the untroubled (but by no means slack) expression on the faces of its citizens. The next is the natural way in which the town has been allowed to grow, the healthy individuality of the houses on the streets, and the absence of any corrosive uniformity. Milton Hershey had a horror of the neat rows of identical houses he had seen in some company towns. He was interested in the Garden City movement in England.

Even the ambitious Hotel Hershey, perched above the town on Pat's Hill, is a strictly individual affair. In the flush of his first multimillions Milton Hershey and his wife planned it to be a replica of the grandiose Heliopolis Palace at Cairo. But the passage of time altered his perspective, and in the end he chose a more modest model. He gave the architect, D. Paul Witmer, a picture postcard showing a small, thirty-room, end-turreted hotel that he and his wife had once enjoyed on the shore of the Mediterranean. He told the archiect to blow it up to 200 rooms. When shown that the hill could not accommodate so many, he reduced the number to the 150 rooms the Hotel Hershey has today. He wanted the lobby to have a Cuban look, to remind him of his beloved plantation, Rosario, near Havana. He wanted the dining room to be without pillars, so that the diners could all enjoy the view of the Blue Mountains on the horizon. Other suggestions came out of a notebook he had kept on his travels. The hotel and the town of Hershey below it may not be the best places in which to study classic architecture, but they are definitely monuments to Mr. Hershey's individualism.

The Milton Hershey School is now the chief beneficiary of the Hershey Chocolate Corporation. Into it Mr. Hershey poured millions for up-to-date buildings, qualified teachers, and the latest equipment, in order to give the boy students the better opportunities he had missed as a child. His own failures and frustrations had not left him bitter. They had given him an overwhelming compassion.

"I would give everything I possess if I could call one of these boys my own," he said to a friend visiting one of the school dormitories with him. His wife was an invalid, and they had no children of their own. Today thousands of "Milton Hershey's boys," graduates of the Milton Hershey School, many of them in high positions, honor him as the man who was more than a father to them.

Hershey was, of course, like all entrepreneurs of the day, something of an autocrat. To get his full flavor, we should not compare him with the "organization man" of today but with the financial tycoons of his own day. He did not fully understand labor problems or the emerging concept of property as being in part the possession of the labor force that helped to create it. He was a hard trader, and not everybody had occasion to like him. But he loved his labor force and did his best, according to his lights, to help them. "Well," said one of his competitors, who had watched him putting millions into his two beautiful towns (Hershey, Pennsylvania, and Hershey, Cuba), "if he *likes* to give money away, that's his affair."

In labor's attempt to unionize the workers of America one of the toughest nuts to crack was the Hershey Chocolate Company. This was in part owing to the unwillingness of the factory workers to join a union, many of them being members of plain sects whose religion forbade them to do so. In part also it was because

Milton Hershey had shown so generous a public spirit that most of his employees, and certainly the Pennsylvania Dutch community behind them, supported his benevolent autocracy.

In the great Hershey sit-down strike of 1937 the farmers of Dauphin and Lebanon counties and the students of Lebanon Valley College in nearby Annville joined forces to break the strike, making a sudden rush into the factory that brought many of the "sit-downers" tumbling out of the windows. This marked the end of an era of sit-down strikes throughout the country. It marked also a change in Mr. Hershey himself. He was bitterly grieved that any of his employees should have turned against him, but he was also led to reappraise the relations between employer and employed, and he came in the end to accept the principle of collective bargaining.

II. ANDREW MELLON

In 1818 Andrew Mellon, a north-of-Ireland farmer, became so discouraged by the high taxes that followed the Napoleonic Wars that he sold his acres at Camp Hill, County Tyrone, and set sail for the New World. With him on the voyage were his wife, Rebecca (of Dutch extraction), his five-year-old son, Thomas, and two hundred guineas sewn in Rebecca's leather belt.

After a twelve weeks' crossing to St. John, New Brunswick, and another week of dropping down the coast to Baltimore, came three more weeks of jolting in a Conestoga wagon over the Allegheny Mountains to the vicinity of Pittsburgh. Though two years earlier that community had received a city charter, it bore little resemblance to the "Smoky City" which the Mellon millions were to help make of it.

Andrew Mellon bought farmland near Turtle Creek, patched up the log house and barn he found there, and fought for the survival of his family during the financial panic of 1819-1820. The price of wheat dropped to forty cents a bushel. Eggs sold two for a penny. In the effort to keep up payments on the farm, little Thomas and his mother spun flax and wove from it grain bags, which they sold for fifty cents apiece.

While the lad Thomas was growing up to be a plowhand in Turtle Creek, his rich and culture-seeking Uncle Thomas, for whom he had been named, put other ideas in his head. Uncle

Thomas, who had made his fortune in New Orleans and retired to the literary environment of Philadelphia, lent books to his nephew, inspiring in the boy a taste that never forsook him. One day the young plowman, searching for good reading in a neighbor's house, found a copy of Benjamin Franklin's *Autobiography* and read it.

"The maxims of 'Poor Richard,'" he wrote afterwards, "exactly suited my sentiments . . . I regard the reading of Franklin's Autobiography as the turning point of my life."

So Thomas Mellon prepared himself for college, attended the Western University of Pennsylvania (now the University of Pittsburgh), studied law with former Judge Charles Shaler, and put up his own shingle on Pittsburgh's Fifth Avenue. Soon he invested successfully in real estate, married a rich wife, Sarah Jane Negley, and became a judge of the county Court of Common Pleas. During this time Sarah Jane bore him sons, Andrew and Richard. Though Mellon was now a rich man, he never forgot the bitter sting of poverty, nor did he let his sons forget it. In 1869 Judge Mellon stepped down from the bench to devote himself to business so that, as he said, he might launch his sons on "the flood tide of business prosperity" which Pittsburgh was then enjoying. In 1870 he opened a private bank, T. Mellon & Sons, which is now the Mellon National Bank.

In such a home atmosphere young Andrew, frail and diffident but in his heart indomitable, grew to manhood with an understanding of money and a genius for acquiring it. Consequently, as Andrew approached graduation after a successful career at Western University in the class of '73, his father approved of his leaving the institution without a degree in order to set up (in company with his younger brother, Richard) a lumber business in the booming town of Mansfield, now Carnegie, on the Panhandle Railroad. The quick success of this business—which after a few months the boys, scenting a depression, sold at a good profit—convinced the elder Mellon of Andrew's financial maturity, and in 1874 the father took his son into the family bank. The young man's success was so phenomenal that in 1882 Thomas Mellon transferred ownership to Andrew, who was then only twenty-seven years old.

After a tour of Europe with the dynamic, art-loving Henry Frick, who opened his eyes to beauty, Andrew came back to

Pittsburgh and immediately fell in love with the charming Adelaide Childs. He was soon to endure the agony of watching his fiancé slowly die of tuberculosis.

After that experience his mind closed tightly on finance. It opened briefly again when at the age of forty-five he was captivated by a vivacious young lady from the British Isles. She was Nora McMullen, daughter of an Irish distiller and granddaughter of Peter Guinness, brewer of stout and ale. The marriage that ensued was a failure. In 1911 they were divorced.

Andrew Mellon's success at banking lay in following the enlightened policy of his father, which was to find a good man— one with initiative, know-how, and a big idea—then give him the capital he needed to put his idea to work and leave him to manage the business without interference. Pittsburgh, center of a great and rapidly expanding industrial area, was the place of all places for a bank with such a program to succeed. Andrew Mellon gave each new project as it came before him a cool, cautious appraisal. Once convinced of the soundness of an idea and of its promoter's competence, he gave quick and generous support —not usually in the form of a straight loan but in shares of the business. It was also his custom, as it had been his father's, to reinvest his winnings in the business that produced them, a plan immensely encouraging to the men he sponsored. Just as Thomas Mellon, by a timely loan given to a young clerk in the Overholt Distillery, launched the spectacular career of Henry C. Frick, so Andrew, by his initial and continuing support of Alfred Hunt and George Clapp in return for a controlling share in their Aluminum Company of America, made an immense fortune. Alcoa's assets rose from $75,000,000 in 1921 to $250,000,000 in 1929. Gulf Oil, which Andrew Mellon helped to found, rose in the same period from $272,000,000 to $761,000,000.

With Henry Frick, who had recently resigned as chairman of the board of Carnegie Steel, Andrew organized the Union Steel Company, which the Carnegie Company was soon constrained to bring into the United States Steel Corporation at a top price. Mellon acquired oil wells in western Pennsylvania and established refineries at Marcus Hook on the Delaware. He then broke the Rockefeller monopoly in Pennsylvania by connecting the two properties with a pipeline. They were later sold to Rockefeller at an enormous profit.

Swiftly the Mellon interests reached into almost every corner of the earth. They included ships, steel, railroads, public utilites, electricity, water power, traction, coal and coke, insurance, locomotives, railroad cars, stationary engines, gun carriages, motor trucks, and the making of many other commodities. The seas placed no bounds on Mellonia.

It was Pennsylvania in particular, however, that was Mellon's oyster. Through direct ownership or through holding companies and subsidiaries the Mellon fortune virtually controlled that state's industry. Through alliance with political machines (Matt Quay and Boies Penrose are said to have counted heavily on his support) it controlled the life of the people as well. Harvey O'Connor wrote in *Mellon's Millions,* "The Keystone State became the patrimony of the Mellons and their allies, as it had once been of the Penns."

Believing, as Andrew Mellon did, in the paramount importance of private business and the necessity of freeing it from heavy taxation and other forms of restraint, he was at home among orthodox Republicans. He contributed money to be used against Wilson in 1916 and against the League of Nations in 1918-1919.

When Republicans in 1920 were looking about for a Secretary of the Treasury and Andrew Mellon was suggested, it was certainly not because his name was then a vote-getter. Few people had heard of him. Even at the height of his business success he remained a soft-spoken, shy man with no desire for the limelight. Warren G. Harding did not even recognize the name when, as Harvey O'Connor tells the story, Harry Daugherty, Harding's campaign manager, proposed it to him.

"Mellon . . . Mellon," Harding muttered. "I don't know him."

Daugherty replied: "A man who can quietly make the millions this modest-looking man has gathered in is little short of a magician. . . . He will make for you the greatest Secretary of the Treasury since Alexander Hamilton . . . if you can get him."

Later Harding was to label Mellon "the ubiquitous financier of the universe."

Certainly a magician—or the equivalent, a man of vast experience, clear head, and organizing genius—was needed by the United States in the postwar emergency of 1921. The national debt had risen to nearly $24,000,000,000 (a big sum in those days), and obligations of $11,000,000,000 were soon to fall due. A heavy and ill-adjusted tax burden lay upon the people. War debts were in a seemingly impossible tangle.

So on March 24, 1921, Andrew Mellon, having divested himself of directorships in over fifty companies in order to qualify for the office, was installed as Secretary of the Treasury.

The problems confronting the nation were not too dissimilar (except in their immensity) from those that had faced his grandparents: debt and taxes. Upon these he now made a frontal attack with such apparent success that seven years later during the political campaign of 1928 he could claim to have reduced the public debt from $23,979,000,000 to $17,604,000,000. By the Revenue Act of 1921 he had reduced taxes by about $663,-000,000.

In a campaign letter he wrote: "The excess profits tax was eliminated, and most of the transportation and some of the nuisance taxes were repealed. On the item of transportation alone, the public saved $273,000,000. Over $48,000,000 was saved by the repeal of the tax on soft drinks, and ice cream nearly $19,000,000, nearly $19,000,000 on life, fire, marine and casualty insurance; $1,332,000 on chewing gum. . . . Within a period of 6 years, the Federal tax per capita has been cut in half, having been reduced from $45.23 in 1921 to $27.17 in 1926."

Despite the emphasis in his letter on such things as soft drinks, ice cream, and chewing gum, the immediate beneficiary of the Mellon Plan (as his tax measures had come to be called) was not the poor workman but the rich industrialist. His conviction that this was not class legislation came from his sincerely held belief that wealth flows best from the top down, and that therefore the government's prime concern should be to encourage the top layers of business, letting money filter down naturally to the lower levels. He scorned the heretical notion of using taxation as a social instrument, a means of equalizing wealth.

He put the war debts (actually the postwar debts, since those contracted during the war had been written off) into a neat series of agreements based on the apparently simple, ethical principle of "ability to pay." The principle proved intractable, however, in the excited postwar atmosphere and the topsy-turvy economics of war-ravaged Europe. To transport coin or bullion in quantities sufficient to pay the debts was clearly impossible. It was necessary, therefore, for the debtor nations to establish large credits in this country, and this could be done only by selling goods here to the value, as has been estimated, of about $20,000,000,000. But Mellon favored high tariffs, which thus diminished foreign trade and prevented the accumulation of foreign credits in this country.

Connected with the war debts was the problem of German reparations. The ability of some debtor nations, notably England, to pay was geared to the reparations they received from Germany. The German economy, however, was too weak to pay reparations without receiving booster shots in the form of loans (under the Dawes and Young plans) from the United States. So the money went round and round, without creating anything but friction. Andrew Mellon is blamed for not having enlightened the American people about the relation of tariffs to international credits or the relation of German reparations to debt settlements. The war debts remained an obstacle to international understanding, until the Second World War blew the whole problem into the void.

Mellon was a thoughtful man, but his thinking was bounded by narrow horizons. He understood the laws of profit and loss as taught in his father's counting house. In the matching of wits within the conventions of the money game he was all but unbeatable. But the range of his sympathies was limited. He kept himself detached from that level of humanity in which the abstract principles of finance, as he understood them, were translated into sweat and sometimes blood.

There was another weakness that marred Andrew Mellon's effectiveness as a public servant. He lacked any great power of imagination. This too limited his human sympathies. That it also limited his foresight as an economist is seen in his ultimate failure with the debt settlements and his unawareness of the impending Great Depression. He did not foresee—any more than the rank and file—the Black Friday of October, 1929, when the stock market broke, so could not give the public any warning.

When the catastrophe of wholesale unemployment burst upon the nation, his palliatives—government retrenchment and citizen self-help—failed to feed the starving. His prestige burned low and went out. President Hoover accepted his resignation in February, 1932, giving him in return the ambassadorship to the United Kingdom. With his daughter Ailsa as hostess in London, he played a hospitable role among England's business and society elite. The defeat of Hoover brought him back to private life and philanthropy.

One of Andrew Mellon's earliest philanthropies had been the founding, with his brother Richard in 1913, of the Mellon Institute for Industrial Research, in his father's memory. Its purpose was to bring science to the aid of industry, not in a paternalistic way, but by encouraging manufacturers to help themselves. The institute offered its facilities to any forward-looking company that agreed to pay the salary of a research fellow for at least a year and to pay for any special equipment the project might call for. In return, the institute provided laboratory space, the use of its library, and the help of its administrative staff. Since its founding it has rendered important service, not only to manufacturers in the form of new products, but also to the public at large. New processes have been discovered, and improvements have been made in the things that people eat, drink, wear, live in, and move about on. Its success has stimulated the creation of research foundations all over the country. Recently it has changed its policy and devotes half of its energies to pure science—the pursuit of knowledge for its own sake, without regard to commercial application.

Mellon's philanthropies were conducted, for the most part, outside the glare of publicity. No rash of Mellon-named buildings sprang up on the nation's campuses. The use of the family name on the Mellon Institute was an exception. When Andrew Mellon gave to the nation his fabulous collection of Old Masters (for which he had spent a fortune of $35,000,000 or more), along with the millions for a building to house it and an endowment to support it, he stipulated that it should not bear the Mellon name.

"My dear Mr. President," he wrote in 1936, "over a period of many years I have been acquiring important and rare paintings and sculpture with the idea that ultimately they would become the property of the people of the United States and be made available to them in a national gallery to be maintained in the city of Washington for the purpose of encouraging and developing the study of the fine arts."

Mr. Roosevelt replied, "My dear Mr. Mellon: When my uncle handed me your letter of December 22 I was not only completely taken by surprise but was delighted by your very wonderful offer."

And so the National Gallery of Art, as it is now called, in Washington, D. C., came into existence.

If there is anything paradoxical about Andrew Mellon, it is to be found in the shyness of a world figure who was, as Allan Nevins calls him in the *Dictionary of National Biography,* "the most powerful personage of the Harding-Coolidge regimes." He was not really a complex person. If he seems to be, considering his various careers as banker, industrial titan, Secretary of the Treasury, art collector, and philanthropist, it is only because events pushed a born banker into all these other roles. Nevins caught the secret when he wrote, "His veiled and reticent personality cloaked an essentially simple, thoughtful, and just nature."

The best of "Andy" Mellon was really the man himself, not the political figure the public saw and fought over. Reputed in his time to be the third richest man in the world, he was by no means a Horatio Alger hero. He was born to wealth and opportunity, bred to aristocratic taste. Yet he won for himself a respected place as a god in the popular rags-to-riches mythology of America. That he accepted this role is proved by his endorsement of the rags-to-riches doctrine and by his solemnly announcing just before the Great Depression: "Any man of initiative and energy in this country can get what he wants out of life."

III. OWEN J. ROBERTS

The career of the late Owen J. Roberts, the "swing man" of the Supreme Court during the heyday of the New Deal, may be said to have brought the wheel of Pennsylvania history to full circle. In many ways he was the image of William Penn. He was a humanitarian and a great administrator. He was also trained in the law, deeply religious, and peace-loving, but zestful in the fight for justice and the protection of the oppressed. His lifelong passion was to preserve democracy and make it effective at home and abroad.

Yet with all his resemblance to the Commonwealth's founder,

Justice Roberts belongs emphatically to our time. He was a typical American of the twentieth century, a living witness to the fact that Penn had planted here the seed of a nation.

"He touched life at many points," recalls his wife, "and he was always busy." His law cases came first. He plugged them up with a savage conscientiousness that paid dividends in court. Opposing counsel admired and feared the intimate ease of manner, the apparently infallible memory, and the quick repartee with which he presented his arguments and, it was said, "hypnotized juries." His family alone understood the long hours of work and the sleepless, worry-filled nights that went to make his knowledge and skill in the end seem so effortless.

Perhaps it was the many absorbing and well-balanced "extracurricular activities" he permitted himself that gave him the respite he needed. He was always interested in his church and for many years served as a vestryman. He was not a bookish man, but he enjoyed the writings of Mark Twain and Dickens. He was a lover of poetry, particularly the work of Shelley and Keats. He could recite Gray's "Elegy" word for word. He treasured *The Oxford Book of English Verse* so highly (especially its poems of chivalrous love) that he took it with him everywhere on his travels.

He was an open-air man, who loved camping, canoeing, and fishing in Maine. He enjoyed the quiet plateau of the Pocono Mountains with their constantly surprising waterfalls. He was a gentleman farmer, priding himself on the breeding of Guernsey cattle and on never losing money on them. He occupied himself delightedly with the Boy Scouts, entertaining them on his farm in Chester County, speaking at their meetings, and serving as a member of the National Council.

He made and kept many friends through the years, men such as Robert T. McCracken, his first law partner. One of his warmest friendships was with Owen Wister, whose living model for the character of the Virginian, Roberts defended successfully against a charge of murder.

His loyalty was proverbial. Writes McCracken, "The absorbing figures in his life were his clients." He had also a touch of hero worship. He admired Justice Brandeis and "adored" Chief Justice Hughes.

He was modest. Justice Frankfurter records that on leaving the bench, Roberts wrote, "I have no illusions about my judicial career. But one can only do what one can. Who am I to revile the good God that he did not make me a Marshall, a Taney, a Bradley, a Brandeis or a Cardozo?"

He was a home-lover, observant of the proprieties, but endowed with too elfish a sense of humor to be bound tightly by convention. He enjoyed a good steak at the Bridge Street Eating House in Phoenixville. He had a repertoire of Calvin Coolidge stories. He loved to see the "plain people's" bonnets and beards displayed at the Lancaster Market. When he traveled in Europe, he spent his spare time not in a dutiful round of galleries, cathedrals, and castles but in his room with a *Baedeker* at hand, composing letters to friends describing the places he had not seen.

His enthusiasm was drawn out by many different organizations: the University of Pennsylvania Law School, of which for a time he was Dean; Lincoln University, of which he was a trustee; the Smithsonian Institution, of which he was a regent; the Personnel Security Board of the Atomic Energy Commission, on which he served; the American Philosophical Society, of which he was president; the Pennsylvania Bar Association, of which he also was president; the Ford Foundation's Fund for the Advancement of Education, on whose board of directors he was chairman; and the Lawyers' Committee for Eisenhower for President.

Truly, as Senator George Wharton Pepper said, "Roberts is properly described as a character in action."

Add to this enormous explosion of energy Roberts' wholesome simplicity, his chivalry ("He was a perfect darling round the house," recalls his wife), and his boyish laughter (as, for instance, when he and Felix Frankfurter stayed up into the small hours of the night swapping yarns), and one can understand why he ranks as the archrepresentative of the open-hearted American type.

Owen Josephus Roberts was born in a house on Fisher's Lane in Germantown on May 2, 1875. His father, Josephus Roberts, was a wholesale merchant dealing in hardware for carriages and wagons. His mother was of Huguenot stock. His grandfather, William Roberts, had come from Wales and settled on a farm on

Perkiomen Creek in Montgomery County. His grandmother Hübner was of Pennsylvania Dutch stock. All in all, Owen was a happy exemplar of Pennsylvania's melting pot.

"His father was a wonderful man," recalls Mrs. Roberts, "with a lovely disposition—kindly, considerate." Though not himself a churchgoer, Josephus Roberts saw to it that Owen's upbringing was strict. As a youth Owen played the cornet in the local Baptist Church and taught Sunday school. His later affiliations were with the Episcopal Church. He rose to become the first layman to serve as chairman of the House of Deputies, which in conjunction with the House of Bishops is the highest ecclesiastical authority in that denomination.

After graduating from the Germantown Academy at the age of fifteen, he waited a year before entering the University of Pennsylvania. There he embarked on a brilliant career in the classics. His graduation thesis was titled "The Agamemnon Myth as Treated by the Attic Dramatists." His plan was to make a career teaching Latin and Greek.

"That is good," said his father, "but I would like you to go to law school first and then make up your mind."

At the University of Pennsylvania Law School he so impressed his professors that, when he graduated in 1898 at the age of twenty-three, they at once put him on the teaching staff. During the twenty consecutive years he spent in that position (though always on a part-time basis), he rose from the rank of instructor to that of full professor.

"He was a born teacher," wrote one of his students, as reported by Dean Edwin R. Keedy in *The University of Pennsylvania Law Review*. "He saw things so clearly himself, that he could only impart them one way—equally clearly. . . . Of course we all admired him. He was so big, so ruggedly handsome, so overwhelming in repartee."

In 1904 he met and married Elizabeth Rogers, a spirited young lady from Connecticut who, in Drew Pearson's words, became "Roberts' pal, inspiration, and goad"—a trinity he needed, for Roberts was not a contemplative man, who fed his mind best when alone, but an active and sociable one, who was healthiest when acting upon, and being acted upon by, others. Mrs. Owen was a lively-minded, independent, outspoken companion who gave him the shock and stimulus he sometimes needed.

"That woman will be the end of me," he used to say laughingly to his friends (in her presence); but she took him to the heights.

As Philadelphia's assistant district attorney under John C. Bell he saw plenty of action in courtroom battles, acquiring a reputation for a memory that played him no tricks and a wit that gave his enemy no quarter. Important clients came his way, such as John Wanamaker, the Pennsylvania Railroad, and Bell Telephone. He became known as a successful corporation lawyer. The new affluence this brought him enabled him to indulge his taste, not for luxuries, but for the simple life. He bought five properties in Chester County near Phoenixville and turned them into a nine-hundred-acre farm to which he gave the Welsh name of Bryncoed. He remodeled the farmhouse. R. Brognard Okie, famous for colonial reconstructions, was his architect; and a young Philadelphia historian, C. B. Montgomery, scoured the countryside in search of handmade nails and old locks and hinges to make the house additions authentic. Bryncoed became the center of Roberts' private life.

Roberts refused to take cases in which he saw no merit. His reputation for integrity spread beyond Pennsylvania. In 1924 President Coolidge turned an eye in his direction when looking for someone fearless and incorruptible to serve as special counsel in the investigation of the Teapot Dome oil scandals. Certain public oil lands reserved for the navy had been improperly leased to private individuals—in return, it was suspected, for financial favors extended to a former member of President Harding's cabinet, Albert Bacon Fall, Secretary of the Interior.

When Owen J. Roberts, who had been recommended by Senator George Wharton Pepper, called at the White House and was asked by President Coolidge what he knew about public land laws, he replied with his characteristic frankness, "Nothing whatever," but added that he did not think he would have much trouble familiarizing himself with the subject. Then began six and one-half years of hair-raising detective work and prosecutions, undertaken in partnership with Senator Pomerene. Records of the work he accomplished would furnish any number of popular "who-done-its." After years of ingenious investigation and tantalizing man-tracking (some witnesses disappeared, even into the farthest reaches of Africa), Roberts recovered for the United States its oil lands. Some of the smaller sharks got away, but the former Secretary of the Interior went to prison. Owen J. Roberts found himself a national figure.

In 1930 President Hoover made one of the wisest decisions in his career when he appointed Roberts to the Supreme Court. The steady, balanced judgment of such a man, in whom the country already had cause for confidence, was never more needed. This was a time of transition in American thinking, and the Supreme Court found itself in the position of umpire between two conflicting modes of thought, conventionally called liberal and conservative. Cases involving government price-fixing, minimum wage laws, the Wagner Labor Relations Act, and the unemployment provisions in the Social Security Act came before it. It was a stirring time for lawyers, an anxious time for the public.

The court when he entered it was divided four to four on fundamental issues. On the conservative side were Justices Van Devanter, McReynolds, Sutherland, and Butler. The liberal wing was led by Justice Brandeis with Chief Justice Hughes and Justices Holmes and Stone in support. Roberts, understanding both sides and respected by both, served as a bridge between them. He was inclined to be conservative himself and was suspicious of Roosevelt's New Deal, but he was too self-critical and honest to "vote his prejudices." What Justice Frankfurter (a most perceptive analyst of Roberts' character) calls his "sensitiveness for those procedural safeguards which are protective of human rights in a civilized society" served as the catalyst which, on important occasions, gave a 5-4 decision in favor of liberal laws.

He was not a crusader. His decisions, on whichever side of the line they fell, right or left, were those of a "lawyer's lawyer," based on solid, individual points and buttressed with common sense. It was the small word *of* that settled the case of *Poe* v. *Seaborn,* and *common parlance* cleared up the Old Colony Railroad case.

Though he was at first unconscious of his determining role in these decisions and their impact on national life, it is certain that, as Erwin N. Griswold, Dean of the Harvard Law School, has put it, he "eased the transition" from old ways to new because of "his way of looking at Law." Justice Roberts helped to tide the nation over what has been called the most far-reaching revolution in its history.

He voted to declare invalid the so-called Minnesota gag law, which would have restricted the freedom of the press. In writing the decision on the Nebbia case, he pronounced what Justice Frankfurter calls "the epitaph on the misconception, which had gained respect from repetition, that legislative price-fixing as such was at least presumptively unconstitutional." His vote saved the Wagner Labor Relations Act.

His wife and his friends helped him to realize the importance of what he was doing. In congratulating him on his appointment to the Supreme Court, Francis Biddle wrote to him on May 13, 1930: "More and more it seems to me that the Supreme Court fundamentally affects the great economic questions of the day. In this sense it shapes thought over long term swings far more than those in executive power."

When in the winter of 1935-1936 he was being talked of for the presidential nomination on the Republican ticket, Mrs. Roberts advised against it. In the Supreme Court, she felt, her husband was in his right place and, through his influence there, exercised greater power in the long run than he could as President.

He was a great stabilizer. He exercised this function directly on the Supreme Court and through that body on the nation. After the shock of Pearl Harbor, President Roosevelt's appointment of Justice Roberts, a lifelong Republican, to head a commission to investigate the disaster at the naval base on Oahu did much to steady an anxious people. Roberts and his staff took evidence on the spot, finding that the commanding officers in Hawaii had been careless but not criminal. The unanimous report of the commissioners was against a court-martial.

During those anxious days in December, 1941, came an example of his consideration for less important people. It came to light in a letter written by the justice to his wife from Hawaii, December 28, 1941: "It looks as if we *might* finish the testimony here this week, but I'm not sure. I would insist on night sessions, if our stenographic staff could stand it; but they can't, nor do I think some of the members could."

Roberts was an excellent presiding officer. Quick to recognize the good in other men's ideas, he had also the administrative wisdom and social tact to see them well carried out. It was during his presidency of the American Philosophical Society that the society's two most important recent projects were successfully launched: the building of a great new library and the partnership with Yale University in the publication of a comprehensive edition of the writings of Benjamin Franklin.

Justice Roberts had an infectious sense of humor, and he loved telling a story against himself. One of his best came from the time he was appointed to defend a man charged with stealing a watch during the Mummers Parade in Philadelphia. He got the man off. As they left the court together and walked down the corridor, Roberts pulled out his watch to see the time.

"Is that the best watch you've got?" asked the man.

"Yes," replied Roberts.

"Well, wait till the next Mummers Parade and I'll get you a better one."

In addition to his Coolidge repertoire, he had a good many stories to tell about the Pennsylvania Dutch, whose blood he shared. One was about a little Pennsylvania Dutch boy who, with his mother, was halted at a railroad crossing while a long, slow freight train rumbled by. When at last the caboose hove in sight, the boy cried, "When the little one comes like so, Ma, it's all."

His appearance was arresting. Writes Robert T. McCracken, "Tall, robust, with strongly cut features, under a great shock of black hair, possessed of a flashing eye, a lightning comprehension and response, and a carrying yet pleasing voice, he was a striking figure in any assembly."

Everyone recognized his attractive public qualities: energy, integrity, precision of thought tempered by common sense, modesty, chivalry, and humor. Behind these were other qualities unseen and unguessed at by most. Justice Frankfurter writes in the *University of Pennsylvania Law Review:* "His was, on the whole, a hidden rather than an obvious nature—hidden, that is, from the public view. His loyalties were deep, as was his devotion to his convictions. Both were phases of an uncompromising honesty. They constituted the most guarded qualities of his personality, and he would not vulgarize them by public manifestation."

When at the age of seventy he retired from the Supreme Court, his mail was flooded, as it had been on his appointment, but this time with letters welcoming him back to private life. Lewis M. Stevens wrote, "It is good to think of you breezing down Fifteenth Street from Delancey in the early morning, amidst the smoke and sparks of a briar pipe."

He had not retired to rest, however. In no time at all he was deep in a hundred affairs, chief among which were the farm in Chester County and the cause of world peace. When he became Dean of the University of Pennsylvania Law School, he received a delightful letter from Harold L. Ickes: "I have come to the conclusion," it ran, "that you are the most 'un-inactive' person within my knowledge. When you haven't been passing recommendations for medals and citations, you have been helping to organize a United States of the World, or actively advocating universal military service. All this, I suppose, in addition to farming. Now here you take on the University of Pennsylvania Law School."

Much of his time was taken up with the cause of Atlantic Union, which he defined in 1949 as "a federal union of democracies and the progressive inclusion of other nations as their people adjust their governments to perpetuate liberty under law." He was co-author with Clarence Streit of *The New Federalist* and contributing editor of *Freedom & Union*. He devoted his clear, terse, pungent English style to advocating what he thought to be the best way of fighting atheistic communism: the union of the Free World.

To those who inveighed against any diminution of national sovereignty he replied: "We have carried over into the relations of nations the concept of absolute monarchy. Though we are a democracy, we have arrogated to ourselves collectively as a nation the independence of an absolute monarch."

Clarence Streit wrote in the *University of Pennsylvania Law Review*, "I believe that history will find that General Marshall was right when he gave first importance to what Justice Roberts did for Atlantic Union."

The *London Observer* had this to say of Justice Roberts at the age of seventy-five: "Physically, with his broad and craggy features, and spiritually, in his disciplined idealism, he is the sort of American who makes one remember that even elderly Americans live in a young country."

Early in 1955 his great energies came to an end. He suffered a heart attack. When they took him to the hospital, he was incredulous. "There *can't* be anything the matter with me," he kept saying. When at length the truth dawned on him, he took it gamely and made one last wager with himself: he would go back to the Chester County farm or die in the attempt. When the exhausting journey was completed and they carried him through the doorway at Bryncoed, his face lit up with something of the old compelling smile as he said, "Well, I made it."

He died a few days later, May 17, 1955—two weeks and a day after passing his eightieth birthday.

In an address on the tercentenary of William Penn's birth, Justice Roberts said of the Commonwealth's founder:

I think of him as the busiest man of his time. To a strong and adequate physique he added a virile and fertile mind and a deep spiritual nature. He was a man of scholarly attainment, of good birth, and of pleasing personality. Throughout his life his spirit seems to have driven him to exercise all his faculties to the limit.

In thus describing William Penn, Owen J. Roberts painted his own best portrait.

32   *Pittsburgh*

Pittsburgh was born in war, bred in industrial conflict, and brought recently to maturity in a battle for survival that has won the admiration of the world.

To say that citizens of the great Steel City are proud of their civic brawn is to state the obvious. To call them materialistic is, however, another matter. If Pittsburgh is materialistic, it is not because it has no soul but because it is a town of producers, as it has been from the days when James O'Hara set up his first "glass manufactory" down to the latest Westinghouse atomic energy plant.

Pittsburghers are proud of their origins, as Philadelphians are of theirs, but in a different way. Pittsburghers had no William Penn to lay out their city for them and pray over it. The pride of Pittsburghers is in the possession of the Forks of the Ohio, which during the eighteenth century was one of the pivots in a war that decided the fate of the continent.

Point State Park is their chief monument to this distant past. Its thirty-six acres are set on a tip of land that looks like a spearhead, located at the point where the Allegheny River from upstate New York joins the Monongahela River from West Virginia to produce the Ohio—parent stream of the Mississippi, the Mother of Waters. Here was once the junction of Indian trails and canoe routes from north, south, east, and west. If a fort were set up here, the French reasoned, and supported by a string of smaller forts from Lake Erie south to Redstone on the Monongahela, it would block the way of Pennsylvania's aggressive Indian traders and preserve the interior of the continent for King Louis.

The dominating situation of Point Park brings vividly to mind the nine years of world crisis during which the Forks of the Ohio played a key role. To forestall French plans to occupy the Forks, a body of Virginians arrived to build a fort there for the British. A covering force was led by young Colonel George Washington, who only a few months before had nearly lost his life nearby in the wintry Allegheny River. Work on the British fort was suddenly stopped by the arrival of a superior French force, which drove out the Virginians and erected the powerful Fort Duquesne. Colonel Washington's subsequent skirmish at Jumonville Glenn and his surrender at Fort Necessity provided the American overture to the Seven Years' (i.e., French and Indian) War.

The British reply was the Braddock expedition, which reaching a point halfway between the present McKeesport and Pittsburgh's Golden Triangle, suffered the greatest debacle in American military history. Three years later the overconfident Major Grant with his bagpipers skirled themselves into disaster at what is now known as Grant's Hill. But that defeat was of little consequence to General Forbes, who proceeded to march his overwhelming forces down to the Point, where he found a smoking ruin, the French having destroyed Fort Duquesne and departed. Forbes built Fort Pitt to hold the Forks for the British.

During Pontiac's War the Indians, disputing the British claim to the western lands, as they had earlier disputed the French, attempted to capture Fort Pitt. Colonel Henry Bouquet with his relieving army won the two-day Battle of Bushy Run and made sure that the Forks of the Ohio should remain an Anglo-Saxon gateway to the west.

Forty years later, in 1803, Thaddeus M. Harris found the situation of Pittsburgh "so commanding that it has been emphatically called 'the key to the Western Territory.'" The town itself, however, during the first century of its existence was less impressive than the site, and the praise it received was mostly of a statistical kind. Thaddeus Harris, commenting on its rapid increase in population, observed that it had three churches, forty-nine stores, and "upwards of four hundred houses, several of them large and handsomely built of brick."

Today when Pittsburghers look back over their city's two centuries, they are reminded by street names of the Braddock, Forbes, and Bouquet expeditions. They like also to remember James O'Hara, who established the first glass factory there and whose granddaughter, Mary Schenley, gave the city its first park, the beautiful Schenley Park. They like to conjure up pictures (as evidenced in *A Pittsburgh Album, 1758-1958*) of a Conestoga wagon carrying settlers through Pittsburgh to the West; the crowd in 1852 welcoming the first through train from the east on the tracks of the Ohio and Pennsylvania Railroad, now the Pennsylvania; the Rodman gun, produced during the Civil War by the C. Knapp Foundry, now Mackintosh-Hemphill; the H. C. Frick and Company coke ovens; the George Westinghouse air brake; George W. Ferris's wheel, designed for the Columbian Exhibition at Chicago in 1893, which was 250 feet high and had 36 coaches carrying 38 persons each; shipping on the Monongahela; portraits of Andrew Carnegie, Andrew Mellon, and Richard King Mellon; and of course the University of Pittsburgh's Cathedral of Learning, in which Pittsburghers have good reason to take pride, not only because of the beauty of its aspiring Gothic lines, but also because it is really their own possession. "In the campaign of 1925," writes Arthur M. Young in *The Voice That Speaketh Clear,* "seventeen thousand people and almost a hundred thousand school children contributed to the proposed multimillion-dollar structure which was to tower 535 feet into the air in 42 stories."

During the nineteenth and twentieth centuries Pittsburgh's industrial development turned the frontier outpost into what Frank C. Harper calls exultantly the "Forge of the Universe." Of its "phenomenal industrial expansion," he writes that "for two or three decades after the discovery of oil at Titusville, Pittsburgh was the greatest oil center in the world with fifty-eight refineries," and "in the 1870's and 1880's Pittsburgh was the greatest glass manufacturing center in the world with 73 factories."

Today its greatest strength is in steel. It produces one-fifth of all the steel made in the United States. As the folksong says:

> Pittsburgh is a great old town,
> Made of steel from McKeesport down.

"Pittsburghers are seldom zealots about anything but production," writes George Swetnam in *Where Else but Pittsburgh?* His description of the city at night is a classic of its kind:

It lies low down in a hollow of encompassing hills, gleaming with a thousand points of light, which are reflected from the rivers. . . .

Around the city's edge, and on the sides of the hills which encircle it like a gloomy amphitheatre, their outline rising darkly against the sky, through numberless apertures, fiery lights stream forth, looking angrily and fiercely up toward the heavens while over these settles a heavy pall of smoke. It is as though one had reached the outer edge of the infernal regions, and saw before him the great furnace of Pandemonium with all the lids lifted.

Smoke formerly blackened the sky at Pittsburgh, as well as the sidewalks and the walls of the buildings, and at the same time half-choked the inhabitants. Today the sun shines again on the city, as it did before Andrew Carnegie's day. Sunlight is reflected from the walls and windows of shiny skyscrapers. The transformation of the Smoky City into a thing of beauty is one of the most heartening stories of modern times.

The fact is that Pittsburgh's greatest glory is not in her steel inventory but in the spirit of her people. They possess great reserves, not only of strength and stamina, but also of wisdom, imagination, and beauty. Giving practical effect to these qualities is a new-found social consciousness and civic solidarity that have brought an all but miraculous renaissance to a city which twenty-five years ago seemed headed for hopeless decline.

The Second World War brought Pittsburgh a resurgence of prosperity, but it was known to be only temporary. *The Wall Street Journal* gave the city Class D rating, which as George Swetnam observes, meant "on the skids." Hearing talk about refurbishing the city, the architect Frank Lloyd Wright observed, "It would be cheaper to abandon Pittsburgh than to try to make it beautiful." High taxes, labor troubles, a tired and worn-out business district, smoke, flood, slums, and antiquated roadways accounted for these adverse judgments. It was nationally known that Pittsburgh was a sad case. She illustrated only too clearly, it seemed, the inescapable laws of urban obsolescence in a modern, industrialized society.

But the image of Pittsburgh has changed. One of the comforts of man in this revolutionary age of the atom and automation is the knowledge that *there will always be a Pittsburgh*. The city awoke to the danger not only to herself but to all industrial communities and met it. Her renaissance, as it nears completion, can best be likened to a golden-winged Phoenix rising from its own smoke and ashes. With a spurt of her old-time jauntiness she set out to make herself the nation's exemplar of industrial urban recovery and at the same time "the most beautiful city in the country." She was right about the first project. Who shall say she may not someday prove to have been right about the second?

Under the lead of Richard K. Mellon, nephew of Andrew Mellon, and with the support of Mayor David L. Lawrence, there came into being a great experiment in civic renewal which William Penn would surely have called holy.

In 1943 the Allegheny Conference on Community Development was organized, receiving in 1944 a state charter. Its purpose, as stated in a public report in 1956, was to make "a comprehensive unified plan for the region as a whole" and provide "civic leadership to carry it forward." It set in motion a complex of civic authorities and commissions that have torn down, dug up, refurbished, rearranged, rebuilt, or turned into parks and parkways the business center as well as certain other sections of Pittsburgh and its environs. They have done it so successfully as to bring back into the city both capital and suburbanites and at the same time to dazzle plane travelers by the sight of the flashing blue-and-gold skyscrapers turning their faces toward Point State Park and the historic river junction.

To serve its general objective of "economic growth and urban renewal," the Allegheny Conference undertook many individual projects, among which were: cleaner air, clean rivers and streams, flood prevention, highway improvements, more and better housing, ample parking facilities, adequate airports, expanded health and welfare facilities, greater educational opportunities, increased educational resources, and enriched cultural opportunities.

> Pittsburgh is a hilly old town;
> The roads and streets go up and down.

The city is still a fighting community, and its citizens, whether Democrats or Republicans, believe fervently in free enterprise—with, of course, a little government support in the right places.

The renewal of Gateway Center (business heart of the city and foremost of the many sections being rehabilitated) is a good example of the Pittsburgh way of doing things. The Urban Redevelopment Authority (created in 1946), whose members are appointed by the mayor, acquired fifty-six acres of downtown land, transferred them to the Equitable Life Assurance Company at cost, and left the redevelopment to Equitable—subject to certain land-use controls. The success was astounding. A bevy of gay and colorful skyscrapers, their steel frames resplendent in glass and aluminum, had by 1956 increased the Golden Triangle's rental office space by a million square feet.

The importance of Pittsburgh's achievement can hardly be exaggerated. *Fortune* magazine in February, 1947, saw in Pittsburgh's experiment "the test of industrialism everywhere to renew itself." Looking back fourteen years later, Governor David L. Lawrence (whose election to the governorship of Pennsylvania was largely on the strength of his Pittsburgh achievement) could justly say that "Pittsburgh's dramatic Gateway Center Program was the forerunner of urban development work, not alone in Pennsylvania but throughout the nation."

So it has come about that Pittsburgh—cocky, philanthropic, unpredictable, unbeatable Pittsburgh—has given the industrialized American nation a key to the continued pursuit of happiness even in this revolutionary age.

33 *Philadelphia*

"The Quaker City," "the Athens of America," "the City of Brotherly Love," "Penn's green country town"—these are some of the
titles that have been given to the great industrial complex, with
its more than two million inhabitants, which spreads west from
the Delaware River to beyond the Schuylkill and south from
Manayunk and Tacony to the junction of the rivers at Tinicum.

Old Philadelphia, the original Quaker city, stands side by side with New Philadelphia, the commercial metropolis; and the new takes pride in the old. This is a city of paradoxes. "Philadelphia was always the city with a country heart," wrote Cornelius Weygandt in *Philadelphia Folks*. No less true is the statement by a writer in *Historic Philadelphia* that the city "never had the characteristics of a frontier town." In that paradox lies the secret of the best loved (if not always the most admired) city in the United States.

William Penn desired that it should always remain a "green country town," and he took steps to keep it so. His plans for the city made room for five squares. The largest of these, covering ten acres, is now occupied by the City Hall. The others, each of eight acres, are still open: Franklin Square, Logan Square, Rittenhouse Square, and Washington Square. Penn desired also that every house be set in a good-sized lot, with land around it for gardens and trees. That his wishes have not been forgotten is attested by Philadelphia's tree-lined streets, her many parks, and the neighborhood garden clubs throughout the city. It is true that in 1782 the corporation of Philadelphia ordered all trees cut down because they obstructed "prospect and passage"; but it is also true that the law was repealed before too much damage was done.

About 1731 John Bartram planted his Garden of Delight on the banks of the Schuylkill and kept on adding to it for forty years. The pleasure he provided there for himself and his friends from Philadelphia—and indeed from all parts of the world—has continued to be enjoyed for more than two centuries. He grew plants that he had gathered himself on travels from Florida to Canada, and he grew other plants that friends sent him from many lands across the seas. He had a "green thumb": everything grew for him. John Faris writes in *Old Gardens in and about Philadelphia:* "Once he returned from a trip into Delaware with a cypress riding-whip. This he placed in the ground. It became a tree, one hundred and fifty feet high, and eight feet in diameter." His "Dark Walk" was shadowed by many species of oak, and he had also many species of boxwood. Among his treasures were the silver-bell tree, the red buckeye, the fringe-tree, the Kentucky coffee-tree, and a gingko tree from Japan.

At Stenton, John Bartram's friend James Logan—president of

the Council, chief justice, translator of Cicero's *Cato major* or *de Senectute* ("Of Old Age")—laid out and tended an elaborate garden. The same fashion swept the suburban estates. In the nineteenth century a number of these gardens on both banks of the Schuylkill were purchased by the city and combined into what is now Fairmount Park. There, with the aid of a French gardener, Robert Morris, "Financier of the Revolution," had established the gardens of Vineyard Hill (The Hills), later named Lemon Hill by Henry Pratt. Among other estates drawn into the park were John Penn's Solitude, with its secret passageways running from the house out under the garden to the river and the hills; John MacPherson's Clunie, which John Adams called "the most elegant seat in Pennsylvania"; Woodford, established by William Coleman, first president of the Library Company of Philadelphia; Joseph Galloway's Ormiston, set on the edge of a glen; William Peters' (and after him his son, Judge Richard Peters') Belmont, so named because of its situation on a 243-foot eminence overlooking the Schuylkill River. To the cultivated color pattern of these lawns and flower beds and blossom trees was added the astonishing valley of the dark and elfish Wissahickon, with its miles of "wild rock garden" and the Hermit's Glen where Johannes Kelpius wrote his songs and taught his school.

When the City of Philadelphia acquired, piece by piece, these sophisticated private gardens and joined them to the broken natural grandeur of the Wissahickon, she became possessor of the loveliest of city parks, while at the same time performing an act of piety to the memory of William Penn by providing the city with the thing he treasured most: "a Sweet and Natural Retreat from Noise and Talk, [allowing] opportunity for Reflection."

"Urban yet Sylvan," wrote Whittier in praise of Philadelphia in the nineteenth century, and the words are still apt in the twentieth. Frank Brookhouser in *Our Philadelphia* calls it admiringly "the biggest small town in the world." Francis Daniel Pastorius used to get lost in the woods between his riverbank cave and the house of his Dutch baker, Bom, at the corner of Third and Chestnut streets. Yet this young German who dwelt in a cave was by no means a frontiersman,—"one who lives beyond the borders of civilization." He brought civilization with him. His cave contained trunks full of books, and he dined frequently with William Penn, who loved to talk with him about literature and religion. Pastorius, James Logan, and not a few others like them planted strong intellectual roots in the colony. Not only was Philadelphia the first planned city in the country; it was also the first city of broad culture where men of European learning easily found congenial company.

If Philadelphia is, as Dr. Cornelius Weygandt has suggested, "the most American city from Portland to Los Angeles," it is not chiefly because of her trees and parks, nor because of the lead she once gave to American science and art. It is rather because of her wealth of quiet, cultured, middle-class people, religious but not bigoted, neither reforming zealots nor blind reactionaries, who represent the least publicized but most influential element in the American population.

Those were the people who in 1669 erected Gloria Dei (Old Swedes Church). They were the people who organized Christ Church, Episcopal, in 1695 and began construction in 1727 on the present church building on Second Street near Market, a building which George B. Tatum in *Penn's Great Town* finds to be "one of the handsomest and certainly one of the most elaborate Palladian churches in America."

They were the people who in 1731 watched the laying of the cornerstone of the State House, now Independence Hall. In the park behind it on July 8, 1776, four days after the signing, they heard the reading of the Declaration of Independence. They amused themselves by attending the Southwark Theater (first theater in America, erected in 1766) at the corner of South and Apollo streets, or by watching displays of horsemanship and acrobatics at Rickett's Circus. They took their children to see Charles Willson Peale's museum, the "Repository for Natural Curiosities," in a hall provided by the American Philosophical Society. They borrowed books from the Library Company, and they polished their manners by attending the dancing assemblies held every two weeks from January to May. Between the years 1790 and 1800, when Philadelphia was the capital of the United States, they sent representatives to Congress Hall, which adjoined the State House. During that decade the Bill of Rights was added to the Constitution, and Vermont, Kentucky, and Tennessee were added to the Union.

It was a city of merchants and scholars, artists and artisans. It was the city of James Logan, classicist and statesman, who made himself a fortune in the Indian trade. It was the city of David Rittenhouse, clockmaker and astronomer, who improved the telescope and served as director of the Mint. Above all, it was the city of middle-class Benjamin Franklin, creator of Poor Richard, inventor of the harmonica, founder of the American Philosophical Society, who played with kites and brought electricity (if not philosophy) down out of heaven to dwell among men.

In material wealth and population growth the city made a quick start and for many years maintained its lead. Dr. William E. Lingelbach writes, "Although founded sixty years after New York and half a century after Boston, it soon outstripped them, and became the first city of the American Colonies, with a population of forty thousand . . . at the beginning of the Revolution."

Travelers found there the best accommodations in America. Philadelphia's inns and taverns were famous, especially the Indian Queen, Oellers, and the City Tavern. It is fitting that, after the recent removal of the "Chinese Wall" (bearing the Pennsylvania Railroad tracks west from the old Broad Street Station), there should have risen in its place a handsome array of business offices and, topping them all, the dazzling twenty-two-storied Sheraton Hotel with its thousand rooms.

Before the Erie Canal was opened, giving the port of New York access through the Mohawk Gateway to the interior of the continent, Philadelphia was the commercial leader of the country. She still ranks high: fourth in shipping, fourth in manufacturing. It has been calculated that eighty-seven per cent of all categories of manufacturing are represented here. She is famous, among other things, for her textile mills, producing carpets, rugs, and clothing; for her coal wharves and sugar refineries, her metal products, her printing and publishing houses, the fabulous Cramp Shipyards, and the Baldwin Locomotive Works.

There is an immense robustness in Philadelphia. In size of population she yields among American cities only to New York, Chicago, and Los Angeles; in port tonnage, to New York, Houston, and New Orleans; and in historic interest, to none. In this last respect, Boston alone vies with her.

Philadelphia does not shout her quality from the housetops, but she is not unaware of it. Among her citizens there is a pride in her past and a pride approaching exultation in her future. Yet

Philadelphians have too strong a sense of humor to be smug. They enjoy jokes on themselves and their esteemed ancestors. They laugh and bear no resentment when others poke fun at their city—incurring thereby in these self-advertising days some misunderstanding of their quality. A vaudeville gag once went the rounds about Philadelphia restaurants failing to put snails on the menu simply because they could not catch them. The truth is (though Philadelphians do not talk much about this) that their street traffic is so fast it has been known to shock visitors from New York.

Philadelphians are not contemptuous of the old-fashioned traditions of good breeding. Their courtesy is warm but unobtrusive, their patience strong but not everlasting. Violate their sense of fair play—especially in dealings with subordinates—and you awake a tartar. They are individualists who have caught the spirit of William Penn in that they are tolerant of other people's individualities. If they seem leisurely, it is not because they are inactive but because they do not live always in fear of someone's overtaking them.

Above all, Philadelphians have, as Mayor Dilworth once said, "a fierce loyalty" to their city, a determination to keep it not only a business and administrative center but also an "intellectual market place" and "a preserver of tradition where historical inheritance is nurtured." The speed and quality of Philadelphia's renaissance attests the truth of his words.

It all began in 1947 as a revolt by some returned service men after World War II—a revolt against Philadelphia's time-honored machine government. Richardson Dilworth (a marine) and Joseph S. Clark, together with Robert K. Sawyer, set out to enlist independent voters of both parties in an attempt to rid the city of the two adjectives Lincoln Steffens had pinned on it when he called it "corrupt and contented." In 1947 Dilworth ran unsuccessfully for mayor, but Clark was elected city controller. In 1951 the Philadelphia Charter, streamlining the city government, was put through and next year Joseph Clark took office as the first mayor under its terms. Dilworth at the same time became district attorney. His subsequent years in the mayor's office, when added to those of Joseph Clark, produced a decade of such profound changes in Philadelphia as had not been seen since 1682–1683, when Penn superintended the first year's growth of his city.

Meanwhile the war, which had raised the specter of destruction by air raids, had created a national movement for the preservation of historic buildings. Dr. William E. Lingelbach, Professor Emeritus of History at the University of Pennsylvania and Editor and Librarian of the American Philosophical Society, became chairman of the Pennsylvania Committee on the Conservation of Cultural Resources, With Dr. S. K. Stevens, the State Historian, as secretary. Together they soon realized that the principal area for the conservation of cultural resources in Pennsylvania was in Philadelphia where neglect and the encroachment of city slums was threatening the very existence of the Cradle of Liberty. Dr. Stevens took the initiative in getting the co-operation of the federal government, without whose help the demolition of buildings on any large scale in downtown Philadelphia and the restoration of historic properties would have been impossible.

Happily Philadelphia's patriotic and historical societies had also been deeply aroused during the war. The Fairmount Park Art Association, Sons of the Revolution, Society for the Preservation of Historic Landmarks, and others met in the Hall of the American Philosophical Society in 1942 and organized the Independence Hall Association with Judge Edwin O. Lewis as chairman. Under his leadership public opinion was gradually aroused. Two projects developed. One was the construction by the Commonwealth of a mall or parkway leading to Independence Hall so that, the buildings that formerly surrounded it having been removed, the nation's foremost historic shrine might be seen in its proper proportions and full beauty.

The second project was the establishment, by the federal government, of Independence National Historical Park "for the purpose," as Public Law 795, 80th Congress, reads, "of preserving for the benefit of the American people . . . certain historical structures and properties of outstanding national significance located in Philadelphia, Pennsylvania, and associated with the American Revolution and the founding and growth of the United States. . . ."

The American Philosophical Society ("oldest scientific and learned society in the country" and symbol of her intellectual life as Independence Hall is of her political life) contributed to the rehabilitation program a great new library, Library Hall, on the site once occupied by Benjamin Franklin's Library Company at the corner of Chestnut and Library streets and in close proximity to Independence Hall and its own Philosophical Hall on Independence Square.

The front of Library Hall is Georgian, conforming with William Thornton's design for the old Library Hall built by Franklin and friends for the Philadelphia Library Company in 1790. The interior is modern, fire-proof, dust-proof, air-conditioned. All in all it is a symbol, in Dr. Lingelbach's words, of "Franklin's intuitive respect for the dynamic force of *ideas* and the records of civilization, preserved in libraries and archives."

There they stand—Independence Hall, Philosophical Hall, Library Hall, and a hundred other historic sites and buildings in Old Philadelphia—a joint memorial to the Holy Experiment in which William Penn planted the seed of a nation.

And thou, Philadelphia, the virgin settlement of this province, named before thou wert born, what love, what care, what service and what travail has there been to bring thee forth and preserve thee from such as would abuse and defile thee. . . . My soul prays to God for thee that thou mayest stand in the day of trial, that thy children may be blest of the Lord, and thy people saved by His power.

WILLIAM PENN, 1684

Bibliography—for the General Reader

The second edition of the *Bibliography of Pennsylvania History,* published by the Pennsylvania Historical and Museum Commission in 1957, runs to 709 pages without the index. A great deal more has been written about Pennsylvania since that time. The present short list attempts no more than to provide a not-too-difficult introduction to the vast body of literature pertaining to Penn's initial experiment and all that came out of it.

Chapter 1. *Three Rivers*

Davis, William Morris. "The Rivers and Valleys of Pennsylvania," *National Geographic Magazine,* v. 1 (1889).

Harshberger, John W. "Nature and Man in the Pocono Mountain Region, Pennsylvania," *Geographical Society of Philadelphia Bulletin,* v. 13, No. 2 (April, 1915).

Keir, R. Malcolm. "Causes for the Growth of Philadelphia as an Industrial Center," *Geographical Society of Philadelphia Bulletin,* v. 13, No. 3 (July, 1915).

Martin, Helen M. *"Ne-Saw-je-won," as the Ottawas Say: A Tale of the Waters that Run down from Lake Superior to the Sea* (Cleveland, 1939).

Murphy, Raymond E., and Marion. *Pennsylvania: A Regional Geography* (Harrisburg, 1937).

Myers, Richmond E. *The Long Crooked River* (*the Susquehanna*) (Boston, 1949).

Chapter 2. *"We Came out of This Ground"*

McNickle, D'Arcy. *They Came Here First: The Epic of the American Indian* (Philadelphia, 1949).

Penn, William. "Letter . . . to the Free Society of Traders, 1683," *Narratives of Early Pennsylvania . . .,* Albert Cook Myers, ed. (New York, 1912).

Smith, Capt. John. *A Map of Virginia: With a Description of the Country . . .,* in *Narratives of Early Virginia 1606-1625,* Lyon Gardiner Tyler, ed. (New York, 1952).

Speck, Frank G. *The Celestial Bear Comes Down to Earth* (Reading, Pa., 1945).

Speck, Frank G. *The Delaware Indian Big House Ceremony* (Harrisburg, 1931).

Wallace, Paul A. W. *Indians in Pennsylvania* (Harrisburg, 1961).

Chapter 3.   Enter the European

Hale, Nathaniel C. *Pelts and Palisades: The Story of Fur and the Rivalry for Pelts in Early America* (Richmond, Va., 1959).

Johnson, Amandus. *The Instruction for John Printz Governor of New Sweden* (Philadelphia, 1930).

Louhi, E. A. *The Delaware Finns: The First Permanent Settlement in Pennsylvania . . .* (New York, 1925).

Sawyer, William E. *The First Hundred Years of Delaware County* (Chester, Pa., 1957).

Weslager, C. A. "Log Houses in Pennsylvania During the Seventeenth Century," *Pennsylvania History,* v. 22, No. 3 (July, 1955).

Chapter 4.   The Beaver Wars

Benson, Evelyn A. *The Story of the Susquehannocks* (Lancaster, 1958).

Hale, Horatio, ed. *The Iroquois Book of Rites* (Philadelphia, 1883).

Hunt, George. *The Wars of the Iroquois: A Study in Intertribal Trade Relations* (Madison, Wis., 1960).

Wallace, Paul A. W. *Indians in Pennsylvania* (Harrisburg, 1961).

Wallace, Paul A. W. *The White Roots of Peace* (Philadelphia, 1946).

Chapter 5.   William Penn

Comfort, William Wistar. *William Penn, 1644-1718. A Tercentenary Estimate* (Philadelphia, 1944).

Dobrée, Bonamy. *William Penn, Quaker and Pioneer* (New York, 1932).

Dolson, Hildegarde. *William Penn: Quaker Hero* (New York, 1961).

Peare, Catherine Owens. *William Penn: A Biography* (Philadelphia, 1957).

Remember William Penn, 1644-1944: A Tercentenary Memorial (Harrisburg, 1945).

Tolles, Frederick B., and Alderfer, E. Gordon, eds. *The Witness of William Penn* (New York, 1957).

Chapter 6.   *The Holy Experiment*

Beatty, Edward Corbyn Obert. *William Penn as Social Philosopher* (New York, 1939).
Janney, Samuel M. *The Life of William Penn* (Philadelphia, 1852).
Penn, William. *Some Fruits of Solitude in Reflections and Maxims,* and *More Fruits of Solitude . . .,* reprinted in *Remember William Penn* (Harrisburg, 1945).
Tributes to William Penn: A Tercentenary Record 1644-1944 (Harrisburg, 1946).
Vulliamy, C. E. *William Penn* (New York, 1934).

Chapter 7.   *Peace without Pacifism*

Drinker, Sophie Hutchinson. *Hannah Penn and the Proprietorship of Pennsylvania* (Philadelphia, 1958).
Tolles, Frederick B. *James Logan and the Culture of Provincial America* (Boston, 1957).
Tolles, Frederick B. *Quakers and the Atlantic Culture* (New York, 1960).

Chapter 8.   *The Melting Pot*

Bressler, Leo A. "Agriculture among the Germans in Pennsylvania During the Eighteenth Century," *Pennsylvania History,* v. 22, No. 2 (April, 1955).
Crary, Catherine S. "The Humble Immigrant and the American Dream: Some Case Histories, 1746-1776," *Mississippi Valley Historical Review,* v. 46, No. 1 (June, 1959).
Dodd, A. H. *The Character of Early Welsh Emigration to the United States* (Cardiff, Wales, 1953).
Dunaway, Wayland Fuller. "The English Settlers in Colonial Pennsylvania," *Pennsylvania Magazine of History and Biography,* v. 52 (1928).
Dunaway, Wayland Fuller. "The French Racial Strain in Colonial Pennsylvania," *Pennsylvania Magazine of History and Biography,* v. 53 (1929).
Dunaway, Wayland Fuller. *The Scotch-Irish of Colonial Pennsylvania* (Chapel Hill, N. C., 1944).
Jenkins, Howard M. "The Welsh Settlement at Gwynedd," *Pennsylvania Magazine of History and Biography,* v. 8 (1884).
Klees, Fredric. *The Pennsylvania Dutch* (New York, 1950).
Wood, Ralph, ed. *The Pennsylvania Germans* (Princeton, 1942).

306 PENNSYLVANIA

Chapter 9.   *The Capital and the Frontier*

Bridenbaugh, Carl. *Rebels and Gentlemen* (New York, 1942).

Rothermund, Dietmar. *The Layman's Progress: Religious and Political Experience in Colonial Pennsylvania 1740-1770* (Philadelphia, 1961).

Stevens, Sylvester K. *Pennsylvania, the Keystone State,* v. 1 (New York, 1956).

Wainwright, Nicholas B. *George Croghan, Wilderness Diplomat* (Chapel Hill, N. C., 1959).

Wallace, Anthony F. C. *King of the Delawares, Teedyuscung, 1700-1763* (Philadelphia, 1949).

Chapter 10.   *George Washington Wins His Spurs*

Cleland, Hugh. *George Washington in the Ohio Country* (Pittsburgh, 1955).

Darlington, William M., ed. *Christopher Gist's Journals* (Pittsburgh, 1893).

Freeman, Douglas Southall. *George Washington: A Biography,* v. 1 (New York, 1948).

Wallace, Paul A. W. "George Washington's Route from Franklin to Fort Le Boeuf, 1753," *Pennsylvania History,* v. 27, No. 4 (October, 1961).

Chapter 11.   *The Fight for the Forks*

Gipson, Lawrence Henry. "The Disaster at the Monongahela," Chapter 4 of *The Great War for the Empire: The Years of Defeat* (v. 6 [New York, 1946] of *The British Empire before the American Revolution*).

Hunter, William A. *Forts on the Pennsylvania Frontier, 1753-1758* (Harrisburg, 1960).

Hunter, William A. "Victory at Kittanning," *Pennsylvania History,* v. 23, No. 3 (July, 1956).

Wallace, Paul A. W. *Conrad Weiser, Friend of Colonist and Mohawk* (Philadelphia, 1945).

Chapter 12.   *Western Pennsylvania*

Buck, Solon J., and Elizabeth Hawthorn. *The Planting of Civilization in Western Pennsylvania* (Pittsburgh, 1939).

Peckham, Howard H. *Pontiac and the Indian Uprising* (Princeton, 1947).

Silver, James W., ed. "Frontier Days: An Autobiographical Sketch of Chauncey Brockway," *Pennsylvania History,* v. 25, No. 2 (April, 1958).
Theiss, Lewis E. "The Pioneer and the Forest," *Pennsylvania History,* v. 23, No. 4 (October, 1956).

Chapter 13.   *1776 and What Came of It*

Brunhouse, Robert L. *The Counter-Revolution in Pennsylvania 1776-1790* (Harrisburg, 1942).
Gipson, Lawrence H. *The Coming of the Revolution 1763-1775* (New York, 1954).
Muhlenberg, Henry A. *The Life of Major-General Peter Muhlenberg* (Philadelphia, 1849).
Selsam, J. Paul. *The Pennsylvania Constitution of 1776: A Study in Revolutionary Democracy* (Philadelphia, 1936).
Stevens, Sylvester K. "William Penn," *American Heritage,* v. 3, No. 1 (Fall, 1951).
Stillé, Charles J. *Major-General Anthony Wayne and the Pennsylvania Line in the Continental Army* (Philadelphia, 1893).
Wallace, Paul A. W. *The Muhlenbergs of Pennsylvania* (Philadelphia, 1950).
Wildes, Harry E. *Anthony Wayne, Trouble Shooter of the American Revolution* (New York, 1941).

Chapter 14.   *Constitutional Conventions: Federal and State*

McDonald, Forrest. *We, the People. The Economic Origins of the Constitution* (Chicago, 1958).
McMaster, John B., and Stone, Frederick D. *Pennsylvania and the Federal Constitution* (Philadelphia, 1888).
Stevens, Sylvester K. *Pennsylvania, the Keystone State,* v. 2, *Documentary* (New York, 1956).
Van Doren, Carl. *The Great Rehearsal* (New York, 1948).

Chapter 15.   *Some Angle Shots of Benjamin Franklin*

Franklin, Benjamin. "Remarks Concerning the Savages of North America," *Benjamin Franklin: Representative Selections,* Chester E. Jorgenson and Frank Luther Mott, eds. (New York, 1962).
Nolan, J. Bennett. *General Benjamin Franklin: The Military Career of a Philosopher* (Philadelphia, 1936).
Van Doren, Carl. *Benjamin Franklin* (New York, 1938).

Chapter 16. *Robin Hood Was at Home Here*

Kinietz, Elenore Loring. "Robin Hood in Pennsylvania," *Keystone Folklore Quarterly,* v. 2, No. 3 (Fall, 1957).

McReynolds, George, ed. *The Doan Outlaws; or Bucks County Cowboys in the Revolution* (Doylestown, Pa., 1897).

The New Doane Book: Bucks County's Bandittories of the Revolution (Doylestown, Pa., 1952).

"Reminiscences of the Robber Lewis," *Notes and Queries,* Third Series, v. 1, page 337.

Sharpe, J. W. "Lewis, the Robber and Outlaw," *Kittochtinny Historical Society* (1901).

Chapter 17. *Some Pennsylvania Utopias*

Bestor, Arthur Eugene. *Backwoods Utopias* (Philadelphia, 1950).

Duss, John S. *The Harmonists. A Personal Story* (Harrisburg, 1943).

Hinds, William Alfred. *American Communities* (New York, 1961).

Klein, Walter C. *Johann Conrad Beissel, Mystic and Martinet* (Philadelphia, 1942).

Shepard, Odell. "Utopias in America," *The American Story,* Earl Schenck Miers, ed. (New York, 1956).

Wallace, Paul A. W. *Conrad Weiser, Friend of Colonist and Mohawk* (Philadelphia, 1945).

Chapter 18. *The Moravian Indian Mission*

Davis, Rose M. " 'The Tents of Grace' in Longfellow's *Evangeline:* Their History and Fate," *Pennsylvania History,* v. 18, No. 4 (October, 1951).

De Schweinitz, Edmund. *David Zeisberger, the Western Pioneer and Apostle of the Indians* (Philadelphia, 1870).

Gray, Elma E., and Leslie R. *Wilderness Christians: The Moravian Mission to the Delaware Indians* (Ithaca, N. Y., 1956).

Hamilton, Kenneth Gardiner. *John Ettwein and the Moravian Church During the Revolutionary Period* (Bethlehem, 1940).

Smith, DeCost. *Martyrs of the Oblong and Little Nine* (Caldwell, Idaho, 1948).

Wallace, Paul A. W. *Thirty Thousand Miles with John Heckewelder* (Philadelphia, 1958).

Chapter 19. *The Growth of Political Parties*

Baldwin, Leland D. *Whiskey Rebels: The Story of a Frontier Uprising* (Pittsburgh, 1939).

Buck, Solon J., and Elizabeth Hawthorn. *The Planting of Civilization in Western Pennsylvania* (Pittsburgh, 1939).

Higginbotham, Sanford M. *The Keystone in the Democratic Arch: Pennsylvania Politics 1800-1816* (Harrisburg, 1952).

Rosenberg, Max. *The Building of Perry's Fleet on Lake Erie, 1812-1813* (Harrisburg, 1950).

Tinkcom, Harry Merlin. *The Republicans and Federalists in Pennsylvania 1790-1801* (Harrisburg, 1950).

Chapter 20.   *Breaking the Mountain Barrier*

Barton, Edwin M. "Living and Working on the North Branch Canal: Reminiscences . . .," *The Columbian,* v. 1, No. 2 (October, 1960).

Burgess, George H., and Kennedy, Miles C., *Centennial History of the Pennsylvania Railroad Company* (Philadelphia, 1949).

Cummings, Hubertis M. "The Allegheny Portage Railroad," *Historic Pennsylvania Leaflet* No. 19 (Pennsylvania Historical and Museum Commission, Harrisburg, 1957).

Cummings, Hubertis M. "Pennsylvania: Network of Canal Ports," *Pennsylvania History,* v. 21, No. 3 (July, 1954).

McGill, Caroline Elizabeth. *History of Transportation in the United States before 1860* (Washington, D. C., 1917).

Rhoads, Willard R. "The Pennsylvania Canal," *Western Pennsylvania Historical Magazine,* v. 43, No. 3 (September, 1960).

Schusler, William Kenneth. "The Railroad Comes to Pittsburgh," *Western Pennsylvania Historical Magazine,* v. 43, No. 3 (September, 1960).

Chapter 21.   *A Game without Rules*

Klein, Philip S. *Pennsylvania Politics, 1817-1832: A Game Without Rules* (Philadelphia, 1940).

Snyder, Charles McCool. *The Jacksonian Heritage: Pennsylvania Politics 1833-1848* (Harrisburg, 1958).

Chapter 22.   *The Underground Railroad*

Arnold, I. C. "An Underground Station in Drumore Township and Other Incidents of Slavery Times," *Lancaster County Historical Society Papers,* v. 55 (1951).

Gara, Larry. *The Liberty Line: The Legend of the Underground Railroad* (Lexington, Ky., 1961).

Mast, C. Z., and Simpson, Robert E. *Annals of the Conestoga Valley in Lancaster, Berks, and Chester Counties, Pennsylvania* (Elverson, Pa., 1942).

Smedley, R. C. *History of the Underground Railroad in Chester and the Neighboring Counties of Pennsylvania* (Lancaster, 1883).

Smith, Joseph Hutchinson. "Some Aspects of the Underground Railway in the Counties of Southeastern Pennsylvania," *Bulletin of the Historical Society of Montgomery County,* v. 3, No. 1 (October, 1941).

Still, William. *The Underground Railroad* (Philadelphia, 1883).

Chapter 23.   *Abraham Lincoln in Pennsylvania*

Catton, Bruce. *This Hallowed Ground: The Story of the Union Side of the Civil War* (New York, 1956).

Churchill, Winston S. *The Great Democracies* (New York, 1958), v. 4 of *A History of the English-Speaking Peoples.*

Coddington, Edwin B. "Rothermel's Painting of the Battle of Gettysburg," *Pennsylvania History,* v. 27, No. 1 (January, 1960).

Conquest, Robert. "The Battle of Gettysburg," *History Today* (March, 1958).

Duff, James H. "David Wilmot, the Statesman and Political Leader," *Pennsylvania History,* v. 13, No. 4 (October, 1946).

Fortenbaugh, Robert. "Lincoln as Gettysburg Saw Him," *Pennsylvania History,* v. 14, No. 1 (January, 1947).

Haskell, Franklin. *The Battle of Gettysburg,* Bruce Catton, ed. (Boston, 1958).

Higginbotham, Sanford W., Hunter, William A., and Kent, Donald H. *Pennsylvania and the Civil War. A Handbook* (Harrisburg, 1961).

Stackpole, Edward J. *They Met at Gettysburg* (Harrisburg, 1956).

Williams, T. Harry. *Lincoln and His Generals* (New York, 1952).

Chapter 24.   *The Industrial Revolution*

Bining, Arthur Cecil. *Pennsylvania Iron Manufacture in the Eighteenth Century* (Harrisburg, 1938).

Bining, Arthur Cecil. *Pennsylvania's Iron and Steel Industry* (Gettysburg, 1954).

Handwork, Edna M. "First in Iron: Berks County's Iron Industry, 1716 to 1815," *Historical Review of Berks County,* v. 25, No. 4 (Fall, 1960).

Klein, Frederic S. "Robert Coleman, Millionaire Ironmaster," *Lancaster County Historical Society Papers,* v. 64, No. 1 (Winter, 1960).

Miller, Frederic K. *The Rise of an Iron Community* (Lebanon County Historical Society, Lebanon, Pa., 1950-1952).
Moore, E. E. "Pittsburgh and the Steel Industry," *Pennsylvania History,* v. 26, No. 1 (January, 1959).
Stevens, Sylvester K. *Pennsylvania, Titan of Industry,* v. 1 (New York, 1948).

Chapter 25.   *Dusky Diamonds*

Billinger, Robert D. *Pennsylvania's Coal Industry* (Gettysburg, 1954).
Eavenson, Howard N. *The First Century and a Quarter of American Coal Industry* (Pittsburgh, 1942).
Korson, George. *Black Rock: Mining Folklore of the Pennsylvania Dutch* (Baltimore, 1960).
Korson, George, ed. *Pennsylvania Songs and Legends* (Philadelphia, 1949).
Murphy, Raymond E., and Marion. *Pennsylvania Landscapes* (Harrisburg, 1938).
Myers, Richmond. *The Long Crooked River* (*The Susquehanna*) (Boston, 1949).

Chapter 26.   *Greentop Gold*

Defebaugh, James Elliott. *History of the Lumber Industry of America* (Chicago, 1906).
Horn, Stanley Fitzgerald. *This Fascinating Lumber Business* (New York, 1951).
Kenderdine, Thaddeus S. "Lumbering Days on the Delaware River," *Bucks County Historical Society Papers,* v. 4 (1917).
King, Samuel A. "A Log Drive to Williamsport in 1868," *Pennsylvania History,* v. 29, No. 2 (April, 1962).
Swetnam, George. "On the Trail of Cherry Tree Joe" and "More About Cherry Tree Joe," *Keystone Folklore Quarterly,* v. 7, Nos. 1-2 (Spring and Summer, 1962).
Taber, Thomas T. "Logging Railroads and Logging Locomotives in Eastern Pennsylvania," *Now and Then,* v. 12, No. 10 (January, 1960).
Tonkin, Joseph Dudley. *The Last Raft* (Harrisburg, 1940).
Tonkin, R. Dudley. *My Partner, the River: The White Pine Story on the Susquehanna* (Pittsburgh, 1958).
Wheeler, Reginald. *Pine Knots and Bark Peelers: The Story of Five Generations of American Lumbermen* (La Jolla, Cal., 1960).

When Timber Was King. A special issue of *Pennsylvania History,* v. 19, No. 4 (October, 1952) devoted to lumbering in Pennsylvania.

Chapter 27. *Black Gold*

Bone, J. A. *Petroleum and Petroleum Wells . . . of Pennsylvania . . .* (Philadelphia, 1865).

Dolson, Hildegarde. *The Great Oildorado* (New York, 1959).

Giddens, Paul H. *The Beginnings of the Petroleum Industry* (Harrisburg, 1941).

Giddens, Paul H. *Pennsylvania Petroleum, 1750-1872, A Documentary History* (Titusville, 1947).

Giddens, Paul H. "The Significance of the Drake Well," in *Oil's First Century* (Cambridge, Mass., 1960).

Leonard, Charles C. *The History of Pithole* (Pithole City, 1867; reprinted, Baltimore, 1945).

Miller, Ernest C. *Pennsylvania's Oil Industry* (Gettysburg, 1954).

Wright, William. *The Oil Regions of Pennsylvania* (New York, 1865).

Chapter 28. *The Labor Movement in Pennsylvania*

Adams, James Truslow. "The Age of the Dinosaurs," Chapter 12 in *The Epic of America* (Boston, 1931).

Beard, Mary. *A Short History of the American Labor Movement* (New York, 1924).

Dulles, Foster Rhea. *Labor in America, a History* (New York, 1949).

Gutman, Herbert G. "Two Lockouts in Pennsylvania 1873-1874," *Pennsylvania Magazine of History and Biography,* v. 83, No. 3 (July, 1959).

Heilbroner, Robert L. "Epitaph for the Steel Master," *American Heritage,* v. 11, No. 5 (August, 1960).

Hendrick, Burton J. *Life of Andrew Carnegie* (New York, 1932).

Palmer, Gladys L. *Philadelphia Workers in a Changing Economy* (Philadelphia, 1956).

Sullivan, William A. *The Industrial Worker in Pennsylvania 1800-1840* (Harrisburg, 1955).

Chapter 29. *Return to Democracy*

Clepper, Henry. "Rise of the Forest Conservation Movement in Pennsylvania," *Pennsylvania History,* v. 12, No. 3 (July, 1945).

Fausold, Martin L. *Gifford Pinchot, Bull Moose Progressive* (Syracuse, N. Y., 1961).
McGeary, Martin Nelson. *Gifford Pinchot, Forester-Politician* (Princeton, 1960).
Stevens, Sylvester K. *Pennsylvania, the Keystone State* (New York, 1956).

Chapter 30.   *A Glance at the Arts*

Dickson, Harold E. *A Hundred Pennsylvania Buildings* (State College, Pa., 1954).
Dickson, Harold E. "Pennsylvania Painters: An Exhibit for Historians," *Pennsylvania History,* v. 23, No. 4 (October, 1956).
Klees, Fredric. *The Pennsylvania Dutch* (New York, 1950).
Lichten, Frances. *Folk Art of Rural Pennsylvania* (New York, 1946).
Mahr, August C. "Origin and Significance of Pennsylvania Dutch Barn Symbols," *Ohio State Archaeological and Historical Quarterly,* v. 54 (1945).
Oakley, Violet. *The Holy Experiment: Our Heritage from William Penn* (Philadelphia, 1950).
Porter, Fairfield. *Thomas Eakins* (New York, 1959).
Sellers, Charles Coleman. *Charles Willson Peale, 1741-1827* (Philadelphia, 1947).
Stoudt, John Joseph. *Pennsylvania Folk-Art* (Allentown, 1948).

Chapter 31.   *Some Pennsylvania Profiles*

Milton Hershey
Shippen, Katherine B., and Wallace, Paul A. W. *Milton S. Hershey* (New York, 1959).
Snavely, Joseph R. *The Hershey Story* (Hershey, Pa., 1950).

Andrew Mellon
Love, Philip H. *Andrew W. Mellon, the Man and His Work* (Baltimore, 1930).
Mellon, William L., and Sparkes, Boyden. *Judge Mellon's Sons* (Pittsburgh, 1948).
O'Connor, Harvey. *Mellon's Millions, the Biography of a Fortune . . .* (New York, 1953).

Owen J. Roberts
Roberts, Owen J. *The Court and the Constitution* (Cambridge, Mass., 1951).
University of Pennsylvania Law Review, v. 104, No. 3 (December,

1955). A memorial issue containing appraisals of Justice Roberts by Felix Frankfurter, Edwin R. Keedy, Robert T. McCracken, Erwin N. Griswold, John J. McCloy, Clarence K. Streit, William E. Lingelbach, George Wharton Pepper.

Werner, M. R., and Starr, John. *Teapot Dome* (New York, 1959).

Chapter 32.   *Pittsburgh*

Allegheny Conference on Community Development Presents—Pittsburgh . . . (Pittsburgh, 1936).

Baldwin, Leland D. *Pittsburgh: The Story of a City* (Pittsburgh, 1937).

Harper, Frank C. *Pittsburgh: Forge of the Universe* (New York, 1957).

James, Alfred Proctor, and Stotz, Charles Morse. *Drums in the Forest* (Pittsburgh, 1958).

Swetnam, George. *Where Else but Pittsburgh?* (Pittsburgh, 1958).

Chapter 33.   *Philadelphia*

Brookhouser, Frank. *Our Philadelphia: A Candid and Colorful Portrait of a Great City* (New York, 1957).

Lingelbach, William E. "Philadelphia and the Conservation of the National Heritage," *Pennsylvania History,* v. 20, No. 4 (October, 1953).

Lippincott, Horace Mather. *Philadelphia* (Philadelphia, 1926).

Riley, Edward M. "Philadelphia, the Nation's Capital, 1790-1800." *Pennsylvania History,* v. 20, No. 4 (October, 1953).

Weygandt, Cornelius. *Philadelphia Folks: Ways and Institutions in and about the Quaker City* (New York, 1938).

Index

About the Author

Paul A. W. Wallace, a resident of Pennsylvania since 1925, has made his hobby—Pennsylvania history—into a full-time profession. Born in Ontario, he received his B.A. and Ph.D. degrees from the University of Toronto, then served as Professor of English at Lebanon Valley College in Annville, Pennsylvania, for twenty-four years.

In 1949 Mr. Wallace joined the Pennsylvania Historical and Museum Commission as editor of the magazine *Pennsylvania History*. He is presently engaged on a comprehensive study of Pennsylvania's Indian trails.

His books on Pennsylvania include *Indians in Pennsylvania; Conrad Weiser, Friend of Colonist and Mohawk; The White Roots of Peace;* and *The Muhlenbergs of Pennsylvania. Pennsylvania: Seed of a Nation* is the result of twenty-five years of research.

Format by Stanley M. Wheatman
Set in Linotype Times Roman
Composed, printed and bound by The Haddon Craftsmen, Inc.
HARPER & ROW, PUBLISHERS, INCORPORATED

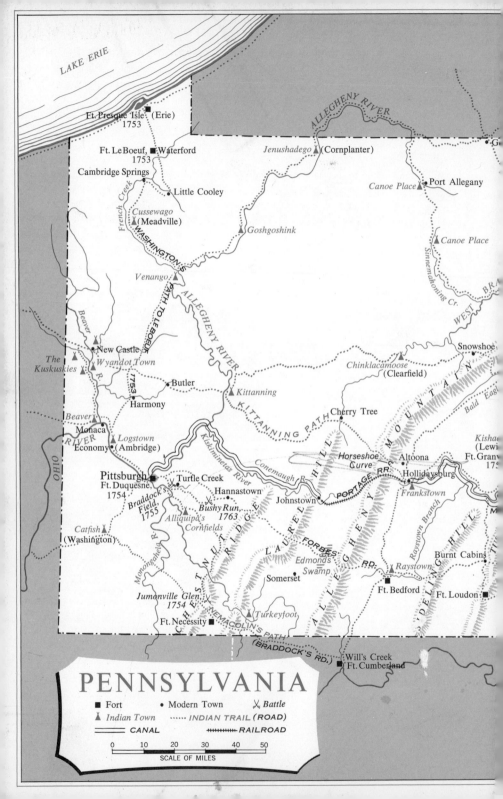

LAKE ERIE

Ft. Presque Isle (Erie)
1753

Ft. Le Boeuf,
1753 • Waterford
Cambridge Springs

French Creek

• Little Cooley

Cussewago
▲ (Meadville)

Goshgoshink ▲

Venango ▲

WASHINGTON'S PATH TO LE BOEUF
1753

Beaver

ALLEGHENY RIVER

The Kuskuskies ✗
✗ New Castle
▲ Wyandot Town

• Butler

• Harmony

Beaver ✗

Monaca
Economy • (Ambridge)
▲ Logstown

Pittsburgh ■
Ft. Duquesne
1754

Braddock's Field,
1755 ✗ Turtle Creek

• Hannastown

*Alliquipa's
Cornfields*

Catfish
(Washington)

Jumonville Glen,
1754 ✗
Ft. Necessity ■

CHESTNUT RIDGE

NEMACOLIN'S PATH
(BRADDOCK'S RD.)

▲ Kittanning

KITTANNING PATH

Kiskiminetas River

Conemaugh R.

Johnstown

Bushy Run,
1763 ✗

LAUREL HILL

*Edmonds
Swamp*

Somerset

• Turkeyfoot ▲

Monongahela

ALLEGHENY RIVER

ALLEGHENY RIVER

Jenushadego ▲ (Cornplanter)

Canoe Place ▲ • Port Allegany

Canoe Place ▲

Sinnemahoning Cr.

WEST BRA

• Snowshoe

Chinklacamoose ▲
(Clearfield)

• Cherry Tree

ALLEGHENY MOUNTAIN

Bald Eagl

*Horseshoe
Curve*

Altoona •

PORTAGE RR.

Hollidaysburg •

▲ *Frankstown*

Raystown Branch

Kisha
(Lewi
Ft. Gran
175

M

FORBES RD.

Raystown •

Burnt Cabins •

Ft. Bedford ■

SIDELING HILL

Ft. Loudon ■

Will's Creek
Ft. Cumberland ■

G •

PENNSYLVANIA

■ Fort   • Modern Town   ✗ Battle

▲ Indian Town   ••••••• INDIAN TRAIL (ROAD)

══════ CANAL   ┿┿┿┿┿┿ RAILROAD

0   10   20   30   40   50
SCALE OF MILES